STALEMATE!

STALEMATE!

The Great Trench Warfare Battles of 1915–1917

J. H. JOHNSON

ARMS AND
ARMOUR

Arms and Armour Press
A Cassell Imprint
Wellington House, 125 Strand, London WC2R 0BB.

Distributed in the USA by Sterling Publishing Co. Inc., 387 Park
Avenue South, New York, NY 10016-8810

Distributed in Australia by Capricorn Link (Australia) Pty Ltd,
2/13 Carrington Road, Castle Hill, New South Wales 2154

British Library Cataloguing-in-Publication data: A catalogue record for
this book is available from the British Library.

ISBN 1 85409 257 X

Edited and designed by Roger Chesneau/DAG Publications Ltd

Printed and bound in Great Britain by
Hartnolls Limited, Bodmin, Cornwall

In memory of my father
Ernest George Johnson (1890–1931)
Trooper, 2nd Life Guards (Guards Machine Gun Regiment)
and his brother
John Johnson (1887–1921)
2nd Lieut., The Norfolk Regiment
who served in the Great War and died as a result of it in the years that
followed

Contents

Preface

In contrast to the Second World War, the First World War (commonly known in the 1920s and 1930s as the Great War) was, for the greater part of its duration, a static war. In the first days of August 1914 it had opened on the Western Front with a dramatic sweep through Belgium by the bulk of the German Army, forcing the French Army and the tiny British Expeditionary Force back towards Paris. By October, however, the seemingly irresistible German advance had been halted. Several factors contributed to this – the premature diversion of two army corps to the Eastern Front because of the Russian threat, the acute difficulties caused by the extended lines of communication, the exhaustion of the German divisions after the long march through Belgium and the Franco-British counter-attacks at the Battle of the Marne. Thwarted in its attempt to break through the Allies' left wing at Ypres in late October, the German Army concentrated on defeating Russia and settled down to a mainly defensive role on the Western Front, choosing where possible the high ground in a series of trenches stretching from the English Channel near Ostend to the northern border of Switzerland. This situation was to remain essentially unchanged until 1918, the last year of the war, when the great German offensive begun in March brought the deadlock to an end. Thus for over three years a condition of trench (or siege) warfare existed.

Trench warfare had not been foreseen by any of the combatants, but the ending of the war of movement had forced the Franco-British armies to come to terms with the problem of conducting a form of siege warfare, a circumstance for which they were neither trained nor equipped. The normal application of siege warfare is in the investment of a town or fortress so that the defenders have no escape. Clearly this was not the case for the German Army, but the latter's defensive system, initially a line of rudimentary trenches aided by natural obstacles, was eventually to become a formidable barrier with its flanks inviolate. Thus there was no way round what Winston Churchill termed 'Ramparts more than 350 miles long, ceaselessly guarded by millions of men, sustained by thousands of cannon . . .'

It was these 'ramparts' that the Allies sought at such terrible cost to storm between 1915 and 1917. The British contribution was the mounting of six set-

7

piece offensives – Neuve Chapelle and Loos in 1915, the Somme in 1916 and Arras, Ypres (the third battle commonly, although incorrectly, known as Passchendaele) and Cambrai in 1917. These offensives had a combined duration of slightly over three hundred days and, although representing less than a third of the three years, accounted for over 60 per cent of the casualties. Now, nearly eighty years later, they can evoke an image of soldiers ceaselessly climbing out of their trenches into No Man's Land, only to be slaughtered in their thousands. The reality, however, was somewhat different. For the greater part of their time over the three years the infantry had spells in the front line, in support, in reserve and out at rest. It is true that there were bitterly contested attacks of a local nature, and there were also patrols in No Man's Land and frequent trench raids, sometimes in company strength but more likely to be confined to a couple of dozen men. This is not to say that life in the front line, or in support, was much less hazardous than 'going over the top'. By far the greatest danger was from enemy artillery, this apart from the conditions in the trenches where mud at times was thigh deep and where men were always exposed to the elements, afflicted with trench fever and lice and overrun with rats. But there were quiet sectors where, by tacit agreement between those on both sides of No Man's Land, an unofficial 'live and let live' policy existed and where the greatest danger was said to be one of boredom.

But what of the six offensives? Some of them are now virtually forgotten battles, their names inscribed on the colours of regiments who took part in them but otherwise a dim memory. The Somme and Passchendaele, however, are etched on the national consciousness and frequently quoted when it is felt that examples of futility, or profligacy in men's lives, need to be demonstrated. But with one exception each offensive had been planned with an objective – to break through the German front and resume open warfare. Each offensive had drawn upon the accumulated experience of those who had gone before, but, despite the massive increase in strength of the British Army and its armaments over the three years, and the knowledge of factors that had led to past failure, no breakthrough was achieved and no objective realized. The theme of this book is to explore why this should have been so.

Acknowledgements

The idea for this book originated in 1977 when I read the manuscript diary of Edwin Campion Vaughan detailing his experiences as a young infantry officer on the Western Front between January and July 1917. The diary, which was eventually published in 1981 under the title *Some Desperate Glory*, served to rekindle my long dormant interest in the Great War, and from 1979 onwards I paid many visits to the old Western Front in company at various times with

Douglas Ellison, Ian Williams, Cliff Eydmann and Jack Brooks – transport providers, and convivial companions in whatever the weather; their help was invaluable. I am also indebted to my friend Roger Webster, who read through the whole of my draft and offered helpful advice, particularly concerning the avoidance of solecisms. For first-hand descriptions of battlefield conditions and life in the front line I must record my appreciation of the help given to me by the late Harry Taylor (1897–1991), who served as a lance corporal in the Liverpool Scottish (1/10th King's) at the Somme and Ypres. I am also appreciative of the service provided by the staff of my local library in Bexhill-on-Sea, who, regardless of the publication date, never failed to provide the many books I ordered, and of the assistance given by Philip Haythornthwaite in the provision of photographs.

For permission to quote from *The Private Papers of Douglas Haig 1914–1919* I am grateful to Lord Blake and Earl Haig, and similarly to Lord Hankey for his permission to quote from his father's book *The Supreme Command 1914–1918*. Permission to quote from *The War Diary of the Master of Belhaven* was kindly given by the publishers of that work, Wharncliffe Publishing Ltd.

Author's Note

For an understanding of the various British formations mentioned in the text of this book, it might be helpful to give an indication of their approximate sizes. The infantry strength of an army – i.e., excluding cavalry, artillery, engineers and medical personnel – is dependent upon the number of divisions employed. For example, on 1 July 1916 the formation of the Fourth Army was fifteen divisions, giving a total of some 180,000 men. Thus a division would total between 11,500 and 12,000 men. Depending on the circumstances, an army could consist of four or five army corps of some 36,000 men each. From these examples the following simplified table can be constructed using rounded numbers:

Unit	Strength	Rank of commander
Company	250	Captain
Battalion	1,000	Lieutenant-colonel
Brigade	4,000	Brigadier-general
Division	12,000	Major-general
Corps	36,000	Lieutenant-general
Army	180,000	General

It must be stressed that the foregoing figures represent established rather than actual strength. For example, the average strength of a battalion going into action was 800 officers and men; at the Third Battle of Ypres the usual custom was to reduce the total to 676 officers and men.

1

The Gathering Darkness

The great states of Europe had never been so powerfully prepared for war in human and material sources as in 1914. And this was a natural result of the policy which they pursued.—C. R. M. F. Cruttwell, *A History of the Great War 1914–1918*

T HE ORIGINS of the Great War lie deep in the second half of the nineteenth century. Before 1870 the major powers in continental Europe were France, Austria-Hungary, Italy and Russia. The Ottoman (or Turkish) Empire in Europe, once embracing Hungary, Greece and the Ukraine, had been in continuous decline since the eighteenth century and only its Balkan provinces remained, but their struggle for independence was ultimately to have profound consequences. Britain, secure on her island, and with the lifelines to her vast overseas empire guarded by the most powerful navy in the world, stood somewhat aloof from events in Europe; indeed, the only threat perceived from the Continent was from her near neighbour, France. But the map of Europe, and the balance of power, were beginning to change.

Until 1871 Germany comprised a collection of independent states dominated by the largest, Prussia. The objective of its foreign minister, the formidable statesman Otto von Bismarck, had been to establish the pre-eminence of Prussia, and to this end he had embarked on a series of successful campaigns against Denmark in 1863, Austria in 1866 and France in 1870. The war with Austria effectively terminated the latter's influence on the German states, and France had been left humiliated, particularly by being forced to cede Alsace-Lorraine to Prussia. These successes firmly established Prussia's hegemony among the German states, and in 1871 the German Empire was born, with Bismarck its first Chancellor. Thereafter Bismarck, ever mindful of French resentment at the loss of Alsace-Lorraine, confined his efforts to safeguarding the fledgeling empire by a system of alliances. A defensive alliance between Germany and Austria-Hungary was reached in 1879, later becoming the Triple Alliance when Italy joined in 1886, and in 1887 a secret alliance with Russia was negotiated. The effect of the alliances was to secure peace in Europe for over twenty years, but in 1890 Bismarck was forced to resign as a result of a disagreement with the young German emperor, Kaiser Wilhelm II. One of the Kaiser's first decisions was to refuse to renew the secret treaty with Russia, but Russia had no wish to be isolated, and after protracted negotiations a military alliance was reached with France in 1894, the terms of which were that both countries would mobilize their forces in the event of one or the other being threatened by a member or members of the Triple Alliance.

Thus every major European country was allied against a military threat, only Britain standing apart. At the turn of the century an alliance between Britain and Germany had been considered, but it had found little favour with the Germans. Relations over the years between Britain and France had ranged from cool to bitterly hostile, but the French wanted a *rapprochement* and the instrument to achieve this was a formal invitation to King Edward VII to visit Paris. The visit was surprisingly successful and enabled talks to begin in an endeavour to iron out points of difference between the two countries. An Anglo-French agreement was ultimately reached in 1904, establishing what came to be known as the Entente Cordiale. However, this was by no means a military alliance, merely an attempt to remove sources of friction, particularly in colonial affairs.

As the century turned, the European peace engineered by Bismarck began to look increasingly fragile. Germany's aggressive foreign policy in Europe, including her attempts to drive a wedge between Britain and France, only served to bring those two countries closer together. The first real portent of war arose in the Balkans in 1908. Russia had long wished for naval access to the Mediterranean by way of the Bosporus, but the passage of warships through the strait was prohibited by the Treaty of London signed in 1871 by the major powers. On the other hand Austria wanted to annex the two provinces of Bosnia and Herzegovina. Once part of the Ottoman Empire, these territories had been administered by Austria since 1879, but a group of reformist army officers in Turkey known as the Young Turks had brought about a revolution in 1908 and were demanding that the two provinces be represented in the new parliament in the Turkish capital. Both provinces had a large Slav population with ethnic ties to neighbouring Serbia, also once part of the Ottoman Empire but an independent kingdom since 1878. The Russian and Austrian foreign ministers negotiated a secret arrangement whereby, in return for Russia's ignoring Austria's annexation of Bosnia and Herzegovina, Austria would support Russian demands on Turkey for the passage of warships through the Bosporus. The arrangements were planned to be made simultaneously, thus presenting a *fait accompli*, but Austria announced the annexation prematurely. This caused great resentment in Serbia and embarrassment in Russia (particularly in view of her close ties with Serbia) and aroused strenuous opposition from France and Britain. Serbia mobilized her forces, but Germany warned Russia that Austria would crush Serbia and, if Russia came to Serbia's aid, Germany would support Austria.

Russia was unprepared for war and had, perforce, to accept the annexation. Austria rejoiced at the outcome, but Russia, the protector of the Balkan Slavs, had been humiliated.

Some of the tensions that had arisen since Bismarck's dismissal had undoubtedly been brought about by the Kaiser. Although a grandson of Queen Victoria, he had an ambivalent relationship with Britain, particularly with King Edward VII. He was suspicious of his uncle's frequent visits to Europe, particularly his meetings with the Austrian and Russian emperors, and saw in these the formation of a grand design to encircle Germany. The Kaiser, while intelligent, was volatile and unstable and possessed an unshakable belief in the divine right of monarchs not only to govern but also to dictate foreign policy. He revelled in martial affairs, thus encouraging the militarism inherent in the Prussian character, but, like Frankenstein, he had created a monster which he was unable ultimately to control. In the 1890s he embarked on an ambitious programme to build a navy that would, in time, rival Britain's in size and capacity. This could be ascribed partly to his vanity, but the impetus had come from his Navy Secretary, von Tirpitz, whose objective was also to build such a navy, to challenge Britain's maritime supremacy. There was disquiet in Britain when the scale of Germany's expansion of her battleship fleet was eventually recognized: it was regarded as serious threat to the Royal Navy, and in the years up to 1914 each country endeavoured to outdo the other in the rate of warship building.

Further crises arose in the Balkans as a result of the two wars of 1912 and 1913 when Serbia wrested further territory from Turkey and Bulgaria. Austria, worried about Slav aspirations, was deterred by Germany from attacking Serbia, but the seeds of a wider conflict, already sown in 1908, were blossoming into a deadly flowering. Austria's distaste for Serbia sprang from the belief that the latter was at the root of the agitation within Hungary for independence from Austria, and the critical point was reached in June 1914 when Archduke Ferdinand, the nephew of the Austrian Emperor Franz Josef and heir to the throne, was assassinated in Sarajevo, the Bosnian capital. The Austrians suspected that the plot had been hatched in Serbia and they now believed that, at last, a *casus belli* existed for the elimination of Slav ambitions.

Having secured German support, Austria delivered a Note to Belgrade, the Serbian capital, on 23 July containing a number of demands phrased in such a manner (so Austria believed) as to ensure their rejection. The Serbian reply was unexpectedly conciliatory in that all the demands, with only minor reservations, were accepted. Indeed, the Kaiser thought that it was a 'great moral victory for Vienna; but with it every reason for war drops away.' Nevertheless, Austria brushed aside the Serbian reply and declared war on 28 July, bombarding Belgrade with artillery fire from across the Danube the following day.

Events then gathered a fatal momentum. The Austrian declaration of war was greeted with dismay in Russia, and after much heart-searching the Tsar ordered a partial mobilization. In an exchange of telegrams with the Kaiser he entreated him to use his influence to restrain Austria, but in reply the Kaiser insisted on the Tsar's cancelling the partial mobilization, indicating that this action had carried the responsibility for 'involving Europe in the most horrible war she has ever witnessed'. But Russia was determined to avoid a repetition of the humiliation she had experienced six years earlier, and on 30 July general mobilization was ordered. The news was received in Berlin with something akin to relief: Germany could now order its own mobilization in the belief that world opinion would regard the move as a response to the Russian threat. Accordingly an ultimatum was dispatched to Russia demanding that the latter 'suspend every war measure against Austria and ourselves within twelve hours . . .' An ultimatum was also dispatched to France couched in arrogant terms: if France stayed neutral, then, as a guarantee, she should hand over the frontier forts of Toul and Verdun – a demand that, Germany believed, France would be bound to refuse.

Britain viewed these events with growing alarm and on 29 July suggested that Austria halt after occupying Belgrade and accept mediation by Britain, France, Germany and Italy, but with the warning that, should the conflict widen into a German attack on France, then the British Government would 'find itself forced to make up its mind'. This warning caused consternation in Berlin and a brisk exchange of telegrams with Austria ensued, urging acceptance of Britain's proposal. But the time for diplomatic initiatives had virtually run its course: diplomacy would shortly succumb to military expediency. The German ultimata expired on 1 August, and in the evening of that day the Russian foreign minister was handed Germany's declaration of war. On the same day France ordered a general mobilization and informed the German ambassador in Paris that 'France would act in accordance with her interests'. Italy, however, decided on 31 July that, as the war had been brought about by Austria's attack on Serbia, she was not bound by the terms of the Triple Alliance as it did not 'bear the character of a war of defence'.

The implications of the Franco-Russian alliance of 1894 were that, at some future time, Germany might have to fight a war on two fronts – an untenable proposition since French and Russian armies together were superior in numbers to the combined German and Austrian armies. This danger had greatly influenced German military thinking, and the plan – virtually a gospel – formulated by the Chief of Staff, General Count von Schlieffen, was based on the hypothesis that the vast distances and poor railway communications in Russia would mean that Russian mobilization would be slow and, therefore, a token force of less than a fifth of the German Army, in co-operation with the Austrians, would be sufficient to deal with any advance. The bulk of the German Army would be concentrated on the Western Front, but because it was believed that a frontal assault on the French fortress system guarding the common frontier would be too costly, von Schlieffen took another gamble: he would use a small force to resist any French advance on the frontier and deploy the main force in a massive thrust through Belgium which would also involve crossing Dutch territory near Maastricht. Then, having reached the English Channel, it would turn south, one army outflanking Paris on the west, then turn east and drive the French armies up to their eastern frontier and destroy them.

This, then, was the plan handed down after von Schlieffen's retirement in 1906 to his successor, General von Moltke – a plan breathtaking in its brutal disregard of the neutrality of neighbours (although von Moltke subsequently abandoned the plan to enter Holland) but, it was believed, the only one that would prevent Germany's being crushed between the forces of France and Russia. The French, on the other hand, had no intention of violating Belgian neutrality (although they had made some allowance for Germany doing so) but made a fatal miscalculation in believing that the enemy had insufficient strength to penetrate far beyond the line of the River Meuse. The French plan was to push four of her five armies across the frontier in the direction of Metz with the object of pressing the enemy back to the Rhine. The remaining army would be kept in reserve to deal with a German move through Luxembourg and Belgium. Thus the bulk of the French and German armies would move in opposite directions 'like a revolving door'.

In the fateful first days of August the Kaiser had belatedly come to realize the dreadful scale of the forces that were about to be released and made a last-ditch attempt to confine the conflict to a Russo-German war. This had arisen because a telegram from the German ambassador in London appeared to imply that if France was not attacked Britain would remain neutral and at the same time guarantee French neutrality. Excitedly the Kaiser sent a telegram to King George V confirming that if France remained neutral Germany would not attack. The Kaiser persuaded himself that the response would be favourable and went so far as to tell von Moltke that Germany could now go to war against Russia alone. But it was not to be. The German ambassador sent a further telegram to the effect that Britain's reply was unlikely to be favourable, while von Moltke had already told the Kaiser that it was impossible to recast the military timetable and march east instead of west. Germany then declared war on France on 3 August. The previous day Germany had demanded free passage for her armies through Belgium but this was refused and the following day the German armies crossed the Belgium frontier. Until then the British Cabinet had been deeply divided over the question of support for France, but the violation of

Belgium's neutrality, guaranteed in 1839 by Britain, France, Austria and Prussia, was seen as the final provocation. Britain thereupon issued an ultimatum to Germany expiring at midnight on 4 August. No reply was received, and in consequence Britain and Germany were at war.

* * *

The British Army had not fought in a European war since Waterloo in 1815, but in the last quarter of the nineteenth century it had seen considerable active service in the so-called colonial wars in the Sudan, India, Afghanistan and elsewhere. However, the South African war against the Boers (1899–1902) had engaged by far the largest commitment of forces, involving 450,000 by its end, made possible by supplementing the regular (or professional) Army by volunteer forces such as the Militia and the Yeomanry. The Army, whose superior firepower had been the dominating factor in the colonial wars, found the Boers equally well armed and masters of their terrain. They seldom chose to fight a pitched battle but melted away after inflicting casualties to strike elsewhere. General Kitchener, the British Commander-in-Chief, complained that the Boers were 'not like the Sudanese, who stood up to a fair fight. They are always running away on their little ponies.'

The Army had suffered several crushing defeats in the first year of the Boer War, mainly through clinging to the tactics it had used in the colonial wars, and its performance, particularly its leadership, had been found seriously wanting. As a result, a Royal Commission was set up after the war to study the lessons learned. This reported in 1903, and it was swiftly followed by the report of the Esher Committee in 1904 on the organization of the Army. These two inquiries led to far-reaching reforms, including the formation of an Army Council, the abolition of the post of Commander-in-Chief, the setting up of a General Staff and the reconstitution of the War Office. Four years later Haldane, the Secretary of State for War, initiated the creation of a British Expeditionary Force (BEF) for employment overseas in a European war. He also proposed the formation of a volunteer Territorial Army as a second-line support to the Regular Army, which would be mobilized at the same time and 'given systematic training for war'. His proposals swept away the existing auxiliary forces (the Militia and Volunteers), whose training and equipment belonged more to the previous rather than the present century. Although Haldane's proposals met fierce opposition, the Territorial Army came into being in 1908 as a fusion of Yeomanry and Volunteers (the Militia becoming a special reserve to the Regular Army), and by 1910 its strength was approaching 300,000, although, at the time, the terms of enlistment were for home defence only.

Although no formal military alliance existed between Britain and France, the recognition of the growing power and menace of Germany prompted talks between the French and British General Staffs envisaging that, in the event of a German attack on France, a British Expeditionary Force, earmarked at 120,000 (six divisions and one cavalry division), would be positioned on the left wing of the French Army close to the Belgian border. At the outbreak of war the strength of Britain's Regular Army was some 247,000, of which 118,000 formed permanent garrisons overseas, for example in Egypt and India. On 7 August 1914 Lord Kitchener, newly appointed Secretary of State for War, made the first of his appeals for volunteers for the Army, and such was the surge of patriotism (or perhaps the desire for adventure) that a million men had enlisted in the Regular Army and the Territorials by December. This enormous response was almost an embarrassment to the Government. The volunteers had to be accommodated, fed, clothed, equipped and, most important of all, trained, but there was a severe shortage of instructors and it was to be many months before Kitchener's volunteers, entitled the New Army, were ready to take their places alongside the Regular Army.

There was not the overriding control of affairs in the Great War that was to exist in the 1939–45 war through the Chiefs of Staffs Committee headed by the Prime Minister. Commanders in the Great War were largely responsible for strategy in their own theatres of operation, although there was a War Council headed by the Prime Minister. This Council, a Cabinet committee, was formed in November 1914, but during 1915 it was preoccupied with the Dardanelles campaign, even to the extent of its being renamed the Dardanelles Committee. Its meetings at that time tended to be dominated by Kitchener. Lloyd George, then Chancellor of the Exchequer, complained: 'His main idea at the Council table was to tell the politicians as little as possible of what was going on and get back to his desk at the War Office as quickly as he could decently escape.' For example, the Council only became aware of the Neuve Chapelle battle a week after it had ended. In June 1916 Kitchener was drowned while on his way to Russia at the invitation of the Tsar. The British warship on which he was travelling struck a mine in stormy weather off the Orkneys and sank with great loss of life. He was succeeded as War Secretary by Lloyd George, and when the latter became Prime Minister in December 1916 the Council was renamed the War Cabinet and given a much sharper focus. Even so, it could not veto the Passchendaele offensive, despite Lloyd George's deep misgivings.

Field Marshal Sir John French was the Commander-in-Chief of the BEF until he was replaced by General Sir Douglas Haig in December 1915 (appointed Field Marshal in December 1916). Both French and Haig were cavalrymen, but history has not been kind to either, especially French: he had distinguished

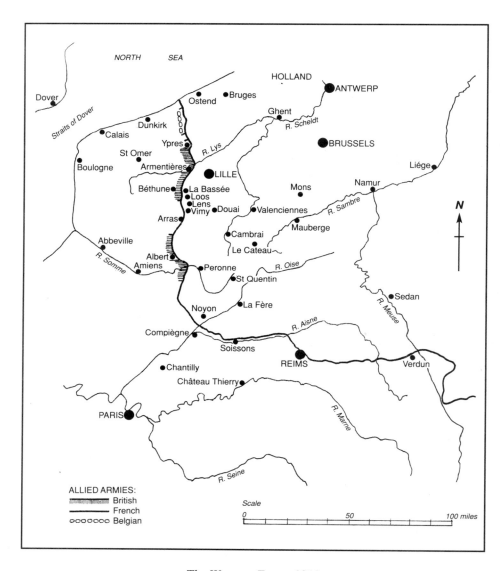

The Western Front, 1915

himself as a daring commander in the South African War, but, at 62 and nine years older than Haig, he was now fighting a very different war. It is possible to have some sympathy for French: his tiny army in 1914 was vastly outnumbered not only by that of the enemy but also by that of his principal ally, and he carried the fearful responsibility of ensuring that it was neither engulfed by the former nor fruitlessly expended by the latter. Part of Kitchener's instructions to French in committing the BEF to his command at the outset of the war included the following caveat:

> It must be recognised from the outset that the numerical strength of the British Force and its contingent reinforcement is strictly limited, and with this consideration kept steadily in view it will be obvious that the greatest care must be exercised towards a minimum of losses and wastage.

Given to moods of optimism when he became over-confident and pessimism when he became indecisive, French was out of his depth. He was ultimately relieved of his command in December 1915 after the Loos offensive and replaced by Haig who, as his subordinate, had commanded the First Army. Haig had always considered French ill-suited to command the BEF, and even went so far as to tell the King shortly after the outbreak of war that he had doubts about his selection.

Whilst there is broad agreement among military historians concerning French's imperfect generalship of the BEF, there are conflicting judgments about Haig. Haig was a thoughtful, meticulous soldier, very ambitious and supremely confident in the belief that his rightful place was that of commander-in-chief – indeed, that God had intended him for the role. He was certainly more intelligent than French, and more temperate. He is generally considered to have been at his best in 1918 after the great German offensive begun in March had finally petered out, but it would seem that it is on his handling of the Somme and Passchendaele offensives that his reputation rests. In public opinion between the wars, these two battles embodied all that was most terrible about the Great War, and it is hardly surprising that his name should have been associated with them in an unfavourable light. His principal antagonist was Lloyd George, who tried unsuccessfully to have him removed after Passchendaele, and a number of historians have criticized him for his stubbornness, his seeming indifference to high casualty rates and his ill-considered decisions not to break off offensives when the result could only mean losses outweighing gains.

Haig, however, has his supporters. Some staff officers who served under him have been generally persuasive in their support, and there is no real evidence that the rank and file of the BEF distrusted his leadership, though the Commander-in-Chief was far beyond the average soldier's perspective. The military historian John Terraine has concentrated single-mindedly on vindicating Haig, particularly in his handling of the Somme and Passchendaele offensives, arguing that many of the weaknesses attributed to him were in fact strengths; that the two controversial offensives correctly demonstrated a tenet of Haig's battle philosophy formulated when he was Chief of Staff in India some years before the war, namely the 'wearing out fight of varying duration'.[1] Haig, writing after the war and perhaps with the benefit of hindsight, referred to the 'wearing out fight' (in other words, attrition) as bringing about heavy losses but carrying within it the price of victory. In the last five years, however, criticism of Haig's generalship has sharpened. For example, Denis Winter's controversial reassessment of his command is forthright in its censure,[2] and the verdict that emerges from a recent biography by the American Gerard J. de Groot is that, 'Though he was the architect of victory, there were flaws in his design . . '[3]

> *And diff'ring judgements serve but to declare*
> *The truth lies somewhere, if we knew but where.*
> —William Cowper, *Hope*

Notes to Chapter 1

1. Terraine, John, *Douglas Haig – The Educated Soldier*, Hutchinson (London, 1963)
2. Winter, Dennis, *Haig's Command*, Viking, (London, 1991)
3. De Groot, G. J., *Douglas Haig 1861–1928*, Unwin Hyman (London, 1988)

2

Neuve Chapelle

THE STRENGTH of the British Expeditionary Force on the Western Front at the beginning of 1915 had been increased to eleven infantry and five cavalry divisions. This had been mainly due to the arrival of Regular divisions from overseas garrisons, enabling Sir John French to reorganize his two corps into two armies, the First commanded by General Sir Douglas Haig and the Second commanded by General Sir Horace Smith-Dorrien. Despite this increase in strength, the British Army was very much the junior partner on the Western Front, and, notwithstanding Kitchener's instructions to Sir John — 'I wish you distinctly to understand that your command is an entirely independent one, and that you will in no case come in any sense under the orders of any Allied General' — for all practical purposes General Joffre, commanding the French armies in the north-east, was the Allied Commander-in-Chief.

Joffre's plans for a spring offensive on the Western Front were aimed at reducing the massive salient in the German line extending from Arras to Reims. He proposed attacks at three points: Neuve Chapelle, east of Lille; Perthes, near Reims; and Eparges, between Metz and Verdun. The attack at Neuve Chapelle was originally planned to be a Franco-British operation (the others being exclusively French) and was dependent on the British relieving the two French corps positioned north of Ypres. However, because of troops being earmarked for the Dardanelles expedition (including the 29th Division originally promised), French was unable to comply, even though the requirement was subsequently reduced to one corps, and, as a result, Joffre decided to abandon the joint offensive.

Sir John then decided to attack alone — a somewhat unwise decision since the prospects of success were not good, particularly because of the shortage of artillery ammunition. He had, however, been stung by French criticism that the British were not 'pulling their weight': the French at that time tended to judge the capability of an army on its offensive ability, and the fiasco of a British attack near Messines in December had led them to believe that the best role for the British Army would be to hold the line while the French did the attacking. Not only was Sir John anxious to prove the French wrong, he was concerned about the condition of the First Army, situated as it was in inadequate and sodden trenches in the valley of the River Lys and enfiladed by the enemy from the salient around the village of Neuve Chapelle:

> No one who was not there can fully appreciate the excruciating agonies and misery through which men had to go in those days before anti-'trench foot' measures were taken, and other similar measures to make trench life more endurable. Paddling about by day, sometimes with water above the knees; standing at night, hour after hour on sentry duty, while the drenched boots, puttees and breeches became stiff like cardboard with ice from the freezing cold air. Rain, snow, sleet, wind and general discomfort all added their bit to the misery of trench life.[1]

The task fell on Haig, as commander of the First Army, to prepare plans for the assault. His original plan, submitted to GHQ on 12 February, was to capture the village and then press on to seize Aubers Ridge and threaten Lille. Meanwhile the French, after capturing Vimy, would merge with the British to disrupt German lines of communication so as to force their retirement from Noyon, the most westerly point of the salient. The plan had to be scaled down because of Joffre's decision to call off the joint offensive, and the new objective became the establishment of a defensive line below the crest of Aubers Ridge in order to provide dry ground secure from observation and a convenient jumping-off position for a future attack. An important factor was that artillery ammunition was sufficient only for three or four days.

Compared with the great battles that were to come, Neuve Chapelle was a very minor affair. Nevertheless, it had a profound impact, out of all proportion to its size, on subsequent offensives on the Western Front. It was the first major British offensive of the war, and although the attack was essentially in the nature of an experiment, there is no doubt that Haig's plans were both meticulous and ingenious. The Official History recorded: 'All subsequent attacks to the end of the war were, indeed, based on the methods developed by the First Army for Neuve Chapelle.' Models of the battleground were constructed and troops rehearsed in the details; aerial photographs were taken over the enemy lines and maps prepared of trench systems and issued, for the first time, to officers; and artillery was positioned with great secrecy, the registration of targets achieved piecemeal so as to allay any suspicion of an impending attack. The attack was to be carried out by the regular 7th and 8th Divisions (including several Territorial battalions) forming IV Corps (commanded by Lieutenant-General Sir Henry Rawlinson) and the Indian Corps (commanded by Lieutenant-General Sir James Willcocks). The attack was to be preceded by a hurricane artillery bombardment lasting thirty-five minutes. It is possible that such a short bombardment (by later standards) was dictated by the shortage of ammunition, but Haig's intentions were in any case to demoralize the enemy by a 'sudden and heavy bombardment'. Because of the converging nature of the assault, the guns were compressed into a frontage of only 1,200 yards, giving an intensity of concentration not reached again until 1917 at Ypres.

In 1915 the little village of Neuve Chapelle consisted of a church, a brewery and a few scattered houses. It had changed hands several times in the fluctuating battles of the previous autumn. It was protected by formidable wire entanglements, numerous machine guns and fortified houses. Because of the high water table, however, the trenches were very shallow, with sandbag parapets. The village itself had no strategic importance, but the German line bent round the village to the west to form a salient presenting a frontage of 2,000 yards. Less than two miles to the east of the village, the Aubers Ridge rises gently to a height of little more than sixty or seventy feet above the flatlands of the Lys valley and the plateau on the summit offers commanding views of the approaches to the cities of the plain of the Scheldt. The enemy position was only lightly held, partly owing to the need to provide reinforcements for the Eastern Front and because no attack was expected from the British in the sector.

The attack was planned for 10 March, and during the night, which was cold and wet, the attacking battalions moved up to their jumping-off positions and were assembled by 4.30 a.m. At 7.30 a.m the bombardment commenced with devastating effect:

> There was no difficulty in making out the German trenches. They had become long clouds of smoke and dust, flashing continuously with shell bursts, and with enormous masses of trench material and bodies sailing high above the smoke cloud. The purely physical effect on us was one of extreme exhilaration. We could have laughed and cried with excitement. We thought that the bombardment was winning the war before our eyes. Incredible that the men in the German front line could have escaped. We felt that we were going to pour through the gap.[2]

At 8.05 a.m the bombardment lifted and moved on 300 yards to the east of the front line; simultaneously, the attacking troops swarmed out of their trenches and advanced across the muddy fields to the enemy lines. The 25th Brigade attacked on a frontage of 400 yards between (but not including) Signpost Lane and the road leading to the village. Fortunately the wire entanglements had been destroyed and the enemy completely demoralized by the intensity of the bombardment. With few losses the Brigade crossed the German front line trenches and pressed on to occupy the support trenches less than 100 yards in the rear. The leading battalions halted while those in support passed through them and went forward to the village, which was occupied shortly before 9 a.m. Having achieved their objective, they waited until the curtain of the artillery bombardment moved on to the area between the village and the Bois du Biez.

The leading battalions of the 23rd Brigade (the 2nd Scottish Rifles and the 2nd Middlesex) attacked on the left of the 25th Brigade immediately north of

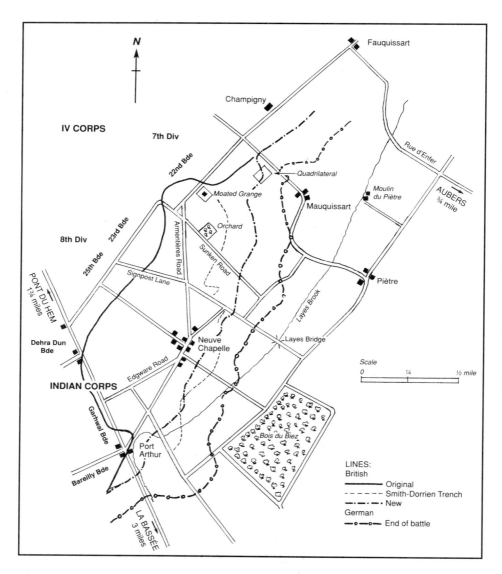

Battle of Neuve Chapelle, March 1915

Signpost Lane with the objective of establishing a front along the Armentières Road. Here disaster struck. This portion of the German front line had been allocated to two siege batteries (6-inch howitzer), but because of a delay of four days in embarkation from England they did not take up their positions until the day before the attack. This caused problems in target registration, with the result that trenches and wire entanglements were not seriously damaged. The reasons for the delay in the embarkation of the two batteries, and the failure of the field artillery to destroy the wire entanglements (where elsewhere they had been successfully cut), are not revealed in the Official History, nor, indeed, is the failure to make alternative arrangements, since the fact that there would be a delay was known to GHQ. The leading waves of the 2nd Middlesex were virtually wiped out, and the Scots had to tear at the barbed wire with their bare hands, meanwhile suffering terrible casualties. Out of 700 men of the 2nd Middlesex, about 400 were killed or wounded in the initial attack.

The attack of the Garhwal Brigade of the Indian Corps on the right of the British line met with mixed fortunes. The three battalions attacking the village itself experienced little opposition: the wire entanglements had been largely destroyed, and by 9 a.m. they had reached their objective, the old Smith-Dorrien trench about 300 yards east of the village. (This was a trench constructed by the British during the fighting for the village in the autumn of 1914.) On the extreme right of the Brigade's attacks south of Port Arthur, the assault of the 1/39 Garhwalis went sadly awry. The two leading companies lost direction and, veering off to their right instead of moving to their front, met German defences not included in the artillery plan and therefore untouched. Under intense fire, the Garhwalis tore down the wire entanglements and eventually gained the trench, albeit suffering severe casualties with all six British officers killed.

In spite of these set-backs, the high point of the attack had been reached: the village was captured by 1 p.m, the enemy was demoralized and any attempt at counter-attacks was thwarted by the curtain of fire laid down between the village and the Bois du Biez. However, few military successes are completely unalloyed, and this was to be the case with Neuve Chapelle. The principal problems had been the failure of the artillery completely to destroy the trenches and wire, and the destruction of all telephone lines by enemy fire, despite being laid in duplicate and even, in places, triplicate. These problems were to become only too familiar in subsequent battles.

The burden of the attack so far had been borne by the 23rd and 24th Brigades of the 8th Division and the Garhwal Brigade of the Indian Corps. The direction of their attacks had been confined to the salient around the village, but to the north of the salient, that is, from Moated Grange, the German line straightened out. This was in the 7th Division's sector, but the leading brigade (the 22nd) had not been in action during the initial assault and its supporting brigades (the 20th and 21st) were in reserve over a mile from the front. Owing to a delay in communication, Rawlinson had not been aware until over an hour afterwards that a key point in the German defence (the Orchard) had been captured soon after noon, but at 1.15 p.m. he ordered the 21st Brigade to be ready to advance towards Aubers Ridge as soon as the 24th Brigade of the 8th Division had come into position. (The latter brigade had been in reserve near Pont du Hem during the attack.) The advance was timed for 2 p.m., but then came further delay. Rawlinson wanted his attack to be synchronized with one by the Indian Corps in the Port Arthur sector, but because of a pocket of enemy resistance Willcocks did not want to move until it had been dealt with. As a result Rawlinson then postponed his attack, but, on learning that the resistance was not as serious as first thought, he gave orders at 2.50 p.m. for the 24th Brigade to advance on the village of Le Piètre and the 21st on its right to move towards the Rue d'Enfer.

The objectives of the two advancing brigades had not, however, been seriously damaged by artillery fire, mainly because they had not been registered. There was undue delay in assembling the 24th Brigade, and the 21st Brigade, which had also moved forward from reserve near Pont du Hem to the Moated Grange, had been halted awaiting the advance of the 24th, which by 3.55 p.m. had been ready to move. Yet more delay ensued finding out if the 21st was ready, and it was not until 5.30 p.m. that the advance finally got under way. By then it was almost dark, and although an advance of several hundred yards was achieved, both brigades came to a standstill after coming under machine-gun fire. The advance of the Indian Corps in the Port Arthur salient suffered from similar delays: the order to advance on the Bois du Biez was late in reaching the Dehra Dun Brigade, and after a further delay of thirty minutes the leading battalions moved along the Edgware Road (thus skirting the enemy still holding out in the salient) and turned south-east towards the Bois du Biez. The wood was reached at about 6.30 p.m. but the advance was enfiladed from the strongpoint at Layes Bridge, causing a hold-up at the northern edge. By this time German reinforcements were entering the wood from the east, and the brigade commander, not wishing to commit his troops to a confused action at night, particularly as the advance of the 7th and 8th Divisions had been halted, decided to withdraw behind the Layes Brook.

Thus ended the first day of the battle – a day of mixed fortunes, with the early successes virtually cancelled out by the delays in maintaining the momentum of the attack. The salient round the village now ceased to exist, but the Aubers Ridge, the prime objective, was still out of reach. From the Germans' point of view the attack had been a serious set-back: nearly all the front line troops had been killed or taken prisoner. When news of the loss of the village reached

German VII Corps headquarters, orders were given for its recapture, but this was out of the question in view of the heavy casualties suffered. Nevertheless, the delay of nearly five hours in the resumption of the British attack had been invaluable in allowing the meagre reinforcements available to strengthen a rudimentary second line trench system to the east of the village. This, together with some scattered strongpoints further east, was all that barred the way to the Ridge itself.

During the day intelligence reached Haig of the movement of German reinforcements, but he was not unduly concerned, believing them to be insignificant in scale. Although this was correct in respect of the immediate area, it failed to take into account reinforcements arriving by train further east under cover of darkness, and he gave orders for the offensive to be resumed at 7 a.m. the following day. The 7th and 8th Divisions were to advance to the Ridge and, on their right, the Indian Corps was to advance through the Bois du Biez. Fifteen minutes before zero hour the artillery was ordered to shell strongpoints around Mauquissart and the Layes Bridge, and then lift to the road that ran from Piètre to Bois du Biez. Meanwhile heavy artillery was to bombard enemy batteries on the Ridge itself.

The artillery bombardment began at 6.45 a.m., but unfortunately the strengthening of the enemy's second line had not been observed and therefore not included in the bombardment. In consequence the morning attacks were doomed to failure, a further contributory factor being a three-hour German bombardment on the whole of the British front. A renewed attempt was made in the afternoon, but the attacks were bedevilled by delays in communication caused by the destruction of telephone lines in the morning's bombardment. The three brigades of the 7th Division were ordered to advance along the Mauquissart road, but the leading brigade (the 21st) came under heavy machine-gun fire and could not make progress. The 8th Division fared little better, confirming doubts expressed earlier to Rawlinson by its commander. Rawlinson, however, was insistent that the Mauquissart–Piètre crossroads must be taken, and the assaulting brigade (the 24th) suffered heavily, with only the doubtful bonus of the capture of some farm buildings on the Mauquissart road. At 2.50 p.m. the 25th Brigade was ordered to attack the Layes Bridge strongpoint in conjunction with the Dehra Dun Brigade, but the latter received orders to attack only five minutes before the zero hour of 2.15 p.m. and on finding that the 25th Brigade knew nothing of an attack at that particular time it was called off. So the day ended with further British casualties and no material gains whatsoever.

Haig ordered that the offensive be renewed at 10.30 a.m. the following day, but during the night the Germans had reinforced their new line with six battalions. At 4.30 a.m. they opened up a bombardment on British positions, the front line escaping serious damage, but there were severe casualties in the rear areas. Then, at 5 a.m., some 16,000 German infantry attacked along the British front from the Moated Grange to Port Arthur, but they were repulsed with significant losses. Despite the counter-attack, Haig's orders remained unchanged, but an opportunity was lost to capitalize on the situation by not following up on the retreating enemy (although the extent of German losses was not then realized). Misty weather, however, made artillery registration difficult and the attack was postponed for two hours, and although conditions were little better by then the artillery bombardment began at noon. The main strongpoint in the German defences, the Layes Bridge, was not affected by the bombardment, and the advance of the 25th Brigade (the only brigade to take any active part in the action on the day) was repulsed with heavy losses. Unfortunately the orders for the postponement of the 10.30 a.m. attack had not reached the leading brigade (the 20th) of the 7th Division, and in consequence it suffered serious losses from machine-gun fire from the Quadrilateral (north-west of Mauquissart). Although the attack was eventually called off, companies of the Scots Guards and the Border Regiment were stranded in the open:

> On the far side of a ploughed field is a shallow depression in the ground. Here, the only available cover, are disposed a number of troops of various companies and regiments. Immediately in front, not under a hundred and fifty yards away, is a group of buildings surmounted by a tall, red-brick chimney – a landmark in all that countryside known as the Moulin du Piètre. . . It fairly bristles with rifles and machine guns. The hail of bullets above our heads increases. We flatten our faces in the muddy ground and lie there for three solid hours under a hell fire that seems to come from every side but one. Shrapnel bursts as regularly as clockwork within twenty or thirty yards and scatters earth over one every time.[3]

The sole success of the day came when the artillery shelled the Quadrilateral with great accuracy, and two companies stormed the position and took several hundred prisoners. After this success, however, came confusion. Reports filtering back to the 7th Division tended to give the impression that the Mauquissart road was now occupied by British infantry, and based on this false information the 21st Brigade was ordered to advance on the Rue d'Enfer, and thence to the villages of Aubers and Le Pluich. The enemy, however, was still entrenched on the northern side of the Mauquissart–Champigny road and in front of Mauquissart itself. The attack came to nothing, although the divisional headquarters were not aware of the true position until the evening. The Indian Corps made a little progress, and some battalions succeeded in reaching the Layes Brook, but fire from the Layes Bridge redoubt caused severe casualties. As the 25th Brigade of the 8th Division had also been halted by fire from the redoubt, no further advance could be made.

The misleading reports of the capture of the Mauquissart road were passed back to First Army headquarters, and Haig, believing that this serious obstacle to progress towards the Ridge had been removed, instructed Rawlinson and Willcocks shortly after 3 p.m. 'to push through the barrage of fire regardless of loss using reserves if required'. Such was the optimism now felt at his headquarters that Haig asked French to release the 2nd Cavalry Division in order to exploit the supposed breakthrough. By the time Haig's orders for the attack reached the infantry it was already dark, but they were ordered to undertake an impossible task. The ground to be covered had not been reconnoitred and units lost their way and became mixed up; moreover, the men were dead-beat after the fighting of the previous days. Postponement followed postponement in an attempt to sort out the confusion. Meanwhile, as chillingly described in the Official History, the men were

> ... exhausted after three days and nights continuously under fire, had fallen asleep, and could only be aroused by the use of force, a process made very lengthy by the fact that this part of the battlefield was covered in British and German dead, who, in the dark, were indistinguishable from the sleepers.

The only attack to be made was by the 25th Brigade north of the village, but this was repulsed as soon as the men left their trenches.

In the darkness and confusion of the night of 12 March, the battle effectively came to an end. Haig proposed to French that a further attack should be postponed for a week, but owing to the shortage of artillery ammunition French wired to Kitchener on 13 March:

> Cessation of forward movement is necessitated today by fatigue of the troops, and, above all, by want of ammunition. The First Army is consolidating and strengthening its new line. Further plans are being matured for a vigorous offensive.

The cost of the battle was almost 13,000 British casualties and about the same for the Germans when nearly 1,700 prisoners are taken into account; as one historian summed up, 'the reward to the victor was a slice of ground no larger than a moderate farm', although in French's official dispatch it was more optimistically referred to as 'the defeat of the enemy and the capture of his position'.

Why had the attack failed to reach its ultimate objective when in the first few days it had held high promise of success, not only for the British whose first major offensive it was, but for all future offensives against entrenched positions? French blamed Rawlinson for not throwing in his reserves at the vital moment, and criticized him for being too cautious. (French's judgement has a certain irony when his own handling of reserves at the Battle of Loos is considered later.) Rawlinson, in turn, blamed the 8th Division's commander (Major-General F. J.

Davies) for failing to advance immediately after the capture of the village, but Rawlinson afterwards withdrew the criticism and admitted responsibility for the delay. His thoughts on the battle were contained in a letter written a fortnight after it had ended:

> The experience of Neuve Chapelle has taught us all a great deal, and I hope that [when] next time we have enough ammunition to undertake a similar enterprise we shall remember what experience has taught us. The losses are the feature most to be deplored . . . These losses might have all been avoided if we had been content with the capture of the village itself, instead of persisting in pressing on in order to get the cavalry through . . . What we want to do now is what I call 'bite and hold'. Bite off a piece of the enemy's line, like Neuve Chapelle, and hold it against counter-attack.[4]

Rawlinson remained constant to his 'bite and hold' doctrine in later battles, but this ran counter to Haig's philosophy of rapid exploitation once a breach had been achieved. This fundamental difference in approach was not to be a happy augury for the future when Haig would be the Commander-in-Chief and Rawlinson an army commander. It was to be further complicated by the fact that Rawlinson felt obligated to Haig after the Davies affair. Haig had defended him against French's displeasure and was instrumental in saving him from being removed.

An analysis of why the attack failed must start with the late embarkation of the 6-inch howitzers from England and, in consequence, their inability to register on targets fronting the 23rd Brigade. This unfortunate delay, combined with the failure of field artillery to destroy the wire entanglements, not only caused grievous casualties to the Middlesex and the Scottish Rifles; it also meant that the advance in this sector came to a standstill instead of resulting in the establishment of a new front along the Armentières road and the clearance of the Orchard. This was a serious check to Rawlinson's plans because, until the Orchard had been captured, he did not believe that an advance was feasible from the Moated Grange. As a result, despite pleas from its commander to push on because of the lack of opposition on his front, the 7th Division remained inactive. There is little doubt that there was hesitation by Rawlinson and Willcocks in putting in their reserves, but this stemmed mainly from the principal problem – that of communication. Information was slow (and occasionally inaccurate) in coming from the forward troops to brigade and divisional headquarters (and vice versa) owing to the destruction of telephone lines by enemy artillery; vital messages had often to be entrusted to runners, many of whom became casualties on their hazardous journeys. It also meant the late registration on, or neglect of, new targets by the artillery. It is hardly surprising, therefore, that information could be hours old, or overtaken by events, by the time it reached army headquarters. The effect of poor communication allowed the enemy several hours in which to bring up reinforcements and establish new entrenchments, and was a significant cause of denying to the British what would otherwise have been a famous victory. As it was, the Germans were seriously concerned about the loss of the village, and realized that the BEF was now a force with which to be reckoned: the front at Neuve Chapelle had been deliberately kept at low strength in the belief that the BEF's role would be purely defensive. Whilst on the one hand the British were encouraged by the initial success of the attack, believing that the lessons learned would materially assist in another offensive, the Germans were not slow in drawing their own conclusions from the battle. These would bring about a bloody rebuff to the British two months later.

*   *   *

On 9 May, at 5.40 p.m., after a bombardment of forty minutes, Haig's First Army was launched again at Aubers Ridge, but this time the Germans were prepared. The defending garrison had been increased from two to three divisions and the front line breastworks strengthened to the extent that only the heaviest calibre shell could make any impression: it was this ammunition that the British lacked in quantity. Moreover, wire entanglements had been broadened and deepened and armoured machine-gun emplacements placed at twenty-yard intervals and at strongpoints positioned in salients in order to enfilade attackers. The result was a disaster: the artillery bombardment (mostly shrapnel) had little effect on the breastworks, the wire was insufficiently cut and the first assault failed with heavy losses. Subsequent attacks met the same result, and at 6 p.m. Haig decided to break off the battle. British casualties in just one day amounted to 11,600, and although German casualties were not revealed they could not have been anything like as severe.

Under pressure from Joffre, yet another attempt was made six days later at Festubert, a village to the south of Neuve Chapelle. Haig had come to the conclusion that a long and methodical bombardment was now necessary owing to the strength of the enemy's defences and the massing of machine guns, setting a pattern that, with one exception, was to be adopted for all future offensives. Because the assault was postponed for twenty-four hours, the bombardment was prolonged to sixty hours and proved to be far more effective than in the previous assault. The battle lasted from 16 to 27 May and achieved some measure of success, the Germans evacuating their front line and committing all their available reserves. Given more artillery ammunition, particularly high explosive to silence machine guns, it is possible that the attack – carried out to assist the French in their operations further south – could have been exploited. But the British suffered nearly 17,000 casualties, the enemy certainly many fewer.

Taking the three battles in the Neuve Chapelle area together, it can be seen that the first of these against the village itself encouraged the British commanders to believe that the hurricane bombardment, followed by a resolute attack (with reserves strategically positioned), was the solution to overcoming the enemy defences. They, however, neglected to take into account that the Germans had learned their lessons too, and the second against Aubers Ridge was a dismal failure: the bombardment made little impression on the strengthened defences and, ominously, the British infantry experienced, for the first time, the dreadful impact of fire from massed machine guns in armoured entrenchments. The third, at Festubert, proved to more successful, the long and systematic bombardment appearing to be the answer to strong defences, but a shortage of artillery ammunition brought the attack to an end. Nevertheless, the British, when viewing the varying fortunes of the three battles in perspective, saw the dawning of the belief that the key to breaking through strongly entrenched positions was, given sufficient resources (particularly in heavy artillery), within their grasp. But it was to prove to be a false dawn. The capture of Neuve Chapelle was achieved by surprise, but the massive and time-consuming infrastructure needed to support future offensives, coupled with long and heavy preliminary bombardments, would give ample notice of an impending attack to the enemy, enabling him to construct several lines of defence beyond the area of bombardment. Apart from two notable exceptions, surprise was not again to be a weapon in the British armoury.

Notes to Chapter 2

1. Baynes, John, *Morale: A Study of Men and Courage*, Cassell (London, 1967)
2. Andrews, W. L., *Haunting Years: The Commentaries of a War Territorial*, Hutchinson (London, 1930)
3. Ewart, Wilfred, *When Armageddon Came*, Rich & Cowan (London, 1933)
4. Maurice, Major-General Sir Frederick, *The Life of General Lord Rawlinson of Trent*, Cassell (London, 1928)

3

Loos

THE EVENTS leading up to the Battle of Loos in September 1915 were marred by serious disagreements between the French and the British. Joffre was still intent upon his grand design for reducing the great German salient between Arras and Reims. The French attack on Vimy Ridge near Arras in May had, after a six-day artillery bombardment, been a tactical success, and although their reserves were too far back to exploit the gains, the French, like the British, believed that they had found the key to the break-through. Experience had shown that a lengthy bombardment could destroy the enemy's front line and that an attack on a wide front could avoid enemy artillery enfilading the flanks of the attacking infantry – one of the reasons for failure when the front attacked had been too narrow.

For the next offensive Joffre proposed a two-prong attack, the French northwards from Champagne and a Franco-British assault eastwards in Artois – in effect, a gigantic pinch. Sir John agreed in principle to an attack north of Lens, in co-operation with the French Tenth Army, between the La Bassée canal and Grenay, but Haig, whose First Army was again to be involved, reported to Sir John on 23 June that the area chosen by Joffre was not suitable for an attack: the ground was flat and bare of cover, and could be dominated by enemy machine-gun fire from strong defensive positions. Indeed, Haig went further and ex-pressed his opinion that the shortage of artillery ammunition precluded any plans for an offensive. (According to the Official History, gun ammunition was only half of establishment, with a particularly serious shortage for 6-inch howitzers at only 15 per cent.)

Shortly before Haig gave his views, a conference of French and British Munition Ministers had taken place in Boulogne on 19 and 20 June with Lloyd George, the British Minister, presiding. One of the significant conclusions drawn was that without heavy artillery there was little hope of destroying the enemy's strengthened defences, and as the supply of ammunition was inadequate the British could see no real improvement until some time in 1916. These factors, coupled with the knowledge that it would not be before the spring of that year that the British Army's strength would be adequate to undertake operations on the scale now thought to be necessary, persuaded the British commanders that the Army could not mount an offensive on the Western Front before then. Joffre was not deterred, however, by these arguments, and one suspects that there must have been a degree of irritation felt by the French General Staff at this display of British caution. It was their country that had been invaded and partially occupied, and Joffre's plan might bring victory before the winter, especially as the French Army was now at its peak in numbers and some 40 per cent of the German Army was preoccupied on the Eastern Front and standing on defence in the west. Joffre's fear (not, however, to be realized until 1917) was that the Russians would collapse, thus releasing a formidable addition to German forces in the west.

In the face of Joffre's determination, Sir John offered a compromise which, in effect, meant that the attack would be as originally proposed, but he wanted the French 10th Army to deal with the problem of enemy artillery around Lens. As a result, planning went ahead for the offensive, now postponed until August. In the meantime the enemy had not been idle. Whilst Sir John and Joffre were bickering over the plans, the Germans had been feverishly constructing a second line of defence some three or four miles behind their front line. The second line was as strong as, and in places stronger than, the front line, protected by fearsome barbed wire entanglements out of range of wire-cutting artillery. This secondary line ran virtually the length of the Western Front. Knowledge of this caused Sir John to waver once again. At a meeting with General Foch (commanding French armies in the north) on 27 July, he suggested, as an alternative, attacks against Aubers Ridge and Messines, but both Foch and Joffre were opposed to this and an impasse had now been reached.

Other events then intruded to force a decision. The news from the Eastern Front was grim: the Russians had evacuated Galicia and Poland in the face of the massive German assaults begun in July, and there was a real fear that she might sue for peace. Kitchener visited France in late August, and after meeting Joffre it appears that he came to the conclusion that the joint offensive should take place. It was a reluctant decision, but the need to take some offensive action in the face of a possible Russian collapse seemed to him to be paramount. Afterwards, in conversation with Sir John, he expressed the view that 'we must act with all energy and do our utmost to help France in their offensive, even though by so doing we may suffer heavy losses.' Kitchener reported accordingly to the British Cabinet, which also came to the conclusion that there was no other option, and Sir John was told by Kitchener on 21 August 'to take the offensive and act vigorously'. The Official History summed up the situation:

> Under pressure from the Lord Kitchener at home, due to the general position of the Allies, and from Generals Joffre and Foch in France, due to the local situation in France, the British Commander-in-Chief was therefore compelled to undertake operations before he was ready, over ground that was most unfavourable, against

the better judgment of himself and General Haig, and . . . with no more than a quarter of the troops, nine divisions instead of thirty-six, that he considered necessary for a successful attack.[1]

During August the six divisions earmarked for the initial assault had been secretly assembling in the area, although Haig still held the view that the heavy artillery available was only sufficient for an attack by two divisions. He proposed, therefore, that the attacks should initially be limited to the village of Loos itself and the Hohenzollern Redoubt and then intensified according to the degree of success achieved. This implied that a two-division assault would only have a narrow front, and he proposed to mislead the enemy by using smoke in the hope that this would conceal the width of the attack and limit the consequences of enemy artillery enfilading his flanks – always provided, of course, that the wind direction was favourable. As these proposals were being made, however, an event occurred that appeared to offer a possible solution. The Germans had used poison gas at Ypres in April 1915, causing heavy casualties and a loss of ground, but had failed to exploit the position. As a result, the production of chlorine gas commenced in England, and at trials in France in August Haig was so impressed that he changed his mind about confining the assault to two divisions in the belief that the discharge of a sufficient quantity of gas would make up for the lack of heavy artillery. He was now persuaded that an attack on a wider front – as in the original plan – was possible.

Although Haig was optimistic about the impact gas would have on the enemy, he was cautious enough to propose that without a favourable wind the attack should not take place, but this was not acceptable to GHQ and he was forced to put forward an alternative. Should the wind be unfavourable, he proposed to revert to the two-division attack, but if favourable the following day then the wider attack would be made or, failing that, then on the day after – or not at all. The proposal, which, on the face of it, seemed sensible, was approved by GHQ. A week before the date of the offensive, fixed for Saturday 25 September, over 5,000 chlorine gas cylinders were distributed among the attacking divisions of I and IV Corps and placed in bays in the front line trenches:

On September 18th the first gas cylinders were carried into the front trench. It was our first sight of these horrid objects, though dark rumours and trial trips had prepared us for the shock, and we handled them with a certain holy dread. They were extraordinarily awkward things to carry up a long and narrow communication trench. Slung horizontally on a pole, they stuck at a sharp corner, and they were abominably heavy. They eventually became by familiarity most unpopular with the troops. On this and the following nights, however, they were safely stored and packed with sandbags in their appointed bays, and the garrison were left to trust that the skill of the experts, and the unwariness of the enemy, would keep the secret safe until the day.[2]

Loos was a coal mining area, and in the autumn of 1915 it presented a forbidding and melancholy landscape dotted with fosses or *puits*, towering *crassiers* and scattered groups of miners' cottages. All these structures had been skilfully converted by the Germans into defensive aids: the gaunt pylons of the fosses made excellent observation posts, the *crassiers* had been tunnelled to form nests for machine guns and the cellars of the cottages had been strengthened to give reasonable protection against shell-fire. Moreover, the Germans had constructed a massive entrenchment protruding some 500 yards into No Man's Land: known as the Hohenzollern Redoubt, this was about 300 yards long and consituted a formidable obstacle. Notwithstanding all these defensive advantages, however, the German position was not strongly held – no more than about 11,000 men against an attacking force of some 75,000.

Haig's plan for his First Army was to break through the enemy's front line between the La Bassée canal and Grenay, and then press on eastwards to the Haute Deule canal (connecting Lens with Douai). This entailed an advance by the infantry of about five miles, but plans for the Cavalry Corps were much more ambitious. After the crossings over the Haute Deule canal had been secured, they were to pursue the retreating enemy and then seize the crossings over the Scheldt between Conde and Tournai – a distance from the British front line of over thirty miles. Meanwhile, on the British right flank, the French 10th Army would advance, as would, further to the north, the British Second Army if its diversionary attacks north of the La Bassée canal brought about the enemy's retirement.

In a letter to Sir John French in July, Joffre had expressed the view that 'your attack will find particularly favourable ground between Loos and La Bassée'. He did not reveal why he considered it to be favourable, and the only conclusion that can be drawn is that it was chosen because the southern edge formed the boundary between the British First Army and the French 10th Army. (A similar conjunction was to be the *raison d'être* for the Somme battle in 1916.) From the La Bassée canal to Grenay, the front was just over six miles long, with the mining areas concentrated to the north and south. In between, on a front of about four miles, lay an extensive stretch of open ground described thus by Lieutenant-General Sir Henry Rawlinson, commanding IV Corps:

> My new front is as flat as the palm of my hand. Hardly any cover anywhere. The lines in many places three hundred yards apart. Easy enough to hold defensively, but very difficult for attack ... D. H. [Haig] tells me that we are to attack 'au fond', that the French are doing likewise and making a supreme effort. It will cost us dearly, and we shall not get very far.[3]

The preliminary bombardment commenced in the morning of 21 September, heavy artillery ranged on strongpoints and battery positions and field artillery concentrated on wire entanglements. Although 47 heavy and 894 field guns were employed, these by no means constituted an overwhelming force. The shortage of ammunition meant a daily average of one round every sixteen minutes for a heavy gun and one every ten minutes for a field gun. This was a derisory figure compared with later battles, but, as mentioned earlier, the effective use of gas would, it was hoped, provide the balance. To quote the Official History,

> Owing to the wide area over which the bombardment was spread, the work was, in fact, only partially accomplished. There were neither enough guns nor ammunition to provide a volume of fire sufficient to destroy effectively either the villages, the strong points, the trenches or the wire entanglements. Reports from artillery and infantry observers showed that practicable passages had been made through the wire at intervals along the front, but that in several places the wire was still thick and not yet passable. This was partly due to the fact that in places the entanglement was on a reverse slope and therefore difficult or impossible to see from British observation posts, and partly due to the fact that many of the batteries had only recently arrived from the United Kingdom, and were not adequately trained for wire cutting, a process for which the greatest accuracy is essential.[4]

As will be seen, the failure to cut the wire effectively was seriously to impede the momentum of the advance.

Weather can play an important part in battles. Excessive temperatures, hot or cold, and rain or snow have an impact sometimes so adverse as to affect the outcome, but the anxiety at First Army HQ on the eve of the offensive about wind direction must be unique in conventional land battles. Meteorological advice at various times during the day had been both pessimistic and optimistic, but at 9 a.m. Haig was told that the twenty-four hour forecast from midnight was 'Wind southerly, changing to south-west or west, probably increasing to twenty miles per hour'. This, at least, was in the right direction, and upon this advice Haig made his fateful decision to launch the offensive the following morning and the assaulting divisions moved into position. Meanwhile the three reserve divisions (Guards, 21st and 24th Divisions – both New Army – making up XI Corps and under the control of GHQ) moved up to within five or six miles of the front. With meteorological advice, zero hour for the discharge of gas was fixed for 5.50 a.m., with the infantry to attack forty minutes later, but at 5 a.m. the wind, which had been somewhat fitful during the night, fell to a virtual calm.

> At 5 he [Haig] came to our office with Fletcher. There was quite a faint breath of wind then, and Fletcher's cigarette smoke moved quite perceptibly towards the Germans. But it died away again in a few minutes, and a little later D. H. sent down a message from the tower to 1st Corps to enquire whether the attack could still be held up.
>   Gough [Lieutenant-General Sir Hubert Gough, Corps Commander] replied that it was too late to change. I was with D. H. when the reply was brought in. He was very upset.[5]

Haig was now in an acute dilemma. The release of gas in the prevailing wind might simply mean that it would hang about in his own trenches, thus rendering the wider attack extremely perilous, but, on the other hand, if the attack were limited to two divisions, then this would mean that his front and communication trenches would be crammed with the non-attacking four divisions and prey to enemy bombardment. Ten minutes before the gas was to be released, however, the wind freshened from the south-west, and at 5.50 a.m., simultaneously with a heavy artillery bombardment, the gas was discharged, although, as will be seen later, not without serious difficulties. The initial objectives for I Corps were Fosse 8, Cité St Elie, Puits 13 and the northern part of Hulluch; and for IV Corps the Double Crassier south-west of Loos village, the village itself, Hill 70, Cité St Auguste (a suburb of Lens) and the southern part of Hulluch. At 6.30 a.m. (or a little later in some sectors owing to problems with the release of gas) the leading brigades of the six divisions left their trenches in the first large-scale offensive launched by the British on the Western Front since the outbreak of the war.

The road from Vermelles to Hulluch bisected the battlefield: IV Corps took the southern half and I Corps the northern. Commencing with the former, that is, on the right of the British line, the three divisions involved were the 1st, 15th (Scottish) and 47th (London), in all comprising an attacking force of thirty-eight battalions against a defending force of a mere six. Initially the assault of the 47th and 15th Divisions probably achieved the most significant success of the entire battle, all the more noteworthy because the 47th was a Territorial division formed of London battalions with such homely names as the Post Office Rifles and the Civil Service Rifles and the 15th a New Army division formed entirely of Scottish battalions.

Forty minutes' worth of gas and smoke had been released, and although some problems were experienced with gas on the left of the 15th Division, the two divisions climbed out of their trenches at zero hour, one battalion of the 47th kicking a football ahead of them:

On the 47th Division front the gas went fairly well. The cloud rolled slowly forward, and its effect was apparent from the lessening force of the enemy rifle fire . . . Forty minutes after zero the infantry attack began. On the right a gallant army of dummy figures, worked with string by the 21st and 22nd Battalions, made progressive appearances in the smoke-cloud, and did their duty in attracting a fair share of fire. The real attack started opposite the Double Crassier, and northwards of this point line after line of men left their trenches. In outward appearance they were hardly more human than the dummies farther south – strange figures, hung about with sandbags and bandoliers of ammunition, with no caps, but smoke-helmets on their heads rolled into a sort of turban, with the mouth-piece nodding by way of ornament over their foreheads. Each line went forward at quick time down into the valley and was lost in the smoke.[6]

By 9.30 a.m. the 47th had achieved its objectives of the Double Crassier and the Loos Crassier and established a defensive flank against the possibility of a threat from Lens, although at a cost of 1,200 casualties.

The objectives of the 15th Division on the 47th's left involved an advance of about four miles. After capturing Loos village, it had to press on to Hill 70, establish a defensive position and then continue eastwards to Cité St Auguste and beyond to Loisin and Annay (north-eastern suburbs of Lens). The two attacking brigades were the 44th and 46th (the third brigade, the 45th, was in support). The 44th, on the right of the advance, swarmed forward to overwhelm the frontal defences of Loos and by 8 a.m. the entire village had been captured. Further north, the 46th had problems with gas hanging about in its own trenches, but the men were rallied by a piper (subsequently awarded the Victoria Cross) and, advancing against strong opposition, overcame the enemy defences in their path:

> It was magnificent. I could not have imagined that troops with a bare twelve months' training behind them could have accomplished it . . . Once in No Man's Land they took up their dressing and walked – yes, coolly walked – across to the enemy trenches . . . I saw one man whose kilt had got caught in our wire as he passed through a gap; he did not attempt to tear it off, but, carefully disentangling it, doubled up to his correct position and went on.[7]

The preliminary bombardment had been successful in destroying the wire in this sector of the front, and it had also had a devastating effect on the enemy, as evidenced by a letter dated 25 September found on a dead German:

> I cannot describe the reality. No one could believe what we endure. In a few hours my company lost 35, of whom 25 were killed . . . We get nothing to drink or eat. Further back the English fire is more terrible still . . . The great shells fall like drops of water.[8]

Eventually both brigades were joined ready for the assault on Hill 70, but the battalions had become mixed up during the severe fighting on the way to the hill and had lost many officers. It was at this point that the attack began to go awry. The ascent of the hill was begun in a somewhat disorderly fashion, giving 'the appearance of a bank holiday crowd', and on reaching the summit the Scottish attacking spirit was fired by the sight of the enemy retreating towards Cité St Laurent. There then began a fatal drift of the attack from the east to the south, compounded by two errors. First, it was thought that the enemy was retreating due east to Cité St Auguste (the division's objective), and second, it was believed that the 47th Division was advancing on his right flank. It was an unhappy coincidence that, viewed from the summit of Hill 70, both Cités looked remarkably similar, but the 47th Division had halted after reaching the Double Crassier and the Loos Crassier, and this had not been made clear in the brigade and battalion orders of the Scottish division. Thus there was no advancing flank, and the Scots were lured inexorably into a trap of their own making. The remaining officers had managed to retain a few hundred men on the crest of the hill, but the bulk of the attacking force (not far short of a thousand men) streamed impetuously down the hill into a re-entrant in the enemy lines between the two Cités, where they met a cross-fire so heavy that, unable to go forward or back, they were forced to scratch what meagre cover they could find in open ground. The wire before the German trenches was uncut (not forming part of the artillery bombardment), and the Germans, believing that the attack was directed at Lens, rushed up reinforcements. Although those remaining on the hill sent messages appealing for artillery support, the situation was so confused that the Corps Commander ordered a bombardment on Cité St Auguste in the belief that the eastwards advance was held up. By the time the true position was known, the enemy, now strongly reinforced and emboldened by the sight of the Scots caught in the open, sprang from their trenches and surged forward to recapture the redoubt on Hill 70. The remnants of the attacking force retained a precarious foothold on the hill, but the attack that had begun so auspiciously had foundered on misunderstandings.

The remaining division of IV Corps, the 1st, had its frontage from the junction with the 15th Division to the Vermelles–Hulluch road, a distance of about 1,400 yards. The two leading brigades had divergent roles, the 1st to advance due east to the southern part of Hulluch village and the 2nd to advance south-eastwards with the ultimate intention of joining up with the 15th Division at Bois Hugo, north-west of Cité St Auguste. The gap in the middle was to be filled by a detachment of two battalions (one from each brigade), known as Green's Force after its commander, Lieutenant-Colonel E. W. B. Green. This detachment, on reaching the Lens–La Bassée road, was to close the gap, and the reserve brigade, the 3rd, would then support a general advance due east to the Haute Deule canal. The attack was slightly delayed because of problems with gas: although troops were issued with gas helmets made of army-shirt cloth with mica eye-pieces, these were extremely uncomfortable to wear, the eye-pieces soon misted up and any exertion, or prolonged use, tended to give a feeling of suffocation.

The 1st Brigade's assault was largely successful, notwithstanding intense fire from trenches around the copses of La Haie and Bois Carré, although a battalion of the Gloucestershire Regiment was almost annihilated during its spirited attack over open ground. Shortly after 9 a.m. the 1st Brigade halted before the northern outskirts of Hulluch and awaited the arrival of Green's Force and the left of the 2nd Brigade before mounting an attack on the village. It was, however, to be a long wait.

The 2nd Brigade's line of advance was in the direction of Lone Tree (the remains of a solitary cherry tree) and the Northern Sap. Immediately it met heavy fire from trenches undamaged by the preliminary bombardment, and in spite of gallant attempts to cut the wire by hand the attack failed and the men had to seek whatever cover they could find in the open ground. A second assault also failed, although for a time it was believed that it had succeeded and, as a result, Green's Force and the 3rd Brigade were ordered forward. The stubborn resistance of the enemy in the Lone Tree area, however, was now beginning to be a serious obstacle and, ultimately, one of the reasons why the battle ended in failure. It was belatedly realized that the position was too strong to be taken by a frontal assault, and another way round was needed. By chance, the 3rd Brigade found the answer. The 2nd Welch, advancing virtually unopposed north of La Haie copse, arrived just short of the Lens–La Bassée road, and in endeavouring to contact the 1st Brigade came behind the enemy trenches holding up the 2nd Brigade (now joined by Green's Force). The gallant defence of the German regiment holding the position was finally ended by its surrender to Green's Force, and by early evening the remnants of the division assembled along the Lens–La Bassée road. It was not realized, however, that the 2nd Brigade and Green's Force, freed at last from the enemy position that had caused so many casualties, had advanced to Bois Hugo, their objective. The other two brigades, believing their right flank to be exposed, partially withdrew from the road, thus exposing a gap of nearly a mile between them and the force in Bois Hugo.

I Corps consisted of the 2nd, 7th and 9th (Scottish) Divisions and held the front from the Vermelles–Hulluch road to the La Bassée canal. After penetrating the German defences facing them, these divisions were to continue eastwards until they reached the Haute Deule canal, an advance of about four miles. On the right of I Corps, the 7th Division's front extended from the Vermelles–Hulluch road to just south of the Hohenzollern Redoubt. The defences facing the 20th Brigade, one of the two involved in the initial assault, although not held in strength, were particularly resistant and had been little damaged by the bombardment. Despite this, some gaps in the wire were found and the defenders surrendered, although the two attacking battalions suffered severely. Nevertheless the survivors pushed on to reach the Lens–La Bassée road, where, after deciding that the Hulluch defences were too strong, they halted, awaiting the arrival of the 22nd Brigade. This brigade, also making the initial assault, had met thick belts of wire (mostly uncut) and suffered severe casualties but eventually reached the Quarries, some 500 yards west of the outskirts of Cité St Auguste, but they were too depleted in numbers to go further. The remaining brigade, the 21st, ordered up to assist the others, could do little more than help consolidate the positions reached. Thus the division's attack was brought to a standstill.

The immediate objectives of the 9th Division were the Dump (the waste from Fosse 8, and strongly fortified) and the Hohenzollern Redoubt. After their

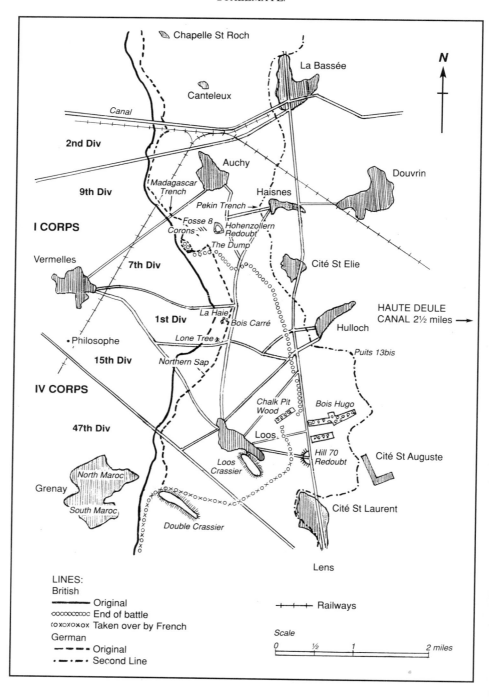

Battle of Loos, September 1915

capture the division was to press on eastwards to the Haute Deule canal. Although initially suffering from the effects of gas and smoke, the 26th Brigade overran the Redoubt, where, during the preliminary bombardment, fire from 9.2-inch howitzers had been most effective in cutting the wire, and within an hour had reached Corons Trench, a few yards east of Fosse 8, where it was ordered to halt.

The 28th Brigade, attacking on the left of the 26th, was seriously affected by gas and, to add to its problems, the enemy positions surrounding Madagascar Trench had not been seriously damaged by the bombardment. The leading battalions could make no headway against strong wire entanglements, and the attacking waves, bunching before the wire, suffered terribly from machine-gun fire in enfilade. The two supporting battalions were thrown in, but they too suffered grievous losses. A bombardment was ordered on the enemy positions, but this was of little avail, and a further attempt made by the remnants of the brigade was repulsed. The failure of the 28th Brigade meant that the 26th advanced on its own towards Haisnes, its next objective being the Pekin Trench. From here it could be seen that the village could, apparently, be taken without difficulty, but the decision was made to await reinforcements. The 27th Brigade, in support, was ordered forward, and although some parties of men managed to reach the Pekin Trench, no attempt was made to send further reinforcements because of extensive enemy shelling of the intervening open ground. The situation of the men in Pekin Trench was now perilous: both their flanks were in the air, and the enemy took advantage of this by bombing their way along the trenches to the north and south of the position. By nightfall the trench had been abandoned and the remnants of the two brigades withdrawn to the Fosse 8 area, now the division's advanced position.

The attack by the remaining division, the 2nd, was a complete failure. Although the objective of its three brigades was limited to providing a defensive flank to the divisions attacking further south, their assaults on strong enemy positions were in vain. South of the La Bassée canal, the attack of the 19th Brigade, with the objectives of the village of Auchy and the railway from Haisnes to the canal, was seriously hampered by gas and smoke drifting into the jumping-off trenches. Advancing without any smoke cover, the men met a merciless fire from the enemy strongly entrenched behind their front line. Further attacks proved fruitless, and the operation was broken off. The 6th Brigade fared little better. Situated immediately south of the La Bassée canal with the same objective as the 19th Brigade, it suffered even more severely from gas and the leading companies met such heavy fire from defences protected by uncut wire that no further attacks were made. The 5th Brigade, attacking north of the canal with the objectives of Canteleux and Chapelle St Roth, was also affected by gas, and a probing attack by the left of the brigade found the enemy defences to be too strong.

By nightfall on the first day of the battle the situation was that only the 2nd Division had failed to penetrate the enemy's first line. Further south the line had been broken, with the Hohenzollern Redoubt, Fosse 8 and Loos village and its *crassier* in British hands and forward troops poised before Cité St Elie and Hulluch. There were significant gaps, however, in the improvised positions held and casualties had been very severe – well over 15,000. The German second line was still intact, and it was at this time, or even earlier, that there was a pressing need for the reserve divisions. The fact that they were not available was to have far-reaching repercussions not only in terms of the Loos battle but also for the future conduct of the war.

A battlefield is more often than not a place of confusion – the so called fog of war, usually caused by problems in communication. Nonetheless, it is difficult to find an excuse for a breakdown in communication – communication not in the physical sense (although this was to come later) but primarily of understanding – between a commander-in-chief and one of his army commanders, particularly when the latter is fighting a battle. On 7 August GHQ had informed Haig that 'The troops available for the operations will be those of your own Army, plus the Cavalry Corps and two divisions held in general reserve under the orders of the Commander-in-Chief.' French subsequently told Haig that these two divisions would be available when required, and Haig's plan of attack included them as immediate support to the assaulting divisions. Only a week before the battle, however, French changed his mind and told Haig that he intended to keep the whole of the general reserve near Lillers as he considered that Haig's six divisions would be sufficient for the assault. Haig protested that Lillers was too far from the front (the distance was about sixteen miles); French's intention, however, was to hold on to them until he judged the time right to put them in. He had moved them from St Omer to Lillers (entailing a series of night marches totalling over forty miles), but after further pressure from Haig he agreed that the two divisions (the 21st and the 24th) should move to between two and three miles west of Vermelles. They arrived exhausted in the early hours of the day of the battle after a gruelling night march in the rain in appalling traffic conditions. The march was graphically described in the Official History as 'like trying to push the Lord Mayor's procession through the streets of London without clearing the route and holding up the traffic'. So chaotic had been the march up that even then the two divisions were not complete: only the leading brigades were in position, with the rear brigades three miles behind. This meant that, on the day of the battle, the reserves were between five and eight miles from the front and hardly in a condition to be thrown into battle. Even then French had still not released them, and, to add to the confusion, he removed himself and a few staff personnel from St Omer to a château near Lillers where he was only in contact with his headquarters by the civil telephone service but not with his armies. French's obstinacy over the release of the two divisions is explained by the fact that they were New Army and had only recently arrived in France after somewhat inadequate training in England. Thus they had no front line experience, and neither, for the most part, had their officers or staff. He did not want to involve raw divisions in support of the initial attack. However, provided this was successful and a breach obtained, his intention was to use them in pursuit of the retreating enemy, when he considered that they would be less likely to be inhibited than 'trench-bound' troops.

Reports reached Haig shortly after zero hour of a breakthrough of the enemy's first line, and a staff officer had to be sent by car to French to request the release of the divisions. At last, at 9.30 a.m., French agreed to move them up, but by then it was too late. The reports received by Haig led him to believe that the situation was better than it was: he was unaware of the heavy casualties; aerial observation of the battlefield had been severely hampered by smoke and mist; and, after the first optimistic reports, communication had been either inaccurate or non-existent. He knew, however, that the French attack on Vimy Ridge had failed and, in consequence, any advance by his First Army would mean that its right flank would be unsupported. Nevertheless, he considered that the British success should be exploited, if only to encourage the French. Accordingly, he ordered the cavalry forward and the 21st and 24th Divisions to follow behind.

It was not until 11.15 a.m. that the leading brigades of the two divisions began their move up, but once again their progress was severely hampered by roads congested with vehicles and columns of wounded. By the early evening they had still not reached their deployment positions, and the decision was made to limit their advance to the Lens–La Bassée road. There then began a nightmarish march in the dark and the rain over the chaos of the battlefield:

> Presently we found ourselves on the battlefield. The roads were broken up, wounded men and abandoned equipment and broken transport lay all over the place. The shelling was considerable and we had several casualties. Often we had to wait for several minutes while other troops passed us from right to left. At last we were ordered to break up into artillery formation. This meant that we shortly lost touch with other units in the Brigade. Someone said that the Brigadier could not find out what artillery was supporting him. We went on, crossed old trenches, by gaps, and threading our way between shell craters, partly destroyed field-work, and other obstacles. All sense of direction was lost, and I think some platoons wandered about for hours. Some of us found a trench held by British troops and got into it, and stayed until we were relieved. The men still had their packs on, there were no orders to take them off, and we had no idea how near the enemy were, or

in what direction. We had no water, and the cookers were far behind. Where officers were wounded, the men did not know what to do, and walked about.[9]

It was not until early morning that the two reserve divisions were in position for their assault.

In dismal conditions on Sunday morning the attack began, preceded at 9 a.m. by an assault on Hill 70 by the 15th Division which was foiled by heavy enfilade fire from the redoubt on the hill. Two hours later, in spite of this rebuff, the ill-fated 21st and 24th Divisions moved off over open ground, believing that the ordeal of the last few days was behind them and that their role was now to pursue a retreating and disorganized enemy. Instead, they were advancing towards an enemy line which had been substantially reinforced during the night and was protected by strong – and intact – wire entanglements and concrete machine-gun emplacements.

The attack of the 24th Division towards Bois Hugo was forestalled by a German counter-attack from the south-east, and a battalion of the 63rd Brigade retreated after suffering severe casualties which, in turn, caused the other battalions in the brigade to retire. Two battalions of the supporting brigade (the 64th), advancing through the retiring troops, met such intense machine-gun fire that they could make no progress. The 24th Division advanced under heavy enfilade fire from Hulluch on its left and Bois Hugo on its right. Despite heavy losses, some units reached the wire, but it was undamaged and, seeing the 21st Division retiring on their right, they too withdrew to their original trenches. A Brigadier of the 15th Division saw, to his astonishment,

. . . large numbers of British troops of another division streaming down the Loos–Philosophe road toward him. They had neither equipment, rifles, nor gas-helmets, and gave out that the Germans were in Loos, and that they had been told to come back. This, of course, was untrue . . . The new and untried troops – a division which later was to win the highest honours – had never experienced anything of this kind before and moreover were utterly famished and exhausted.[10]

They had had no support from their artillery: owing to the difficulties in bringing it up over the ruined battlefield, the batteries had lost their way and fired from an open position, where they were promptly shelled by enemy batteries.

It could not be foreseen by Haig that the retreat of the two reserve divisions and the failure of the 1st Division to capture Hulluch (begun in confusion, owing to a misunderstanding) signalled the failure of the offensive in the sense that the objective of the Haute Deule canal was now unattainable. Other indications of failure were now beginning to emerge. The French, for example, had not succeeded in capturing Vimy Ridge on the 25th and had made no important progress the following day.

With Sir John's agreement, Haig now decided to send in the Guards Division (the remaining infantry division in GHQ reserve), and he directed that the captured enemy trench line between the Béthune–Lens and Vermelles–Hulluch roads be held at all costs. Apart from the Guards Division, the last remaining reserve was the 3rd Cavalry Division, and this was dismounted and sent in to hold Loos village and relieve the 15th Division. The Guards, in moving up to the front, experienced the same problems on the congested roads as the other reserve divisions, and it was not until late afternoon on the 27th that an attack by the 3rd Guards Brigade on Hill 70 was mounted:

> More came over the crest by platoons in artillery formation, and the intensity of shelling increased. Quite quickly the opposite slope took on the appearance of a gigantic moving chess-board as the platoons approached with intervals between them. The steadiness of their march was impressive, and those who thought that Guardsmen were only ornamental soldiers revised their opinion speedily. So inspiring was the sight that scores of 23rd men [23rd London Regiment] of their own accord clambered out of their trenches, and, under machine-gun fire, pulled aside wire entanglements and threw duckboard bridges over the ditches to facilitate the way for the Guards when it was seen that they had to pass through their lines.[11]

The attack ended in failure, and an attack by the 2nd Guards Brigade on Puits 14*bis*, near Bois Hugo, also failed.

On 28 September Foch agreed to relieve the British in the Loos village sector, and from the beginning of October the First Army, with its reduced frontage, was able to concentrate on the original objective of the Haute Deule canal. In the meantime, however, the enemy, now considerably reinforced, had recaptured Fosse 8, and there was fierce fighting around the Hohenzollern Redoubt. With Joffre's agreement, Foch proposed an Allied attack on 3 October, but this was postponed until the 10th owing to bad weather and the necessity for reliefs. A vigorous counter-offensive by the enemy on the 8th was repulsed, but this further delayed the First Army's attack until the 13th. Nevertheless, the French 10th Army again attacked Vimy Ridge on 10 October, without success, and, apart from providing artillery assistance to the British, the French role in the battle came to an end.

On 13 October the British attacked at noon with the objectives of recovering Fosse 8 and consolidating the line of the Lens–La Bassée road between Chalk Pit and the Vermelles–Hulluch road. After a two-hour bombardment and the release of gas (both largely ineffective), the attack met such heavy artillery and machine-gun fire from a well-prepared and a well-entrenched enemy that the Official History was moved to make the stern comment, 'The fighting on 13/14th October had not improved the general situation in any way and had brought nothing but useless slaughter of infantry . . .' This, for all practical purposes, was the end of the Battle of Loos, and, although Haig had proposed a renewed attack on 7 November, the persistent rains and the disruptive effects of enemy shelling caused him to abandon it.

* * *

It is difficult, if not impossible, to find any justification for the battle, undertaken as it was under pressure from Joffre (and Kitchener) without the resources considered necessary, and at a location which the British considered wholly unsuitable. Notwithstanding these factors, however, some measure of success was achieved in the first few hours, tending to reflect more the courage and perseverance of the attacking divisions than on the architects of the battle. There is no doubt that the enemy had been shaken by the breaking of his front line, and the alarm was felt as far back as Douai, where arrangements had been made in the afternoon of the first day of the battle to evacuate the city. Had the reserve divisions been available at the due time, it is possible that the second line would have fallen. Although the gain was the capture of four miles of German front line trenches, involving a penetration eastwards of some two miles, the cost of the battle was grievous: there were over 50,000 casualties in the First Army attack, of which, according to the Official History, 'some 800 officers and 15,000 men were killed, or missing and never heard of again.' When the losses of the French 10th Army and British subsidiary attacks are included, the total rises to 115,000, compared with estimated German losses of 50,000.

There are several imponderables about the battle. The handling of the GHQ reserve divisions by French and ultimately by Haig, the decision to use gas and the problems of communication all interact with one another to make analysis (if hindsight is to be avoided) difficult. In spite of earlier misgivings about the resources available to fight the battle, and the location chosen, it seems that, once the decision was made to employ gas, the general expectation was that it would be successful and effective up to a distance of two miles, which would have included the enemy's second line. Indeed, the statistical evidence regarding the direction and strength of the wind during the days preceding the battle supported this belief. In reality, however, the reliance placed on gas was essentially a gamble.

Having decided on the wider attack (that is, by six divisions), Haig had been obliged to assemble them, some 75,000 men, in the front and support lines, but in the knowledge that if the wind direction was unfavourable then only the two-division assault could take place. He would then have run the risk of the enemy bombarding trenches packed with the four divisions stood down. There is also a strong likelihood that this must have influenced his decision to give the go-ahead shortly before zero hour, even though the speed and direction of the wind were barely favourable. In the event, the release of gas was only partially successful, and not only did it prove to be ineffective just south of the La Bassée canal (where the enemy defences were very strong) but it also lingered in the British trenches, causing casualties. Although Haig, at the last moment, was minded to call off the wider attack, he was told by the I Corps commander that it was too late to countermand the instructions – this despite the fact that quite elaborate precautions had been taken to provide for a short-notice cancellation. It is ironic that, had the limited attack taken place (by the 9th Division against the Hohenzollern Redoubt and by the 15th Division against Loos village), it would have been in the two locations where the gas had been more successful. Although cancellation at such short notice – nearly thirty minutes – would have caused some confusion, there is a case for believing that this might have been the right decision, particularly as the attack by the 2nd Division took place without the assistance of gas (indeed the reverse), achieved nothing and suffered heavy losses.

It is possible to discern a certain logic in French's intended employment of the GHQ reserves, but his vacillations over where and when he would release them cannot be defended. Writing after the battle, Haig complained that, had the reserves been under his orders at the proper time, the attack could have been 'the turning point of the war'. It cannot be denied that French had originally kept the reserve divisions too far back, but the outcome of Haig's pressure was his agreement that 'the heads of the two leading divisions of XI Corps should be on the line Neoux les Mines–Beuvry by daylight on the 25th September'. As mentioned earlier, the leading brigades of the 21st and 24th Divisions were in fact there by 6 a.m., but it would appear that there was a serious miscalculation at First Army headquarters as to the time it would take the troops to cover the five miles to the front in view of the chaotic situation on the roads already described. It is possible, of course, that if the two divisions had been thrown in in support of the assaulting divisions, particularly where progress had been made between Hulluch and Hill 70, the German second line could have been broken. This, in turn, might have drawn enemy reserves from the French 10th Army sector, perhaps enabling Vimy Ridge to be captured. Against this hypothesis, however, must be set the fact that the two divisions were totally inexperienced and at some point would have met German reserves where, in this situation, seasoned divisions might have been more effective: these could have been made available from the quiescent Somme front.

The eventual release of the reserve divisions was directly due to Haig's optimistic reports on the initial results of the attack, leading Sir John to believe that the breakthrough of the weak enemy second line was imminent. The situation, however, was not nearly as favourable as that. Neither commander was aware of the true position – the wrong direction taken by the 15th Division, the gap in the 1st Division's front, the lack of forward momentum on the other divisional fronts where, initially, progress had been made and, above all, the heavy casualties. One can only speculate on what Sir John's reaction might have been had he, in fact, been aware: he might have refused to release them or, alternatively, agreed to their release on condition that the six brigades in the two divisions be loaned to I and IV Corps (two brigades were, indeed, diverted to this end) and used in a reinforcement role.

Of the various threads running through the battle, the most persistent, and ultimately the dominant one, was the difficulty in transmitting and receiving timely and accurate information. The communication problems at the battle of Neuve Chapelle have already been described, but the situation at Loos was no better, and although attempts were made to report progress by the use of ground symbols (strips of white sheeting), these proved to be of little use because the smoke of battle, aggravated by rain and mist, prevented aerial observation. Notwithstanding the elaborate plans for an offensive devised at all levels of command resulting in a cascade of corps, divisional, brigade and battalion operation orders couched in the minutest detail, once the attacking battalions left their trenches, communication as to their success or otherwise was more often than not left to the humble runner. Clad in 'fighting order', encumbered with rifle and bayonet, he picked his way (and frequently lost it) over the debris of a featureless battlefield, sometimes in smoke and darkness, running the gauntlet of enemy fire before arriving, against all odds, at brigade headquarters. It is not surprising that messages sometimes took hours to arrive, and the information they contained had often been overtaken by events. But some never arrived at all. Although telephone communication existed between brigade and division, this could be disrupted by the lines being cut by enemy shelling, and any lines taken forward by battalions would be at much greater risk. Wireless as a battlefield aid was still at a very rudimentary stage. It had been used in static situations at Ypres with only limited success, and it was too unwieldy to be taken forward in an assault. (The age of the 'walkie-talkie' would not dawn until the next war.) The employment of carrier pigeons would have been helpful in reporting information from the forward troops, but battlefield conditions of smoke are far from ideal for their use. A pigeon service had only been authorized in August 1915, and although I Corps had 120 pigeons at the battle it is not known whether any were used. (The usefulness of carrier pigeons on the battlefield can be illustrated by the fact that by 1918 there were 20,000 birds on the Western Front.)

The problems arising from inadequate wire-cutting by artillery had already been demonstrated at Neuve Chapelle, and although it was realized that there was insufficient artillery to cut adequate paths through the wire at Loos, it was hoped that the use of gas would so disorganize the defenders as to ease the passage of the attackers through the front defences. Where the gas failed, and the advancing troops met uncut wire, the attack stalled completely and bloodily. If nothing else, this demonstrated the folly of assaulting strongly wired, entrenched positions without adequate artillery preparation and where the gas had failed to travel. Yet, on 13 October, when the release of gas had been even less successful than on 25 September, the attacks by the First Army went ahead and were consequently repulsed with tragic and unnecessary loss of life.

Loos was a lamentable and unwanted battle, and it ultimately caused the removal of French from his post as Commander-in-Chief in December 1915. The heavy casualties and lack of any tangible success in the offensives at Neuve Chapelle, Aubers Ridge, Festubert and, finally, Loos had seriously damaged his prestige, and he was censured over his handling of the reserve divisions at the latter battle. He was replaced by Haig, who had not been slow to criticize him. In a conversation with the King in October, he expressed his conviction that French should be removed 'for the sake of the Empire'.

It will be clear, however, that the British still had much to learn from the experience of Loos, but once again they were persuaded that, given adequate heavy artillery resources, they could break the German line. But the lessons learned from experience are not confined to the attacker: they equally aid the defender, and the Germans, realizing that they must expect an increase in heavy artillery bombardments in future Allied offensives, set about constructing deep dug-outs (or concrete 'pill-boxes' where the water table made this impracticable), sheltering their machine-guns under reinforced concrete and constructing a heavily fortified second line. They believed in keeping one step ahead.

Notes to Chapter 3

1. Edmonds, Brigadier-General Sir James, (comp.), *Official History of the War: Military Operations, France and Belgium 1915*, Vol. II, Macmillan & Co. (London, 1928)
2. Maude, Alan H., (ed.), *The 47th (London) Division 1914–1919*, Amalgamated Press (London, 1922)
3. Maurice, Major-General Sir Frederick, *The Life of General Lord Rawlinson of Trent*, Cassell & Co., (London 1928)
4. Edmonds, *op. cit.*
5. Charteris, J., *At G.H.Q.*, Cassell (London, 1931)
6. Maude, *op. cit.*
7. Stewart, J., and Buchan, J., *The Fifteenth (Scottish) Division, 1914–1919*, Blackwood (London, 1926)
8. *Ibid.*

9. Mottram, R. H., *Journey to the Western Front*, G. Bell & Sons (London, 1936). Quoted on p.142.

10. Stewart and Buchan, *op. cit.*

11. War History of the 23rd London Regiment.

4

The Somme

A sense of the inevitable broods over the battlefields of the Somme.—Winston
Churchill, *The World Crisis 1911–1918*

THE YEAR 1915 had been a depressing one for the Allies. The French
attacks in Artois and Champagne had been unsuccessful in breaching
the enemy's defences; the British, still the junior partner on the Western
Front, had made no significant progress in the offensive at Neuve Chapelle and
the sequels at Aubers Ridge and Festubert; and Loos, despite the evidence that
the enemy's front could be ruptured, had been little short of a disaster. Elsewhere
the results had been even worse: the Dardanelles expedition had failed, the
Russians were retreating after the loss of Poland, the Serbian Army had been
defeated and the British were coming under increasing pressure from Turkish
forces in the Middle East. Italy had declared war on Austria (but not Germany)
in May, but its army could make little progress against the natural obstacle of
the mountainous Austrian frontier.

The impasse on the Western Front had been foreseen as early as December
1914. In a memorandum produced for the British War Council, its secretary,
Lieutenant-Colonel Maurice Hankey (later Lord Hankey), wrote:

> The experience of the movements of the Allies within the last few weeks seems to
> indicate that any advance must be both costly and slow. Days are required to
> capture a single line of trenches, the losses are very heavy, and as often as not the
> enemy re-captures his lost ground on the following day, or is able to render the
> captured ground untenable. When viewed on a map, the total gains . . . are almost
> negligible, and apparently incommensurate with the effort and loss of life.[1]

This was a remarkably prescient analysis of the situation, not only as it seemed
to him in 1914 but also which was to exist, in effect, for another three years. He
suggested in the memorandum that the impasse could be overcome by a
'diversion elsewhere'. This notion was to cause divided counsels in the British
direction of the war even up until 1918. The differences were more political than
military, however, although early in 1915 both Kitchener and Sir John French
were pessimistic about success on the Western Front and for a time shared the
view that 'it would be desirable to seek new spheres of activity'. By the end of

1915, however, Kitchener's influence was waning, and in December 1915 French was replaced by Haig and Lieutenant-General Sir William Robertson (formerly French's Chief of Staff) was appointed Chief of the Imperial General Staff at the War Office in London. This powerful partnership would ensure dominance of the military view that the war could only be won on the Western Front.

Proposals for 1916 were formulated at a conference of Allied commanders held at Chantilly in December following an earlier meeting between the French and British prime ministers. The main proposal was that the four Allied powers should deliver simultaneous attacks with maximum forces as soon as they were ready to do so, and that only minimum forces should be employed in secondary theatres. These proposals were considered by the War Committee (formerly the War Council) in London at the end of December, and although it agreed that France and Flanders should remain the main theatre of operations, and that a British offensive should take place in the spring 'in the greatest possible strength', the Committee later had second thoughts and added the rider 'although it must not be assumed that such offensive operations are finally decided on'.

The first suggestion that a Franco-British offensive take place on the Somme front emerged from Joffre late in December. He wrote to Haig informing him that he had directed General Foch (commanding the French armies in the north) to examine the possibility of a powerful offensive south of the Somme and that

> Without prejudice to the area where our principal attack will be made, the French offensive would be greatly aided by a simultaneous offensive of the British forces between Somme and Arras. Besides the interest which this last area presents on account of its close proximity to that where the effort of the French Armies will be made, I think that it will be a considerable advantage to attack the enemy on a front where for long months the reciprocal activity of the troops opposed to each other has been less than elsewhere. The ground is, besides, in many places favourable to the development of a powerful offensive.[2]

Three weeks later he proposed to Haig that the British should carry out preparatory attacks north of the Somme in April with the object of wearing down the enemy. Haig would not agree to this, owing to the possibility of unacceptable losses, and Joffre ultimately dropped the idea. Instead, it was agreed that there would be a joint offensive astride the River Somme around the beginning of July. But there was no strategic object, no threat to German communications, only a salient facing west which, if penetrated, would be likely to result in a salient facing east. Haig, however, had other ideas. At the end of December he had met Vice-Admiral Bacon (commanding the Dover patrol), who emphasized the importance to the British of denying the ports of Ostend and Zeebrugge to the enemy. With this in mind Haig asked General Sir Hubert Plumer (commanding

the Second Army) to consider the possibility of offensives in the Ypres sector.
One was an attack north-eastwards towards Roulers (a plan which was to remain
in Haig's mind until it came to fruition in July 1917); another was an attack on
the Messines–Wytschaete ridge. There is good reason to believe that Haig
would have preferred a Second Army offensive, but when appointed Commander-in-Chief of the BEF in December Kitchener had told him that 'the closest
co-operation between the French and British as a united army must be the
governing factor'. So, once again, he was to fight on a battlefield chosen by the
French, but a week later the Allied plans were thrown into serious disarray by
the massive German assault on the French fortress of Verdun.

The Verdun offensive was not an attempt at a breakthrough but a cynical ploy
to destroy French morale. In September 1914 command of the German Army
had passed from General von Moltke to General von Falkenhayn, and in
December 1915 the latter addressed a long memorandum to the German
Emperor expounding his views on the future prosecution of the war. His
rationale for attacking Verdun was that

> Within our reach behind the French sector of the Western Front there are
> objectives [for] the retention of which the French General Staff would be
> compelled to throw in every man they have. If they do so the forces of France will
> bleed to death – as there can be no question of a voluntary withdrawal – whether
> we reach our goal or not. If they do not do so, and we reach our objectives, the moral
> effect on France will be enormous.[3]

This tragic battle drew in more and more French divisions, to the extent of
throwing doubts on the practicability of mounting the joint Somme offensive,
and Haig even considered that the newly formed Fourth Army (commanded by
Lieutenant-General Sir Henry Rawlinson), which was to carry out the attack,
might have to act on its own.

In April Haig had finally secured the Cabinet's approval for a summer
offensive on the Western Front in combination with the French, but according
to Lloyd George's *War Memoirs* it does not appear that the decision was
unanimous, and this is confirmed in Lord Hankey's book *The Supreme Command
1914–1918*:

> The decision, though inevitable, was not given without a good deal of misgiving.
> The attack was to be preceded by an intensive bombardment of several days'
> duration, the object of which was to shatter the enemy's trenches, to destroy his
> barbed wire and machine-gun posts, to silence his guns, and thus to prepare the way
> for an advance by divisions of infantry massed for the purpose. In this way a gap
> was to be made in the enemy's lines, through which was to pour an 'army of pursuit'
> composed of cavalry supported by infantry ... The critics of this plan were frankly
> derisive. They said it had really been tried before by both sides without success.
> Even the German attack at Verdun, terrible as it was for France, was probably

proving no less costly to Germany ... It might be possible, they admitted, at great cost to break through the first line of the enemy's defences. But the range of guns was not sufficient to ensure the destruction of the successive lines of any one section of these defences, which were constructed in depth ... There were some who continued to believe that for the present the best plan was to limit ourselves to a series of operations of a comparatively limited scope.[4]

From Rawlinson's diary entry for 30 March, it appears that one of the critics was Kitchener:

I have had Lord Kitchener here all day, and he was very communicative. He is opposed to our making a big attack, and would prefer us to continue small offensives with a view solely to killing Germans.[5]

By the end of May the French, due to their preoccupation with the defence of Verdun, were not only concerned about their ability to play a full part in the Somme offensive but also beginning to question whether it would lead to a decisive victory. Foch even doubted whether the offensive should take place at all, but Joffre wanted the British to shoulder more of the burden of the fighting on the Western Front and thus relieve the pressure on Verdun. He had, however, begun to believe that the objective on the Somme was not a breakthrough but attrition. He urged Haig to be ready by the beginning of July, to which Haig agreed, although he would have liked to have deferred the offensive until August when more divisions would be available. Because of the uncertainty as to the extent of French participation, Haig, even at this late stage, had not given up the idea of attacks in the Ypres sector. Based upon Plumer's appreciation of the various alternatives put to him in January, Haig had instructed him in April to prepare for an assault on the Messines–Wytschaete ridge, and at the end of May he asked for the preparations to be expedited. It was to be a combined naval and military operation which would include two divisions being landed in Belgium between Nieuport and Ostend in a coastal assault.

Notwithstanding French pessimism about the forthcoming offensive, there was guarded optimism at GHQ. The lessons of the previous battles had shown that a heavy preliminary bombardment spread over a number of days had a significant effect. Now that ammunition was more plentiful, it was felt that, with the massive array of armament available, and provided that the assault were delivered on a wide front, a rupture could be secured in the enemy's line.

On 3 June Joffre finalized the arrangements for the attack, which was now planned for 1 July, and Haig, in his response, sought to know the strength that the French would put in the field as it was evident that their contribution would be diminished because of the demands of Verdun. Joffre replied that the 6th Army, albeit much reduced in strength, would be co-operating on the right of the British Fourth Army. Joffre's original plan for the Somme had envisaged a force of forty French and twenty-five British divisions, but French participation would now only consist of six divisions, with two in reserve, compared with nineteen British divisions, also with two in reserve. In addition there would be three divisions, plus five cavalry divisions, in GHQ reserve. But meanwhile the situation was worsening at Verdun and Joffre asked for the date of the offensive to be advanced to 25 June. However, it was subsequently put back until the 29th.

The Plan

The Somme is not only a *département* of France but also a river (partly canalized) winding its way through Picardy to the English Channel at the Bay of the Somme. The Germans in this sector in 1914 had come to a halt on the Somme, where they had briefly occupied the small town of Albert until driven out by the French. Since then they had settled down on the defensive, occupying the most advantageous positions on the high ground to the east. North of the river the ground rises to a broad, irregular chalk ridge some 400–500 feet high with outlying spurs and deep re-entrants. Running north-eastwards, the ridge is intersected by the ruler-straight Roman road connecting Albert with Bapaume. The ridge descends gradually to the River Ancre, a northern tributary of the Somme, rising again to continue north-westwards in a series of rolling hills. The whole area was (and is) intensively cultivated, with groups of small villages, and, then as now, scattered with woods, many of which were to figure prominently in the battle.

> All the advantages of position and observation were in the enemy's hands, not in ours. They took up their lines when they were strong and our side weak, and in no place in all the old Somme position is our line sited better than theirs, though in one or two places the sites are nearly equal. Almost in every part of this old front our men had to go uphill to attack.[6]

The area made a welcome change for the British from the dreary, battle-scarred flatlands of the north. Ever since 1914 the French and the Germans had operated an unofficial 'live and let live' policy on the front to the extent that men from a British brigade taking over trenches from a French Territorial division were astonished to discover that it had suffered a mere seven casualties in as many months. The Germans, in preparing for the Verdun offensive, had expected that, once it had been mounted, they could expect attacks elsewhere in order to relieve the pressure. At first, the German Supreme Command believed that an offensive would be made on the Alsace-Lorraine front, but by early June the German 2nd Army facing the Allies on the Somme front was reporting on the build-up of British strength and that an attack was expected at Fricourt and Gommecourt. Falkenhayn, nevertheless, still believed in an Alsace-Lorraine offensive and took no material steps to reinforce his 2nd Army.

In the knowledge that no reinforcements would be available to plug any gaps in their line, the 2nd Army embarked on a massive programme of defensive works. They had not only constructed a strong front line protected by hundreds of fortified machine-gun posts (many in reinforced concrete) with the usual support and reserve trenches, but had also established a second, or intermediate, line some two miles behind the front, and even a third line two or three miles in the rear. Perhaps the most significant factor was the construction of a series of deep dug-outs (more like barracks) made possible by the underlying chalk some thirty feet or more below the surface and proof against anything except the heaviest shell. Many were lit by electricity, ventilated with fresh air, provided with piped water and provisioned with emergency rations. They were to play a major role in the battle:

> Covered sunk forts, carefully placed mine fields, machine-gun pits, gigantic quarries, enlarged in the chalk, connected with systems of catacomb-like dug-outs and subterranean works at all depths, in which brigades could lie until the fitting moment. Belt upon belt of fifty-yard-deep wire protected these points, either directly or at such angles as should herd and hold up the attacking infantry to the fire of veiled guns. Nothing in the entire system had been neglected or unforeseen, except knowledge of the men who, in due time, should wear their red way through every yard of it.[7]

Rawlinson submitted his plan of attack to GHQ on 3 April. It was somewhat cautious, demonstrating his 'bite and hold' philosophy:

> It does not appear to me that the gain of 2 or 3 kilometres of ground is of much consequence, or that the existing situation is so urgent as to demand that we should incur very heavy losses in order to draw a large number of Germans against this portion of our front. Our object rather seems to be to kill as many Germans as possible with the least loss to ourselves, and the best way to do this appears to me to seize points of tactical importance which will provide us with good observation and which we may feel quite certain the Germans will counter-attack. These points to be not only ones of special tactical importance with a view to a further advance, but to be such that the Germans will be compelled to counter-attack them under disadvantages likely to conduce to heavy losses, which we can only ensure if these tactical points are not too far distant from our gun positions . . .[8]

Haig was not happy with it, and this was to lead to a fundamental and unfortunate difference of approach. Rawlinson saw the offensive as essentially one of siege warfare – in other words a tactical battle. Haig, on the other hand, had become increasingly optimistic that it would lead to a strategic breakthrough. Rawlinson wanted a two-stage attack – a penetration on the whole front to a depth of about 2,000 yards between Mametz and Serre followed, after an interval, by a further advance of about 1,000 yards taking in part of the German second line around the village of Pozières on the Albert–Bapaume road (the highest point). It was this second line that worried Rawlinson because it was out of range of all but the heaviest guns and the effect of wire-cutting could only be observed from the air, presenting difficulties in the event of bad weather quite apart from interference by enemy aircraft. Haig, however, not only wanted the part of the line around Pozières to be achieved in the first rush but also the capture of Montauban – further east than Rawlinson had proposed. Haig's proposal for a diversionary attack at Gommecourt (the northerly edge of the front), which Rawlinson considered to be beyond his resources, was transferred to the Third Army.

If Haig was not happy with Rawlinson's proposed plan, then neither was Rawlinson with Haig's, which by the middle of April had become formal instructions; he thought them too optimistic and the reports of a decline in the enemy's morale exaggerated. It was something of a paradox that their shared experience of the Loos battle should have impressed them in different ways. Haig believed that there were lessons to be learned when part of the enemy's front line had been overrun, resulting in enemy confusion. Rawlinson, on the other hand, was aware that, despite this success, the second line had remained intact, and after recovering from the initial confusion the enemy had been able to mount powerful counter-attacks. Both commanders knew, however, that the enemy's defences on the Somme were far more formidable than at Loos, but they considered that these would be overcome by a massive preliminary bombardment. But, here again, there were differences. Rawlinson wanted a long bombardment over several days on the ground that it

> ... gives the enemy no chance to sleep; food and ammunition are difficult to bring up; and the enemy is kept in a constant state of doubt as to when the infantry assault is to take place.

Haig, however, wanted a hurricane bombardment such as had been used at Neuve Chapelle, but ultimately the Rawlinson view prevailed. Writing in his diary on 30 April, Rawlinson recorded:

> I am quite clear in my mind now, about the plan. The bombardment is to be deliberate, four or five days, according to ammunition supply. The attack is to go for the big thing. I still think it would be better to proceed by shorter steps; but I have told D. H. I will carry out his plan with as much enthusiasm as if it were my own.

After the preliminary bombardment, Haig's plan was to push through the three successive defensive lines in one rush and seize the high ground between Serre and Montauban, thus gaining good observation to the east. Following consolidation of the ground gained, the reserve of three cavalry and two infantry divisions would advance eastwards into open country around Bapaume then swing north to roll up the enemy's flank as far as Arras. On the day of assault there would be an intense bombardment concentrated on the enemy's front trenches, lifting at zero hour on to the next trench, then lifting again and moving on. The infantry, advancing in line and in waves, 'each line adding impetus to the preceding one', would follow behind each lift at a distance of about a hundred yards.

By early June, however, the involvement of the French in the offensive began to look doubtful, and Haig warned Rawlinson that, if his attack 'should meet with very considerable opposition and involve it in hard fighting before it got the first objectives', then he might decide to close down the offensive and carry out the Messines attack. Haig was still of the same mind, even by the middle of June: if it was found inadvisable to push the cavalry forward on the Somme, the main effort would be transferred to the Second Army in the north.

The Preparation

The preparations for the battle were immense and could be likened to the creation of a vast industrial complex, the end product to be the greatest offensive yet undertaken by the British Army. To cater for the intensive movement of the traffic of war – guns, ammunition and men – the generally inadequate roads leading to the forward areas had to be strengthened; bridges repaired and widened; railways, both standard and narrow gauge, constructed; rail-heads established for the dumping of ammunition and stores; eight casualty clearing stations erected; huts and tents for the billeting of troops provided; miles of communication trenches dug; over 7,000 miles of telephone cables buried; and dug-outs and assembly trenches built. Because of the inadequate water supply, over 120 miles of pipes were laid and over a hundred pumps installed. All this labour was accomplished under the protection of the Royal Flying Corps, which had achieved such dominance that few German aircraft were able to penetrate the area either to observe or to interfere with operations. Nevertheless, the enemy did not fail to note all this activity from captive balloons.

The artillery preparations were on a similar scale. There were 1,010 field guns, 182 heavy guns and 245 heavy howitzers, and, added to this total of over 1,400, there were 100 guns loaned by the French. For the Loos battle over 500 field and heavy guns had been employed for the main assault, and comparisons with the provision of ammunition for the Somme are even more impressive when the amount of artillery ammunition is taken into account. For example, field gun ammunition allocated at Loos was less than half a million rounds, compared with just under three million allocated to the Fourth Army on the Somme. This substantial increase could be accounted for not only by the wider frontage of the attack – eighteen miles instead of six – but also by the great strides made in the manufacture of munitions since September 1915. (The increasing mechanization of the war, however, would mean that in later battles the provision of ammunition for the Somme would look positively frugal.)

The preliminary bombardment was originally planned to extend over five days, 24 to 28 June, with a final bombardment on the 29th, the day of assault. It duly commenced on the 24th with concentration on wire-cutting, but the weather was bad, low cloud and heavy rainstorms interrupting the aerial observation so crucial for determining the locations of enemy batteries. The weather improved the next day but steadily deteriorated over the following three days to the extent that the offensive had to be postponed until 1 July. In consequence, the bombardment was prolonged for a further two days, and over the seven days a total of something over one and a half million rounds were fired, culminating in 250,000 on 1 July. But the extra two days' bombardment had the effect of 'watering down' the ammunition available for the day of assault.

> Day and night the bombardment went on, and the next day, and the day after that, but still no attack took place. To those in the gun-pits, the whole of life seemed to merge into one clanging, clashing roar of sound. Covered with sweat and grime, the slaves of the gun toiled and laboured, ate, lay down and slept, and toiled and laboured again, to the roar and rush and scream of hundreds of hurrying shells. Their horizon was bounded by the vast and insatiable engine which they continuously fed. Their minds were numbed and deafened by the never-ceasing clamour of their gods . . . For seven summer days this tumult of Hell went on, and on the seventh hour of the seventh day gathered in force and volume so that the whole world seemed to rock with sound. Surely no human being could live under that terrible blasting and hammering![9]

This awesome bombardment – it could even be heard in the south of England – wreaked terrible damage on the enemy trenches and constituted a severe ordeal. A German account records:

> A culminating point was reached which was never again approached. What we experienced surpassed all previous conception. The enemy's fire never ceased for an hour. It fell night and day on the front line and tore fearful gaps in the ranks of all defenders. It fell on the approaches to the front line and made all movement towards the front hell. It fell on the rearward trenches and battery positions and smashed men and material in a manner never seen before or since. It repeatedly reached even the resting battalions behind the front and occasioned there terrible losses. Our artillery was powerless against it . . .[10]

The men in the deep dug-outs were comparatively safe, but they existed, day after day, in a state of almost unbearable tension, unable to evacuate their wounded or bury their dead; weary, thirsty and hungry. For the British infantry the ordeal was of a different kind. They were already keyed up, the majority facing battle for the first time, living uncomfortably in flooded trenches or in cramped billets, and the postponement only served to heighten the tension.

There was a sense abroad, however, that the forthcoming attack would at last see the great breakthrough and even, perhaps, the end of the war: the massive and prolonged bombardment led many to believe that nothing could survive it. Rawlinson had told his corps commanders that 'nothing could exist at the conclusion of the bombardment in the area covered by it', the implication being that it would be a walk-over for the infantry. Nevertheless, the reports from patrols sent out at night to explore the damage to the enemy's front were not always encouraging. Despite the damage to the trenches, the reports filtering back on the condition of the wire entanglements were often conflicting. Some patrols reported that the wire was no longer an obstacle, others that it was not properly cut, or that there were only a few gaps and these just a few yards wide. Indeed, in some places the wire was intact, and on the extreme left of VIII Corps' front between Beaumont Hamel and Serre no patrol had succeeded in entering the enemy trenches. Haig had stressed in discussions with Rawlinson that corps were not to attack until their commanders were satisfied that the enemy defences had been sufficiently destroyed, but, as will be seen later, it does not appear that reports of uncut, or insufficiently cut, wire were always acted upon.

During the night of 30 June the assaulting divisions moved up to their assembly trenches:

> The men were in excellent spirits and full of hopes. It was such a change to realize that after so many months in the trenches and taking everything coming our way, without a chance of hitting back, that tomorrow would give us our chance of revenge for so many lost pals. We paraded at 9.45 p.m. and marched to the assembly trenches, which were reached about midnight. We were then ordered to put our ladders and bridges into position, and try to get a couple of hours' rest.[11]

Clad in 'fighting order', that is, with steel helmet, rifle and bayonet, entrenching tool and haversack on back, the infantry also had to carry 200 rounds of rifle ammunition, two empty sandbags and two grenades. The total weight carried, according to the Official History, was about 66lb, making it difficult to climb out of a trench and impossible to move more rapidly than at a slow walk and to rise or lie down quickly.

The British had suggested that the attack should take place at first light, just before 5 a.m., when the Allied line would be in semi-darkness and hindering enemy observation, but this was unacceptable to the French who wanted it at 9 a.m. to enable their artillery to observe the effect of the final bombardment. As a compromise, zero hour was fixed for 7.30 a.m. In the evening of 30 June Rawlinson recorded in his diary:

> The situation at Verdun is critical, and we cannot wait longer if it is to be saved. So the issues at stake in tomorrow's battle are as great, if not greater than any in which has been fought during the war. What the actual results will be no one can foretell,

but I feel pretty confident of success myself, though we shall only get it after heavy fighting. That the Boche will break and that a debacle will supervene I do not believe; but if that should take place I am quite ready to take full advantage of it. We have done all that we can, and the rest is in the hands of the good God . . .[12]

Haig, in a similarly reflective (but perhaps more trusting) vein, wrote to his wife before the battle:

You must know that I feel that every step in my plan has been taken with the Divine help – and I ask daily for aid, not merely in making the plan, but in carrying it out, and this I hope I shall continue to do until the end of all things which concern me on earth.[13]

The Assault

July 1 broke a lovely morning and the birds were singing.—Sergeant A. H. Cook, 1st Somerset Regiment[14]

At 7.30 a.m. the bombardment lifted and passed on to the enemy's second line, and with the shrilling of whistles all along the front tens of thousands of British soldiers climbed laboriously out of their trenches and, with the sun glinting on their bayonets, advanced in line across No Man's Land:

Never before had the ranks of a British Army on the field of battle contained the finest of all classes of the nation in physique, brains and education. And they were volunteers not conscripts. If ever a decisive victory was to be won it was to be expected now.[15]

The German front line can be pictured as like a face in profile: on the extreme right of the front the French 6th Army attacked the 'throat', the British Fourth Army attacked from under the 'chin' to just over the 'nose', while the Third Army carried out a diversionary attack on the 'forehead'. The attack under the 'chin' (from Maricourt to Carnoy) was carried out by XIII Corps and was virtually the only British success of the day. The objective of the Montauban ridge (which Rawlinson had thought to be too far east) had been gained by 4 p.m., although at a cost of 6,000 casualties, but the achievement was all the more noteworthy because the two divisions involved, the 18th and the 30th, were both New Army, with, apart from two battalions, no previous battle experience. The 30th Division had to cross about 500 yards of No Man's Land but was fortunate in finding the wire entanglements almost all destroyed; the 18th Division had only 200 yards to cross and found the enemy cowed by the bombardment. Both divisions could have gone further,but Rawlinson's orders had been specific: 'No serious advance is to be made until preparations have been completed for entering on the next phase of the operations . . .' The French, who attacked side by side with the British, had similarly reached all their objectives and wished to continue the advance, but the opportunity was lost because of Rawlinson's caution.

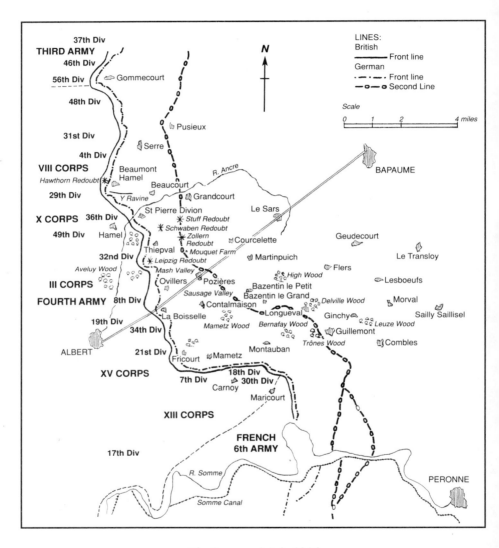

LINES:
British
—— Front line
German
—·—· Front line
—o—o Second Line

Scale

0   1   2   4 miles

THIRD ARMY
37th Div
46th Div
56th Div
48th Div
31st Div
4th Div
VIII CORPS
29th Div
X CORPS   36th Div
49th Div
32nd Div
III CORPS
FOURTH ARMY   8th Div
19th Div
34th Div
ALBERT
21st Div
XV CORPS
7th Div
XIII CORPS
17th Div

Gommecourt
Pusieux
Serre
Beaumont Hamel
Hawthorn Redoubt
Y Ravine
Beaucourt
Grandcourt
St Pierre Divion
Stuff Redoubt
Schwaben Redoubt
Zollern Redoubt
Hamel
Thiepval
Mouquet Farm
Leipzig Redoubt
Aveluy Wood
Mash Valley
Ovillers
Pozières
Sausage Valley
Contalmaison
La Boisselle
Mametz Wood
Fricourt   Mametz
18th Div
30th Div
Carnoy
Maricourt
FRENCH 6th ARMY
R. Somme
Somme Canal

R. Ancre
BAPAUME
Le Sars
Courcelette
Geudecourt
Martinpuich
Le Transloy
Flers
High Wood
Lesboeufs
Bazentin le Petit
Bazentin le Grand
Delville Wood
Morval
Longueval
Ginchy
Leuze Wood
Sailly Saillisel
Bernafay Wood
Guillemont
Trônes Wood
Combles
Montauban

PERONNE

The Somme, 1 July 1916

XV Corps attacked the point of the 'chin' (from Mametz to north of Fricourt), but this was an exceedingly strong position with deep dug-outs and strongpoints nestling in the ruins of houses. Mametz was the objective of the 7th Division, but Fricourt would be bypassed by the 21st Division. In the next phase XV Corps was to move forward and overlook Mametz Wood, in touch with XIII Corps on its right and III Corps on its left; Fricourt would be dealt with later by the reserve division, the 17th. The ruins of Mametz village were captured by the 7th Division, the enemy offering stubborn resistance, but the bastion of Fricourt had not suffered serious damage in the bombardment (owing to defective howitzer ammunition) and machine guns caused havoc among the supporting waves of infantry as they passed to the north of the village. An attack in the afternoon on the village itself by a brigade of the 17th Division was a complete failure, machine guns destroying the advancing infantry within yards of their own trenches. Some progress had been made on either side of Fricourt, but the village still held out. Casualties had been heavy – nearly 9,000, of which almost half had been suffered by the 21st Division.

The task of III Corps was to attack the 'mouth' lying astride the Albert–Bapaume road. The two attacking divisions were the 34th and 8th; the former was a New Army division, but the 8th had fought at Neuve Chapelle and Aubers Ridge. Their ultimate objective was the establishment of a line stretching from east of Contalmaison to north of Pozières, involving an advance of approximately two miles and capturing on their way the two fortified villages of Ovillers and La Boiselle and six lines of trenches. The first objective of the 34th Division was to pinch out the tiny salient formed by the latter village by attacking on either side of it, aided by the firing of two huge mines. (The crater of one, Lochnagar, still exists today.) It was at La Boiselle that the ultimate tragedy of 1 July began to unfold. Made aware of the imminence of the attack by overhearing a telephone message, the Germans, once the bombardment had moved on, swiftly emerged from their dug-outs with their machine guns and virtually annihilated the leading battalions as soon as they left their trenches. Successive waves met the same fate, and although some penetration was achieved by small parties at a few points, the men were either killed or captured. The 8th Division, attacking across the rising ground (bare of any cover) of Mash Valley towards Ovillers, fared no better. Advancing through heavy artillery fire, enfiladed on both flanks and meeting fierce machine-gun fire from the village, they had a hopeless task. Some units managed to enter the front trenches in a few places, but as no reinforcements were available they had no alternative but to withdraw. Their casualties amounted to 11,500, with no significant gains whatsoever.

The assault of X Corps on the 'nose' was even more daunting. It had first to overcome the village of Thiepval, which had been developed into a position of great strength. The village had been all but destroyed in the preliminary bombardment, but nests of machine guns lurked in relative safety under the rubble. In addition, a number of redoubts, bristling with more machine guns, had been constructed around the village as a protection from frontal as well as flanking attacks; the most notable – and infamous – of these was the Schwaben Redoubt. It became evident to the waiting battalions that the preliminary bombardment had not succeeded in silencing the machine guns, and, as the Official History records, 'So far from being cowed by the bombardment and keeping quiet as elsewhere, the Germans on the X Corps front had given ominous signs of life . . .' (These worries, when reported, were dismissed by divisional staff officers as a case of 'wind up'.) After overcoming all these formidable obstacles, the two attacking divisions (the 32nd and the 36th, both New Army) had to press on and establish a line between Mouquet Farm just north of Pozières and the outskirts of Grandcourt village, an advance at its greatest of about two miles. The sole success of the 32nd Division was the capture of one of the redoubts, Leipzig, on the extreme right of the corps front, but attempts at exploitation ended in failure. Elsewhere, attacks on the village were repulsed with heavy losses. However, the 36th Division (raised in Ulster in 1914) gained a conspicuous success. Fifteen minutes before zero hour the leading battalions moved forward under cover of the bombardment to within 100 yards of the enemy's front. Aided by well-cut wire, they overran the Schwaben Redoubt and were established beyond by 8.30 a.m. The battalions advancing on the extreme left of the corps front could not, however, make progress against fire from machine guns in St Pierre Divion and suffered terribly.

Despite the success of the capture of the Schwaben Redoubt, the lack of progress on the flanks meant that only the formation of a narrow salient had been accomplished. Further attempts to storm Thiepval were unavailing and the position of the Ulstermen in the Schwaben Redoubt grew increasingly precarious. They were running short of ammunition, their position ultimately became untenable and at 10 p.m. the decision was made to withdraw. By the end of the day the sole gain had been the capture of the Leipzig Redoubt, but casualties had been severe – approaching 10,000.

The almost unremitting tragedy of the first day reached its zenith with the attack of VIII Corps on the village of Beaumont Hamel (the 'bridge of the nose'). The position overlooked the valley the divisions had to cross and had, like Thiepval, been transformed into a fortress. Skilful use had also been made of the valleys behind the front in order to shelter reserves. One such valley was the Y Ravine:

> Whenever the enemy had a bank of any kind, at all screened from fire, he has dug into it for shelter. In the Y Ravine, which provided these great expanses of banks,

he dug himself shelters of unusual strength and size, he sank shafts into the banks, tunnelled long living rooms, both above and below the valley bottom, linked the rooms together with galleries, and cut hatchways and bolting holes to lead to the surface as well as to the gully. All this work was securely done, with baulks of seasoned wood, iron girders, and concreting.[16]

The objective of the two attacking divisions, the 29th and the 4th (both Regular divisions, the 29th having served at Gallipoli), after overrunning Beaumont Hamel and Beaucourt, was the German second line running south from Pusieux to Grandcourt, involving an advance of over two miles. A third division, the 31st, was to form a defensive flank to the advance of the 4th Division. A controversial factor in the preliminaries to the advance was the time of firing of the large mine under the Hawthorn Redoubt opposite Beaumont Hamel. The corps commander had wanted it fired four hours before zero hour so that the position could be occupied before the assault, but his request was turned down by GHQ on the grounds that the British never 'made a good show' of occupying a crater. It was eventually agreed that the mine should be fired at ten minutes before zero hour: there were worries that, if fired at 7.30 a.m., the advancing infantry could be caught by the falling debris. The mine was fired promptly at 7.20 a.m. and a cameraman recorded his impressions:

> The ground where I stood gave a mighty convulsion. It rocked and swayed. I gripped hold of my tripod to steady myself. Then, for all the world like a gigantic sponge, the earth rose in the air to a height of hundreds of feet. Higher and higher it rose, and with a horrible grinding roar the earth fell back on itself, leaving in its place a mountain of smoke.[17]

It produced an enormous crater, and the artillery bombardment moved on in order to allow the infantry to occupy it, but the element of surprise had been thrown away. The premature firing of the mine had alerted the enemy to the imminence of the attack and fire was immediately brought down from over sixty batteries (whose existence had been unsuspected) on the waiting divisions. Furthermore, the lifting of the bombardment from his front line had enabled the enemy to occupy the near lip of the crater and open a deadly fire on the infantry of the 29th Division. The attack withered in the face of such resistance, and by 10 a.m. the divisional commander had called it off. The wire before the 4th Division had been well cut, but the enemy quickly emerged from dug-outs and the leading battalions came under heavy machine-gun fire:

> Punctually at 7.30 a.m. the attack was launched, the 1st Rifle Brigade [4th Division] advanced to our front in perfect skirmishing order, and the same applied to all troops, left and right, as far as the eye could see. Everything was working smoothly, not a shot being fired. We were supposed to follow up the R. B.'s at 7.40, but we were so anxious to get on with it that we were at once out of our trenches

on our way after the Rifles. The first line had nearly reached the German front line, when all at once machine guns opened up all along our front with a murderous fire, and we were caught in the open, with no shelter; fire was directed at us from both flanks, men were falling like ninepins ... Our guns had made an unholy mess of the German trenches, but very few dead could be seen, owing to the fact that they were safely stowed away in their dug-outs. Scarcely a square foot of ground had been left undisturbed, everything was churned up, [and] there were huge gaps in the wire entanglements, but the dug-outs were all practically safe. These were a revelation to us, being most elaborately made, and down about thirty feet.[18]

Some units managed to enter the front trenches and pressed on to the support lines, but this was ultimately to be of little avail. Reserves sent in two hours later as reinforcements immediately came under a hail of fire, and although some parties managed to reach the support trenches their position was hopeless because of the failure of the 29th Division on their right, and the 31st Division on their left, to make any progress. The latter division, apart from providing a defensive flank to the 4th Division, had the objective of the village of Serre. Although the enemy's front trenches had been extensively damaged, machine guns appeared as soon as the leading battalions had left their trenches and only a few men reached the front trench, where they were either killed or captured. Some parties of men succeeded in reaching Serre, giving rise to persistent but erroneous reports that the village had been captured; no attempt, however, was made to confirm the position because of the heavy losses already incurred. Thus ended a day of disaster for VIII Corps. Apart from a penetration of the enemy's front by isolated parties, none of its objectives had been attained, and its losses, at well over 14,000, were little short of calamitous.

The role of the Third Army's VII Corps at Gommecourt was to create a diversion designed to attract 'against itself the fire of artillery and infantry which might otherwise be directed against the left flank of the main attack near Serre'. The two divisions selected were the 46th and 56th (both Territorial divisions), but, once again, the German position, forming a small salient, was immensely strong and well provided with deep dug-outs. The divisions attacked on both sides of the salient, and although managing to obtain footholds in the enemy's front – particularly the 56th Division, which made some encouraging progress – they eventually had to withdraw because of fierce opposition and a shortage of ammunition. The attack succeeded to the extent of bringing in a German Guards division which might conceivably have been employed elsewhere on the front, but the cost to VII Corps was nearly 7,000 casualties.

So ended a day of catastrophe for the British Army. Total casualties had reached an unprecedented 57,000, with almost 20,000 killed. The only significant gains had been a penetration of the enemy's front on the extreme right, and the capture of Mametz and Montauban. The French had also been successful in the same area: the enemy had not expected them to attack on the Somme, believing them to be preoccupied with the defence of Verdun. Elsewhere, apart from two lodgements, the advance had been repulsed, and a prime factor in the lack of success had been the failure of the preliminary bombardment to destroy the enemy's defences and neutralize his batteries:

> As the day wore on, the intensity of fire died down, and an ever-increasing number of walking wounded began to stream past the battery position. They spoke of failure and disaster, of the accurate and terrible enemy barrage on our trenches before the start, of the withering machine-gun fire which met them as soon as they climbed over the parapet, of the snipers and machine guns hidden in holes and tunnels between the lines, who shot them in the back as soon as they had passed. They spoke of whole companies mown down as they stood, of dead men hung up on the uncut German wire like washing, of the wounded and dying lying out in No Man's Land in heaps.[19]

To compound the failure, there were not enough heavy guns, and there were disturbing amounts of defective ammunition, particularly in heavy shell, and 'prematures'. On the eve of the battle Rawlinson wrote in his diary:

> We are short of 9.2 ammunition, and there is none for the 4.7's . . . We are short of heavy trench mortars, having only about 25, instead of the 200 promised . . .

Although much damage had been done to the enemy trenches – some of them were found to be barely recognizable as such – the deep dug-outs sheltered the enemy in a fair degree of safety and substantial stretches of wire entanglements remained intact. According to the Official History, the deep dug-outs 'came as a surprise to all', but their existence was certainly known to Fourth Army staff through reports from trench raiding parties and the interrogation of prisoners prior to the battle. It does not appear, however, that this knowledge brought about any purposeful effort by heavy artillery to concentrate on them: from the statistics of ammunition fired during the preliminary bombardment, three-quarters were fired by field guns with the main objectives of cutting wire, destroying machine-gun emplacements and interfering with communications. Thus only a small proportion was fired by heavy guns, and, spread over a front of eighteen miles, coupled with the need to seek out enemy artillery in the rear areas, it is evident that there was a severe dilution of heavy shell for dug-out destruction. Nevertheless,

> A much greater intensity and weight of gunfire would have failed then as later to blow in all the entrances to the German dug-outs, and no weight of artillery then available could have wrecked the deeper dug-outs themselves.[20]

Dug-outs were successfully destroyed, however, on the extreme right of the Fourth Army front by the heavy guns of the French 6th Army, thereby materially aiding the attack of XIII Corps on Montauban:

The facts of the fighting on July 1 cannot be accounted for, however, ascribing them to the faulty use of artillery, neither is it fair criticism to allege without explanation that the use the French made of their artillery gave better results than were achieved by ours. On a much narrower front on which the French attacked they concentrated a mass of heavy artillery substantially greater than the total British resources in that essential arm at that date in France. It has been seen that on July 1 there were but some 730 heavy guns on the whole British front from Ypres to the Somme. In support of his attack on an effective front of some six miles, Foch was able to employ no less than 900 heavy pieces . . .[21]

Counter-battery bombardment had been generally successful along the front south of the Albert–Bapaume road, but, in the expectation that the attack would be between Albert and Arras, the enemy's batteries north of the road had remained silent during the preliminary bombardment in order to conceal their existence. It was these guns that caused such havoc among the advancing battalions of VIII Corps and those waiting to form the next wave.

The faith placed in the impact of the preliminary bombardment, and the lack of an effective contingency plan in the event of its failure, led to an inflexible approach in the construction of the artillery timetable for the day of the assault. Provision had been made for re-bombardments in the Fourth Army's Tactical Notes, but the difficulties in arranging them were stressed, and in any case permission had to be obtained from corps headquarters before they could proceed. As these headquarters were located several miles behind the front, and with the ever-present danger of telephone lines being cut, communication was likely to be uncertain. Thus, when held up, the infantry had, perforce, to watch helplessly as the bombardment lifted and went on – no doubt experiencing a frustration somewhat akin to missing a train that had left before time. In a few cases local initiative prevailed and the bombardment was brought back, but otherwise it moved on inexorably beyond recall. In a letter from GHQ to Rawlinson in May, it was stated that,

> As regards artillery bombardment, it should be of the nature of a methodical bombardment and be continued until the officers commanding the attacking units are satisfied that the obstacles to their advance had been adequately destroyed.

As referred to earlier, it is clear that some officers were not satisfied: instances of inadequately cut wire were reported, as were the 'ominous signs of life' in front of X Corps, but these warnings appear to have been disregarded. Rawlinson had said that nothing could exist at the conclusion of the bombardment, and this might have had the effect of stifling complaints.

Some accounts of the failure on the first day have attributed it to the inexperience of the troops themselves. Of the fourteen divisions involved in the initial assault, seven were New Army with little or no previous experience in battle and the other seven were nominally Regular or Territorial. However, their ranks had been much depleted by losses in 1914 and 1915 and made up by wartime volunteers. Thus there were pockets of seasoned troops, but for the most part it was a civilian army. Because of this inexperience, Rawlinson had adopted the wave-formation approach on the grounds that it was less complicated than a rushing tactic: 'Each line of assaulting troops must leave its trenches simultaneously and make the assault as one man. This is of the highest importance.' This inflexible method had its critics among some of the corps and divisional commanders, but they may have been deterred from voicing them by a paragraph in the Tactical Notes already referred to:

> Finally it must be remembered that all criticism by subordinates of their superiors, and of orders received from superior authority, will in the end recoil on the heads of the critics and undermine their authority with those below them.

Hence the attack was to be like a 'vast, complicated parade-ground movement, carried out in slow motion'. The wave-formation approach might have succeeded had the expectation of the destructive power of the preliminary bombardment been realized, but, as it was, when the leading lines of infantry failed to penetrate the enemy wire, there was a 'concertina' effect as successive waves closed up, thereby offering tempting targets. A German eye-witness recorded:

> A few minutes later, when the leading British line was within a few hundred yards, the rattle of machine-gun and rifle fire broke out along the line of shell-holes. Some fired kneeling so as to get a better target over the broken ground, whilst others, in the excitement of the moment, stood up regardless of their own safety to fire into the crowd of men in front of them. Red rockets sped up into the sky as a signal to the artillery, and immediately afterwards a mass of shell from the German batteries in the rear tore through the air and burst among the advancing lines. Whole sections seemed to fall, and the rear formations, moving in closer order, quickly scattered. The advance rapidly crumbled under this hail of shell and bullets. All along the line men could be seen throwing up their arms and collapsing, never to move again. Badly wounded rolled about in their agony, and others, less severely injured, crawled to the nearest shell-hole for shelter.[22]

Nevertheless, the only unalloyed success of the day was achieved by the two New Army divisions of XIII Corps on the extreme right of the front. Only two battalions had been in battle before, and their success was due to the wire entanglements' being mostly destroyed and to severe losses suffered by enemy artillery. It is true that the Germans had not expected an attack astride the river and that their defences were not as formidable as those further north. But even there, where the defences were very strong, another New Army division, the 36th, used its initiative by creeping forward before zero hour to within 100 yards of the enemy's front. The Schwaben Redoubt had been stormed with spectacular success and could have been held had it not been for a lack of progress on the flanks.

The charge of lack of experience should not, however, be confined to the troops: it extended to the staffs of higher formations and even to GHQ itself. Bearing in mind Britain's unpreparedness for a European land war and the massive build-up in Army strength in 1914 and 1915 resulting from Kitchener's call for volunteers, it is not surprising that by 1916 the supply of experienced staff officers had not kept pace. Moreover, as the Official History noted,

> Of the corps commanders on the 1st July only two had commanded as much as a division in peace, and of the twenty-three divisional commanders in the field only three had commanded as much as a brigade before the war.

It might be thought that the outcome of the first day would have persuaded Haig to call off the Somme offensive and transfer it to the north with the assault on Messines by the Second Army. He had, after all, previously warned Rawlinson that, if the attack met strong opposition before reaching its first objectives, he might decide to close it down. On the face of it, the results provided justification for Haig to have taken this decision. The Official History commented:

> There now appears to be little doubt that the Messines attack, carried out so successfully in 1917, would have had in 1916 a far better chance of a decisive result, especially if combined with a coastal attack, than had an offensive astride the Somme. The German defences in the north were not as strong as they were a year later, as very few concrete pill-boxes had been built.

It is unclear why Haig did not make this decision, but it is probable that the success on his far right by XIII Corps and the French was the deciding factor. Apart from this, he was committed to Joffre, and to have transferred the attack to the Messines sector would inevitably have meant delay and undoubtedly have caused serious political and military repercussions.

The Long Ordeal

The battlefields of the Somme were the graveyards of Kitchener's Army.—Winston Churchill, *The World Crisis 1911–1918*

The scale of casualties on the first day had not yet been fully appreciated at GHQ, although Haig recorded in his diary on 2 July that the preliminary estimate of 40,000 'cannot be considered severe in view of the numbers engaged, and the length of front attacked'. This was a somewhat surprising comment, bearing in mind that, apart from the success on the far right, the assault had signally failed to reach the objectives set. Nevertheless, Haig was determined to renew the offensive, and thus began the long travail of the British Army in a series of grim and bloody battles that were ultimately to shatter any illusion that a break-through could be achieved. Instead, it was to experience the sterility and bitterness of attrition, calling forth not only the courage that this demands, but also discipline and, perhaps above all, endurance, for as the summer and early autumn rains turned the underlying chalk into a milky, glutinous swamp, men came to regard the mud as an enemy as great as the Germans. German losses had not been nearly as severe as those suffered by the British, but over the coming months this was to change. On 2 July Falkenhayn instructed that 'the first principle in position warfare must be to yield not one foot of ground; and if it be lost to retake it by immediate counter-attack, even to the use of the last man'. Thus in this tiny corner of northern France was to be enacted a savage struggle for the possession of a single trench, or for the brick-stained mud where once a village had stood or, perhaps most dreadful of all, for the tree-stumped ruins of a wood.

In the evening of 1 July Rawlinson had proposed to renew the attack, not on his right where his only success had been, but on his left where it had failed. It was to be undertaken by three divisions of X and VIII Corps. (These two corps were removed on 3 July and constituted in what was to be known as the 'Reserve Army' commanded by Lieutenant-General Sir Hubert Gough.) Haig, however, scaled this down to a two-brigade operation as he wished the success on the right to be exploited. The attack on the right took place on 3 July and succeeded in capturing Fricourt (although abandoned earlier) and Bernafay Wood and, for a time, the village of La Boiselle, but the Germans counter-attacked and retook part of the village. The scaled-down attack on the left of the front against Thiepval failed. Rawlinson was concerned, however, about pushing on with his right without French support, and on the same day Joffre (accompanied by Foch) met Haig. According to the latter's diary,

> Joffre began by pointing out the importance of our getting Thiepval Hill. To this I said that, in view of the progress made on my right near Montauban, and the demoralised nature of the enemy's troops in that area, I was considering the desirability of pressing my attack on Longueval. I was therefore anxious to know whether in that event the French would attack Guillemont. At this, General Joffre exploded in a fit of rage. 'He could not approve of it.' He ordered me to attack Thiepval and Pozières. [Haig's emphasis][23]

Haig argued that his supply of gun ammunition was not sufficient for him to attack along the whole front: better to capitalize on the success gained on the right. Joffre was not convinced, however, and Haig had to remind him that he was responsible for the operations of the British Army. Joffre was apparently pacified, but the suspicion remained with the French that the British resolve to continue the Somme offensive might be weakening.

The first two weeks in July were the harbingers of things to come. All attempts to push forward were fiercely resisted and, when any progress was made, frustrated by counter-attacks that on occasions even, as it were, preceded the British attacks. And the weather on 7 July, graphically described in the Official History, was appalling:

> Weather conditions were too bad to allow of much co-operation from the air, the trenches became knee-deep, in some places waist-deep, in clinging slime, and, under shell-fire, collapsed beyond recognition. Movement was often an agony; men fainted from sheer exhaustion whilst struggling through deep mud; in some localities a team of fourteen horses was required to bring up a single ammunition wagon.

Trônes and Mametz Woods were attacked and the former was briefly occupied until shelling caused a withdrawal. Mametz Wood was ultimately captured, but the confused fighting in the undergrowth and fallen trees was particularly savage:

> I reached a cross-ride in the Wood where four lanes broadened out into a confused patch of destruction. Fallen trees, shell-holes, a hurriedly dug trench beginning and ending in an uncertain manner, abandoned rifles, broken branches with their sagging leaves, an unopened box of ammunition, sand-bags half filled with bombs, a derelict machine-gun propping up the head of an immobile figure in uniform, with a belt of ammunition drooping from the breech into a pile of red-stained earth – this is the livery of war. Shells were falling, over and short, near and wide, to show that somewhere over the hill a gunner was playing the part of blind fate for all who walked past this well-marked spot. Here, in the struggle between bursting iron and growing timber, iron had triumphed and trampled over an uneven circle some forty yards in diameter. Against the surrounding wall of thick greenery, the earth showed red and fresh, lit by the clean sunlight, and the splintered tree-trunks shone with a damp whiteness, but the green curtains beyond could conceal nothing of greater horror than the disorder revealed in this clearing.[24]

These attacks, however, were only the preliminary operations to secure strategic points prior to the main assault planned for 14 July.

Rawlinson had decided that this should take place at dawn, which would entail moving five divisions half a mile in the dark to assemble them ready for the assault. This was to be the first tactical innovation of the Somme offensive. He had not, however, reached this decision on his own: it was made in agreement 'with the whole body of infantry opinion'. Haig objected to the proposal on the grounds that troops were not experienced in this kind of manoeuvre; the French, believing it to be madness, would have nothing to do with it. In spite of this discouragement, Rawlinson's plan remained in being, and after further representations Haig relented. On 12 July the final decision was made: the attack would take place at 3.25 a.m. on the 14th.

The preliminary bombardment opened on the 11th, but another innovation was that in order to achieve surprise the final bombardment before zero hour would last a mere five minutes. Moreover, for the first time, the infantry would advance under cover of a creeping barrage – a rolling curtain of shell-fire (usually shrapnel) proceeding about a hundred yards before the advancing infantry with the object of keeping the enemy's heads down until the last moment. This was in contrast to the bombardment on 1 July when the infantry left their trenches only after the bombardment had lifted in accordance with its pre-arranged timetable and moved on to the next objective. Its principal drawback was the assumption that the infantry would be keeping up with artillery timetable. The creeping barrage had been tried unofficially, and successfully, on the right of the Fourth Army's attack on the first day. Rawlinson's objectives were part of the German second line, Longueval to Bazentin le Petit and, in the event of a breakthrough, four cavalry divisions were to be used to exploit the position with the objectives of High Wood, Leuze Wood and the village of Martinpuich.

The night movement went with barely a hitch, and at 3.20 a.m. on the 14th 'the whole sky behind the infantry of the four attacking divisions seemed to open with a great roar of flame'. The suddenness of the assault found the enemy unprepared, and although resistance ultimately stiffened, the British advance could not be stayed. Within a few hours the German second position on a front of 6,000 yards had been taken; both Bazentin le Petit and the neighbouring village of Bazentin le Grand had been captured, as had Trônes Wood, but part of Longueval still held out. The tide of the advance had even lapped at the edges of Delville Wood and High Wood, both soon to be of evil memory, but the pockets of resistance in Longueval, now strongly reinforced, remained the stumbling block. As early as 10 a.m. the 3rd and 7th Divisions stood before High Wood, which appeared to be unoccupied. Their orders were not to go beyond their set objectives; a proposal by the commander of the 7th Division to push through the wood using a reserve brigade for the purpose was turned down by XV Corps on the grounds that the wood was a cavalry objective. But the cavalry had been at Morlancourt over ten miles away, and although they had set off at 8.20 a.m. their advance was at little more than walking pace over the muddy, cratered ground. As they had not arrived by noon, permission was given by Fourth Army headquarters for the 7th Division to advance into the wood, but the move was postponed because the enemy still held out in Longueval. An incorrect report was later received that Longueval had fallen, and the division was ordered to move at 5.15 p.m., but delays in communication held up the advance until 7 p.m. Little opposition was encountered at first, but thick undergrowth made progress difficult and eventually the advance was brought to a halt by enemy fire. By nightfall all operations had ceased and the weary divisions set about consolidating their gains.

Rawlinson's plan had been largely successful: most of the objectives allotted had been gained in a remarkably short time, but there was disappointment that Longueval still held out, and attempts to clear Delville Wood had been strongly resisted. However, an excellent opportunity was unquestionably missed at High Wood. At 10 a.m. the way through the wood was open, but there was a delay of nine hours before it was eventually entered, and by that time the enemy had brought up reinforcements. Had the capture of the wood been effected in the morning, it could possibly have caused the enemy to withdraw from Longueval, and it is conceivable that, had this occurred, Pozières and Delville Wood would have been threatened. In fact, two months were to pass before High Wood was finally taken, and at a cost of many casualties.

It is ironic that this was the first real opportunity since 1914 to use cavalry in the role for which they had been so expensively retained. The capture of the wood had been the objective of the 2nd Indian Cavalry Division, but they were too far back to take advantage of the rapid advance of the infantry. Some advanced squadrons did, however, charge between High Wood and Delville Wood in the early evening, causing some casualties to the enemy, but they were withdrawn the following day. The other cavalry divisions were not called on to take part in the battle. A cavalryman expressed the frustration in his memoirs:

> We trained all we knew for the impending battle in our normal role, while our chiefs talked of a 'gap' through which we were to be rushed as cavalry when the enemy line was pierced by artillery and infantry. Looking back now I cannot recall many signs of faith in this scheme on the part of the 'other ranks'. Not that we were not prepared, and even glad at the prospect of a chance, to play our part. We were determined, should the opportunity actually arise, to put up a good show ... The ensuing weeks proved that the men in the ranks were right. The 'gap' did not materialise. The infantry, who in the first few days cheered us we rode up to our kicking-off point, soon ignored us completely, if they did not actually jeer at us ...[25]

The rest of July saw attempts to take the villages and woods that had resisted capture on 14 July, but any progress made was immediately subjected to intense artillery fire followed by counter-attacks. The struggle for Delville Wood was particularly bitter. The South African Brigade entered the wood on 15 July and suffered appalling casualties in endeavouring to obey the order to take it 'at all costs'. At first their advance all but cleared the wood, but strong counter-attacks forced them back, and over six days and five nights, without relief or reinforcements, they had to endure a bombardment, almost unparalleled in its intensity, from hundreds of batteries and determined counter-attacks from fresh troops:

> As the Germans came on they were mown down; every shot must have told. Our rifles smoked and became unbearably hot, but though the end seemed near it was not yet. When the enemy wavered and broke they were reinforced and came on

76

again. We again prevailed and drove them back . . . The lip of our trench told more plainly than words can how near they came to not failing. Beyond, in No Man's Land, we could do something to estimate the cost of their failure. Exhaustion now did what shell-fire and counter-attacks had failed to do, and we collapsed in our trench, spent in body and at last worn out in spirit. The task we had been set to do was too great for us.[26]

According to the Official History, out of 3,000 officers and men in the brigade who went into the wood, only 800 answered the roll call six days later.

Ovillers was finally captured on 15 July, and towards the end of July the 1st Australian Division succeeded in capturing Pozières, but only after suffering grievous casualties. The northern edge of Longueval was also taken, and Delville Wood was virtually cleared. High Wood, however, still resisted capture, and the village of Guillemont was entered but could not be held. Attacks by the French north of the river were initially successful, but much of the ground gained was retaken. The French, like the British, were now meeting a changed defence strategy on the part of the Germans, where the front was only lightly held but strong formations waited in the rear to carry out the inevitable counter-attack. Although British losses in July had been very heavy, Falkenhayn's orders that ground lost should be recaptured had caused German losses to mount. The Allied attacks on the Somme were now causing so much anxiety that on 11 July Falkenhayn decided to call off the Verdun offensive and remain there on a 'strict defensive', thereby facilitating the transfer of units not only to the Somme but also to the Eastern Front, where the Russians had achieved a spectacular success against the Austrians. Thus the Somme offensive, planned before the German onslaught on Verdun, had performed a vital role which could not have been foreseen at the time it was conceived.

Haig now realized that his hopes of a breakthrough were disappearing and that, at least for August, it would be a time of 'wearing out' the enemy, but he had hopes for late September, by when, he considered, the crisis would be reached. At the end of July, however, he received a letter from a somewhat worried Robertson:

> The Powers that be are beginning to get a little uneasy in regard to the situation. The casualties are mounting up and they were wondering whether we are likely to get a better return for them. I do my best to keep the general situation to the front, and to explain what may be the effect of our efforts – more especially in regard to our allies . . . But they will persist in asking whether I think a loss of say 300,000 men will lead to really great results because if not we ought to be content with something less than what we are doing . . . In general, what is bothering them is the probability that we may soon have to face a bill of 2–300,000 casualties with no very great gains additional to the present. It is thought that the primary objective – relief of pressure on Verdun – has to some extent been achieved.[27]

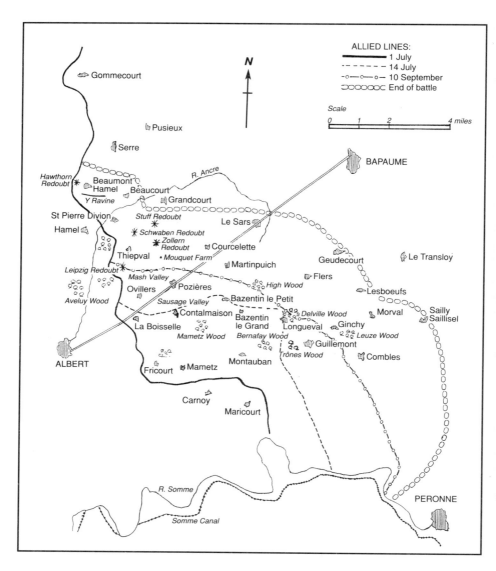

The Somme, July–November 1916
Stages of the Battle

Haig, in his response, referring to the heavy losses that had been suffered by the enemy, remarked that 'in another 6 weeks the enemy should be hard put to find men', and that 'maintenance of a steady offensive pressure will result eventually in his complete overthrow'. He was cautious enough, however, to state that he could not see this occurring 'without another campaign next year'. Robertson replied, ' I read it to the War Committee today (Aug. 5th) and it pleased them very much indeed'. So the battle dragged on during August with a series of attacks on Guillemont and some particularly bloody fighting around Pozières, in which the Australians again suffered severely, and the casualty lists grew even longer. The conditions in the trenches were dreadful:

> The trench had been blown to pieces in many places and one had to climb out and run across the mounds of thrown-up earth. In many places the men who had been killed a week or ten days ago were lying in the bottom of the trench, and one had to walk and crawl over them. Many had been half buried by the shells, and only their faces or hands or feet could be seen. They had been trampled into the soft earth by the many reliefs who had passed along the trench since they were killed. Many of the bodies were not complete: in one place a pair of legs were lying in a heap with no signs of the rest. To add to the horror of it all, there were millions and millions of flies everywhere. As we climbed along the heaps of corpses they rose in dense black clouds round us, with a hum like an aeroplane. I was nearly sick with the stench and the sights.[28]

It seemed as though a position of deadlock, at least for 1916, had been reached on the Somme. Haig still hoped, however, that the extent of enemy casualties, coupled with the evidence of a deterioration in morale, might mean that a crisis point would be reached by late September. The anxieties were indeed mounting for the Germans: the Russians had had successes on the Eastern Front, the Italian offensive on the Isonzo had been successful, and the Romanians had entered the war on the side of the Allies at the end of August.

During the month Haig formulated plans for yet another great assault, timed to take place in mid-September, but this would be an assault with a difference: he intended to employ tanks. The notion of an armoured, caterpillar-tracked vehicle had been conceived some years before 1914, but European General Staffs had seen little use for it because none had envisaged a static trench war. It remained, ultimately, for the British to pursue the idea, but this was not until the end of 1914 when the implications of trench warfare had become evident. Even then the War Office had not been enthusiastic, but, due chiefly to the exertions of Colonel Hankey, Colonel Swinton (a regular officer in the Royal Engineers) and Winston Churchill (then First Lord of the Admiralty), the project eventually came to fruition. Tanks were initially known as 'landships', but because of the secrecy surrounding their development the name 'tank' was suggested because of the vehicles' passing resemblance to water containers. The Mark I tank was rhomboidal in shape and weighed nearly thirty tons, the armour was between 6mm and 10mm in thickness and the armament consisted of two 6pdr guns or two machine guns. It could achieve nearly 4mph at maximum speed, but on cratered ground this was drastically reduced to a crawl of barely 1mph. After the final trial in February 1916 Lloyd George, as Minister of Munitions, placed an order for 100 and Haig became increasingly impatient to lay his hands on them, but it was not until August that the first tanks began to arrive in France.

Haig saw his September offensive as the decisive blow, and he was fortified in the knowledge that the War Committee had assured him 'that he might count on full support from home', although in other quarters there was disquiet about the extent of British casualties on the Somme – over 196,000 by the end of August – and the meagre gains achieved. Haig's plan was to

> . . . press the main attack south of the Albert–Bapaume road with the object of securing the enemy's last line of prepared defences between Morval and Le Sars with a view to opening the way for the cavalry.

It was expected that fifty or sixty tanks would be employed against objectives likely to cause obstacles to the advancing infantry, and 'operate as a general rule in groups of 3'. This flew in the face of the 'Notes on the Employment of Tanks' prepared by Colonel Swinton. In particular,

> Since the chance of success of an attack by tanks lies almost entirely in its novelty and in the element of surprise, it is obvious that no repetition of it will have the same opportunity of succeeding as the first unexpected effort. It follows, therefore, that these machines *should not be used in driblets* (for instance as they may be produced), but the fact of their existence should be kept as secret as possible until the whole are ready to be launched, together with the infantry assault, in one great combined operation.[29]

Haig was aware of this caveat, having earlier approved the Notes, but he felt that time was not on his side: autumn was approaching and, despite the sacrifice of surprise, he was determined to use every tank available in what he saw as being his last great effort in 1916 to achieve a breakthrough.

Rawlinson's plan was an attack on 15 September by XIV and XV Corps on a frontage of nearly six miles; five cavalry divisions would be on hand to exploit the breakthrough. Preliminary attacks were made on 3 September when Guillemont was finally captured; Ginchy was taken the following day, although losses were heavy. Gough's Reserve Army also attacked astride the Ancre on the same day, but with no success. Zero hour was 6.20 a.m., with the ultimate objective of the line Morval–Gueudecourt, thereby having the effect of driving an enormous wedge into the German defences. The preliminary bombardment commenced on the 12th, gradually increasing in volume until zero hour on the 15th with a concentration of fire double that delivered on 1 July. Forty-eight tanks had arrived from England and 34 of these were allocated to the two corps making the main assault, the remainder being distributed among III Corps and the Reserve Army. At dusk on the 14th the infantry moved up to their assembly trenches, the tanks meanwhile making their ponderous way to their points of departure for the assault, but of those allocated to the main attacking force only 23 arrived, mainly because of mechanical problems. The preparations were now complete for what was to be the most powerful assault launched by the British since 1 July, and hopes ran high that this time the breakthrough would succeed.

The attack commenced under cover of a light mist but was only partially successful. The villages of Martinpuich and Courcelette were taken and High Wood finally cleared, but the main thrust towards the line Morval–Lesboeufs–Gueudecourt made little progress beyond the first objective, a notable exception being the capture of Flers, where tanks achieved a spectacular success. Tanks provided some assistance elsewhere, although their full potential was by no means realized because only eleven succeeded in crossing the enemy's front line, thanks mainly to a chain of mishaps suffered when starting from their departure points. As an example, of the ten tanks allocated to the Guards Division, only five arrived at their departure points; one of these failed to start and the remainder lost direction, and the result was that the Guards attacked without their assistance.

The battle was resumed on the following two days, but it was limited to local operations in which some ground was gained in the face of heavy artillery fire and counter-attacks. It was already clear that a breakthrough was not realizable and, as if to underline this, the rain fell day after day, turning the already sodden battlefield into a sea of mud and making any sustained movement one of the utmost exertion. The rain caused constant postponements to operations, and there was concern about stocks of gun ammunition. Nevertheless, it was agreed that the French and the British would carry out a combined assault on 25 September, while an attack by the Reserve Army on Thiepval was fixed for the following day. The Fourth Army's objectives for the attack were those not reached on the 15th, that is, Morval, Lesboeufs and Gueudecourt. Zero hour was 12.35 p.m., and once again the cavalry were to be employed, provided that the first two villages were captured. After two days of bombardment, the attack by XIV Corps on Morval and Lesboeufs was completely successful and Gueude-court was taken (and the outskirts were reconnoitred by a squadron of cavalry that was forced to withdraw after being shelled), and on the following day the enemy evacuated Combles. The French, however, could make only slow progress against Sailly Saillisel, thus holding up any further advance by the British right.

This hold-up caused the initiative to be passed to the Reserve Army with the objective of clearing Thiepval and the surrounding redoubts and gaining the

Thiepval ridge – an objective originally set for 1 July. Zero hour on the 26th was 12.35 p.m., the preliminary bombardment having commenced three days earlier. In the event, the attack was only partially successful. The 1st Canadian Division on the right of the attack almost reached the crest of the ridge but suffered heavily in the process. On the left, the attack by II Corps succeeded in clearing Thiepval except for the north-west corner, but the main obstacles to further progress were the Schwaben and Zollern Redoubts, where the enemy still stubbornly held out. Tanks were again employed, but of the two allocated to the Canadians one ditched and the other was totally destroyed by a direct hit. Eight tanks were to assist II Corps, but only one was able to render any assistance. Thus the Germans still held the ridge, but they withdrew from the Zollern Redoubt on the 27th and Thiepval was finally subdued the following day. The Schwaben Redoubt – initially overrun by the 36th Division on 1 July – still held out.

Although the Allied attacks on the Somme during August and September had gained little ground, the impact on the enemy had been severe. Falkenhayn's policy of uncompromising defence, with immediate counter-attacks where positions had been yielded, had brought about serious casualties. By the end of August the rumblings of discontent had surfaced over Falkenhayn's defence strategy and the German Emperor was prevailed upon to remove him. On 29 August he was replaced by Field Marshal von Hindenburg, with General von Ludendorff as his Chief of Staff. Together they had achieved striking successes against the Russians on the Eastern Front, but they were faced with a grave situation on the Somme, which deteriorated even further in September. In particular, the British attacks on the Flers–Courcelette line, followed by the assault on Morval, had caused heavy losses, and there was a desperate need for reinforcements and reliefs for the battle-weary divisions. Coupled with Russian and Italian successes against the Austrians in August, the need to find troops to deal with Romania and maintain the defence at Verdun, the German Army was under such pressure that a tactical withdrawal on the Somme in order to shorten the front was being given serious consideration.

Undeterred by the onset of autumn, with the possibility of further unfavourable weather, Haig decided to continue operations and at the end of September he instructed his army commanders to make preparations for the next assault. This would take the form of a combined attack by the Fourth, Reserve and Third Armies, to be launched on 12 October. The plan was ambitious in its scope. It would have the effect of moving his entire Somme front some three to four miles north-eastwards, straightening it in the process and ultimately threatening Bapaume. But Haig's hopes for reasonable campaigning weather were to be dashed. Although preliminary operations commenced on 1 October for the main assault, rain set in on the 2nd and fell continuously for the following two days, causing a postponement of preliminary operations until the 7th, but the only success was the capture of the village of Le Sars on the Albert–Bapaume road. The main assault took place on the 12th, but the Fourth Army achieved little against determined resistance. The French attacking astride the River Somme fared no better: any advance was vigorously counter-attacked and some ground won had to be given up. The Reserve Army had captured Stuff Redoubt on the 9th and finally cleared the Schwaben Redoubt five days later. But the constant rain made the conditions appalling :

> The roads, which at the best of times were ill-founded, had long since ceased to possess any stable foundation. Into the deep mud which formed their surface tree trunks and balks of timber were thrown to support the unceasing wheeled traffic. But, think with pity on the men who staggered and slithered, their feet often trapped between heavy sleepers, as the unseen road bottom, on which they trod through twelve inches of slime, rocked and swayed beneath the weight of passing wagons. The agonies of the battlefield were not alone due to the terrors of shell-fire and the lash of machine guns, nor even to the piteous wail of the wounded, but they were increased a hundredfold by the exertions required in going up to the line, and retreating therefrom when relieved. Often men would have preferred to risk the peril of the front line to the almost intolerable journeys back to comparative sanctuary. These roads, registered to an inch by the enemy artillery, were under incessant shell-fire, their scuppers and banks heaped with corpses of mules and horses and with shattered waggons.[30]

Haig would not release his grip on the offensive, despite the dreadful conditions. He knew that the Germans had suffered severely (as indeed had his own armies), but he remained optimistic that the enemy's morale was weakening and that one final push would bring about the longed-for breakthrough. To a certain extent he was right: there is little doubt that the German Army on the Somme was not now of the same quality that had faced the Allies at the beginning of July. There is also little doubt that German morale had been shaken both by the unremitting attacks and by the use of tanks. With the prepared defences and the deep dug-outs of 1 July now relics of the past (except in the Beaumont Hamel salient), the infantry, in particular, had suffered increasingly from Allied heavy artillery. Short of reinforcements, which were denied to them at the last moment because of indications that the French were about to go over to the offensive at Verdun, the enemy was tired and dispirited. However, notwithstanding the over-optimistic reports fed to Haig by GHQ Intelligence, the Germans were still a formidable fighting force and, indeed, would remain a force to be reckoned with even in the last months of 1918.

On 18 October Haig issued orders for the Reserve Army to complete the capture of Thiepval ridge and attack astride the Ancre; the Fourth Army, in concert with the French, was to attack Le Transloy. The Reserve Army gained the Thiepval ridge on the 21st, but the other attacks proved fruitless. Rain fell again on the 19th and after a brief lull returned once more, with no improvement until 3 November. The attack against Le Transloy had been planned for the 5th but the appalling conditions at last moved the commander of XIV Corps to protest to Rawlinson:

> No one who has not visited the front trenches can really know the state of exhaustion to which the men are reduced. The conditions are far worse than in the first battle of Ypres; all my General Officers and Staff Officers agree that they are the worst they have seen, owing to the enormous distance of the carry of all munitions – such as food, water and ammunition.[31]

As a result the attack was called off, and the Fourth Army's role in the offensive came to an end. The struggle, however, was not quite over. Gough's Reserve Army (renamed the Fifth Army at the end of October) launched an attack against Beaumont Hamel at 5.45 a.m. on the 13th. The advance began under a creeping barrage and the right of the attack succeeded in taking the village (a 1 July objective) but the left failed. The attack was renewed the following day and Beaucourt (near Beaumont Hamel) was captured, but although Gough had hopes of renewing the offensive, the failure of his left and the need for fresh troops meant that the Battles of the Somme had come to an end. The final attack was made on the 18th in terrible conditions: snow had fallen overnight, turning to driving sleet and then rain as the advance began. Meeting heavy machine-gun fire, and suffering many casualties, the attackers gained some ground, but they could go no further.

* * *

What lessons had been learned by the British Army and its commanders since the disaster of 1 July? In the four and a half months that the battles had lasted, the attack on 14 July initially held high promise of an overdue change from the rigidity of previous strategies: assembling the troops in the dark and advancing before dawn under cover of a creeping barrage (after a preliminary bombardment of only five minutes), the attack took the Germans completely by surprise. Here was a strong indication that, given a flexible and imaginative plan, the infantry, in particular, could do all that was demanded of them. Indeed, on the left of the attack, they could have done more and were eager to do so, but the wait before High Wood for the cavalry (whose objective it had been) effectively brought to a halt what could have been a promising development. The refusal to allow the infantry to proceed was made at corps headquarters and is illustrative of staff rigidity in not delegating decisions to the men on the spot.

The attack on 15 September against the Flers–Courcelette line saw the first use of tanks in a combat role. Relatively few German infantry encountered the eleven tanks that managed to penetrate the front, but the shock caused was out of all proportion to the numbers involved. A German eyewitness described the scene:

> When the German outposts crept out of their dug-outs in the mist of the morning and stretched their necks to look for the English, their blood was chilled in their veins. Mysterious monsters were crawling towards them over the craters. Stunned as if an earthquake had burst around them, they all rubbed their eyes, which were fascinated by the fabulous creatures ... One stared and stared as if one had lost the power of one's limbs. The monsters approached slowly, hobbling, rolling and rocking, but they approached. Nothing impeded them: a supernatural force seemed to impel them on. Someone in the trenches said, 'The devil is coming,' and the word was passed along the line like wildfire.[32]

Notwithstanding the impact on its troops, the German High Command was not impressed by the performance of tanks, noting the ease in which they became ditched in cratered ground and how easily they could be put out of action by shell-fire. (It was only after the Battle of Cambrai in 1917 that the Germans changed their views.) Apart from the capture of Flers, where tanks gained a much publicized success, the operations on the day were only partially successful, and the Fourth Army plan, in the words of the Official Historian, 'actually "gambled" to a considerable extent on the success of tanks'. In terms of the objectives planned, it was a gamble that did not come off. (This, indeed, was the case with the use of gas at Loos, indicating that there was still a tendency to place too much reliance on a key element in a plan without providing a contingency for its failure.)

Much controversy followed Haig's decision to use the small number of tanks available in driblets. It was argued that the majority failed to reach their objectives because they were in a poor state mechanically owing to extensive trials and demonstrations; that the crews were inexperienced; that the ground was unsuitable; and that he should have waited until many more were available and have used them over ground suited to their capabilities, that is, not heavily cratered. All these are reasonable arguments, but there are counter-arguments equally reasonable. Until tanks had been tried in battle, it could not be known how they, or their crews, would perform, nor what modifications or improvements would be necessary, nor what their future should be in collaborating with advancing infantry. Furthermore, delaying their use until several hundred had become available would have been difficult to keep secret, thus giving time to the enemy to develop counter-weapons. It is suggested here that although the arguments might be considered to be evenly balanced, a marginal case could be made in support of the decision to use them on the Somme on the grounds of the need to gain experience of their performance in battle, both in terms of design and the need for crew training, and to make the improvements necessary to improve reliability. It is clear that tanks had by no means reached their potential, and many staff officers doubted their value, but Haig did not lose confidence in them and asked the War Office to order 1,000 of an improved design.

The opportunities for attacks of an innovative nature, however, were fast disappearing by the end of September. As a departure from dawn attacks, the French practice was adopted of not attacking until good daylight observation could be obtained of the impact of the preliminary bombardment. It was used in the successful assault against Morval and Lesboeufs on 25 September, but when adopted in subsequent attacks it was found that the Germans had not been slow to note the change and were consequently prepared. Instead of manning a definitive front line, they were positioning forward troops in shell-craters, with machine guns sited further back, making the task of observation more difficult and, in consequence, the artillery bombardment less effective. Haig and his commanders had run out of ideas and so, until the offensive came to an end in November, attempts to push forward lapsed into the familiar grind of bombardments followed by costly assaults against an enemy fiercely resisting where his defences were strong and yielding ground only slowly elsewhere.

The Reckoning

The Somme was the muddy grave of the German field army . . .—Captain von Hentig, Guards Reserve Division[33]

The Battle of the Somme tends to be associated with the disaster on the first day, but it will be apparent that it was not one battle but a series, commencing on a hot summer's day and ending in the snows of early winter. It was the greatest battle yet fought by the British Army, and undertaken not by a highly trained, disciplined and experienced army but, for the most part, by civilians in khaki hastily and inadequately trained and thrown into battle by a directing force hardly more competent:

> Almost the whole of the 500,000 British troops who . . . according to calculations made before the battle . . . were available for expenditure in casualties, were duly expended; and the question arises, how far that sacrifice was justified by results.[34]

The results, viewed subjectively, could be measured simply in terms of whether a breakthrough, which was Haig's objective, had been realized. Clearly this had not been so: the maximum depth of penetration was about seven miles on the British right, but on the extreme left, facing Serre, there had been none at all. Moreover, the ground lost by the Germans was of little strategic importance to them, and of not much more to the British having gained it:

The folly of the last phase, from September 25th onwards, was that, having at last won the crest of the ridge, and its commanding observation, the advantage was thrown away by fighting a way down into the valley beyond. Thereby the troops were doomed to spend the winter in flooded trenches. 'Somme mud' was soon to be notorious.[35]

Another subjective measure, viewed in the stark terms of a profit and loss account, could be whether the casualties suffered by the defenders were so much in excess of those caused to the attackers that the imbalance represented an undoubted victory. This is a much more difficult proposition because there has never been consensus, only controversy, on the actual figures, particularly those of the enemy, who excluded the lightly wounded from casualty statistics. Nevertheless, there appears to be a greater measure of reliability concerning the statistics of French and British casualties where the losses in killed, wounded and missing total some 600,000, with the British loss at around 420,000. On the other hand, estimates of German losses have ranged between 400,000 and 600,000: the figure generally quoted in German histories between the wars was 500,000. (German records were apparently destroyed in the 1939–45 war.) Nothing is to be gained, however, by attempting to throw any fresh light on the problem because the means to do so no longer exist. This being so, it is suggested that it would not be unreasonable to assume a total of 1,200,000 casualties shared more or less equally between the participants.

It will be obvious that the number of casualties sustained by an army in battle is of considerable importance, but there are other factors to be borne in mind in when considering the results of the Somme battles. Writing after the war, Ludendorff considered that 'the German Army had been fought to a standstill and was worn out'; other German accounts lament the irreparable loss of so much of their trained army, and the fall in morale brought about by the increasing evidence of Allied superiority in *matériel*, particularly in heavy artillery. The loss to the British was not of its professional army – this had virtually ceased to exist by 1915 – but of those who had flocked so enthusiastically to enlist in 1914 and 1915 in response to Kitchener's call for volunteers. Thus, if the German Army was not the same at the end of the Somme battles, then neither was the British. It had certainly gained experience, at inordinate cost, but its morale had also been shaken, not in the same sense experienced by the German Army but in the realization that 'walk-overs' and 'breakthroughs' were illusory. Although the resolve to finish the war was not in doubt, there had been, in a sense, a loss of innocence, particularly by those (and there were many) who had enlisted out of patriotism. The mood had undergone a perceptible change: there was now the belief that there had been a needless sacrifice of many lives, and the early idealism was tinged with bitterness. The places of those who had not survived would be taken up by reluctant conscripts: 'the Somme had eaten up the volunteers, the cream of Britain's manhood.'[36]

The question then arises, what was to be gained by attacking on the Somme? There was no great strategic prize to be won: the offensive was chosen by Joffre simply because the British and French Armies had a common boundary in this sector. Haig would have preferred to have attacked in Flanders, but his instructions were to co-operate with the French unless by so doing he endangered his own armies. Joffre had always regarded the attacks by the four Allied powers in 1916 as a means of wearing out the enemy, in other words attrition. 'Wearing out' was certainly part of Haig's philosophy, but increasingly he saw the opportunity for a breakthrough and this was reflected in his plan for the offensive. He never relinquished the hope that German morale would break. Had the weather not been so adverse, there is no doubt that he would have continued the battle, and he was criticized by the French for not doing so – Joffre considered that Germany would then have suffered 'a complete defeat'.

This, then, poses the next question: would a unified command on the Western Front have been an advantage? This expedient had to be adopted in the crisis caused by the German offensive in March 1918, but it is questionable whether it would have been beneficial in 1916. It would seem almost inevitable that Joffre, despite his waning prestige in French government circles, would have been the generalissimo, and in his anxiety to maintain pressure on the enemy he might well have decided to employ British forces in attacks over Haig's objections, which would have brought about a serious political crisis. But it is also questionable whether, at this stage in the war, the Allies possessed a commander of sufficient experience and stature to fulfil the role. Although Haig had disagreements with Joffre, sometimes to the extent of refusing to co-operate with his tactical proposals, he did his utmost to support him. Even so, the experience of a unified command is not always without its difficulties; certainly there were problems in 1918 when Foch took over the supreme command, and they certainly existed in the 1939–45 war. Haig has been much criticized for continuing the offensive beyond September, but his decision to do so was partly a result of his optimism that German morale was on the verge of crumbling and partly a result of pressure from Joffre and Foch. It was this pressure that caused Haig to embark on his autumn offensives in the rain and mud. These ill-considered attacks, even allowing for the capture of Beaumont Hamel, pushed the infantry, in particular, to the limits of endurance. With his constant preoccupation with the enemy's morale, it does not readily appear that he gave due thought to that of his own troops.

When all the strands of this great series of battles are drawn together, it ought to be possible take an objective view, but it would seem that the Somme inhibits this – it is, as it were, a picture that goes continually in and out of focus. One notable historian wrote that 'Strategically [that is, for the Allies] the battle of the Somme was an unredeemed defeat',[37] and another has written, 'The Somme was an Allied, and in particular, a British disaster'.[38] Lloyd George, soon to be prime minister, was so outraged at the extent of British casualties for so little gain that his anger was to sour his relations with Haig for the rest of the war. And yet there is another point of view: 'Nevertheless, within the terms of reference of the 1914–1918 War, the Battle of the Somme was an unquestionable Allied victory, mainly a British one, because it laid the essential foundation for the final defeat of the Germans in the field.'[39] It was a defeat if only the events of 1 July are considered, but a victory if its primary purpose was the relief of Verdun – and this had been gained by the middle of July. For the remainder of the offensive, despite British hopes for a breakthrough, it was a battle of attrition, leaving all the participants exhausted by the end of it.

But perhaps an objective view is not possible. Perhaps the battle should be regarded in the much wider perspective of the war as a whole, which was Haig's approach when writing at the end of the conflict. The losses by the Germans on the Somme (and at Verdun), which they were less able to withstand than, in particular, the British, brought about their fateful decision in the following January to engage in unrestricted submarine warfare. Hindenburg had said, 'We must save men from a second Somme battle'. It was realized that the decision would be likely to bring the United States into the war, but it was a calculated risk that, before her Army could make any substantial impression on the Western Front, Britain, now seen as the principal enemy, would within a matter of months have been starved into seeking a negotiated peace. This desperate gamble misfired, but Haig could hardly have foreseen his Somme battle as bringing it about, leading to the conclusion that he was ultimately to be proved right for the wrong reasons.

Notes to Chapter 4

1. Hankey, Lord, *The Supreme Command 1914–1918*, Vol. 1, Allen & Unwin (London, 1961)

2. Edmonds, Brigadier-General Sir James, (comp.), *Official History of the War: Military Operations, France and Belgium 1916*, Vol. I, Macmillan & Co. (London, 1932)

3. Quoted in Horne, Alistair, *The Price of Glory: Verdun 1916*, Macmillan & Co. (London, 1962)

4. Hankey, *op. cit.*

5. Maurice, Major-General Sir Frederick, *The Life of General Lord Rawlinson of Trent*, Cassell (London, 1928)

6. Masefield, John, *The Old Front Line*, Heinemann (London, 1917)

7. Kipling, Rudyard, *The Irish Guards in the Great War*, Macmillan & Co. (London, 1923)

8. Edmonds, *op. cit.*

9. Severn, Mark, *The Gambardiers*, Ernest Benn (London, 1930)

10. Edmonds, *op. cit*

11. Cook, A. H., (Sergeant, 1st Somerset Regt), *I Was There*, The Amalgamated Press (1938–39)

12. Maurice, *op. cit.*

13. Quoted in de Groot, G. J., *Douglas Haig 1861–1928*, Unwin Hyman, (London, 1988)

14. Cook, *op. cit.*

15. Edmonds, *op. cit.*

16. Masefield, *op. cit.*

17. Malins, G. H., *How I Filmed the War*, Herbert Jenkins (London, 1920)

18. Cook, *op. cit.*

19. Severn, *op. cit.*

20. Dewar, G. A. B., and Boraston, J. H., *Sir Douglas Haig's Command*, Constable (London, 1922)

21. *Ibid.*

22. Edmonds, *op. cit.*

23. Blake, Robert, (ed.), *The Private Papers of Douglas Haig 1914–1919*, Eyre & Spottiswoode (London, 1952)

24. Griffith, L. Wyn, *Up to Mametz*, Faber (London, 1931)

25. Lloyd, R. A., *A Trooper in the 'Tins'*, Hurst & Blackett (London, 1938)

26. Lawson, G. A., *I Was There*, The Amalgamated Press (London, 1938–39)

27. Quoted in Farrar-Hockley, A. H., *The Somme*, Pan Books (London, 1966)

28. Hamilton, The Hon. R. G. A., *The War Diary of the Master of Belhaven*, John Murray (London, 1924; republished by Wharncliffe Publishing, Barnsley, 1990)

29. Edmonds, *op. cit.* The italics are Swinton's.

30. Hutchison, G. S., *Pilgrimage*, Rich & Cowan (London, 1935)

31. Quoted in Travers, Tim, *The Killing Ground*, Allen & Unwin (London, 1987)

32. Quoted in Cooper, Bryan, *The Ironclads of Cambrai*, The Souvenir Press (London, 1967)

33. Edmonds, *op. cit.*

34. Bean, C. E. W., *The Official History of Australia in the War of 1914–1918*, Angus & Robertson (Sydney, 1921)

35. Liddell Hart, A. H., *A History of the World War 1914–1918*, Faber & Faber (London, 1934)

36. Horne, Alistair, *Death of a Generation*, Macdonald, (London, 1970)

37. Taylor, A. J. P., *The First World War: An Illustrated History*, Hamish Hamilton (London, 1963)

38. Winter, J. M., *The Experience of World War I*, Macmillan (London, 1988)

39. Terraine, John, *Douglas Haig – The Educated Soldier*, Hutchinson (London, 1963)

5

Arras

ON EASTER Monday, 9 April 1917, in intermittent storms of sleet and snow, the British First and Third Armies attacked the German positions around Arras and for the first time in nearly three years achieved a brilliant success. As the attack proceeded, however, the hopes roused were slowly to dissolve until, at its conclusion, it was destined to be one of the most costly offensives ever launched by the British Army in France. This was as much due to mistakes on the battlefield as to the repercussions of political and military events that had their roots in the previous year.

On 15 November 1916 Joffre and Haig, together with military representatives from Russia, Italy, Belgium, Romania and Serbia, had met at Chantilly to review the events of the year and make plans for 1917. It might be thought that the heavy losses at Verdun and the Somme, in particular, would have created a mood of disillusionment, but, according to the Official History, 'The atmosphere of the Conference was one of sober optimism, reflected in the geniality in which General Joffre greeted the assembly'. This optimism could be ascribed to the heavy losses by the Germans at Verdun and the Somme and the impact on their morale; to the successful Russian offensive in June against the Austro-Hungarian Army, which had drawn troops from the west; to the partial success of the Italians in their attacks on the Isonzo; and to the fact that the British Army on the Western Front now numbered over one and half million men with more to come. But the clouds of what was to become a year of calamity for the Allied powers were already gathering. Romania would seek an armistice within weeks of the Conference, and the days of Joffre's command were already numbered.

The main conclusions reached at the conference were that, during the coming winter of 1916–17, the Allies would pursue offensive operations on their respective fronts within the limits imposed by the weather, and were to be ready from the first fortnight in February to launch attacks 'with all means at their disposal'. Plans for future operations were not discussed in any detail. So far as the Western Front was concerned, Joffre and Haig had already agreed that the French would attack between the Oise and the Somme (with two secondary attacks later on elsewhere) and the British between Bapaume and Arras. Haig was still intent, however, on his operation to deny the ports of Ostend and

Zeebrugge to German submarines. Joffre was sympathetic to the proposal, but he thought that it should not be carried out before the Allied offensive already agreed upon had begun.

The optimism felt by the military was not, however, shared by either the public or the politicians in France and Britain. The great battles of Verdun and the Somme, with their enormous casualty lists, had fuelled a growing frustration with the direction of the war, and in some circles there was even talk of a negotiated peace. This undercurrent of dissatisfaction surfaced first in Britain with the resignation of the Prime Minister, Asquith, and his replacement on 11 December by Lloyd George. In France the criticism was centred on Joffre. He was blamed for the inadequate state of the Verdun defences and the failure on the Somme, and as a result of Cabinet changes he was made 'technical adviser' to the Government whilst still remaining Commander-in-Chief of the French armies, although effectively in name only. A hitherto little-known general, Robert Nivelle, who had distinguished himself in the French counter-attacks at Verdun in the autumn, was more to French taste, and he was promoted over the heads of the other army group commanders to be Commander-in-Chief of the Armies of the North and North-East. Joffre soon found the situation intolerable and resigned on 26 December, to be superseded by Nivelle. These changes were to lead to incidents of high drama.

Haig had first met Nivelle at Cassel (headquarters of the British Second Army) on 20 December and was impressed, noting in his diary that 'He was, I thought, a most straightforward and soldierly man'.[1] The day after the meeting Haig received a letter from Nivelle setting out his views on the 1917 offensives. They represented a radical change from the plans previously agreed between Joffre and Haig. Instead of an increasing burden of future offensive operations being carried out by the British (which had been Joffre's intention), Nivelle's proposals were that the enemy should be pinned down in the Bapaume–Arras sector by attacks delivered by the British, with the French operating similarly between the Oise and the Somme – basically the original Joffre/Haig conception. Nivelle's strategy, however, was to deceive the enemy as to where the main blow was to fall, and he proposed what he termed 'a mass of manoeuvre' involving twenty-seven divisions ready to be flung in a sudden attack on another part of the French front. After the enemy's front had been ruptured, both the French and British Armies would exploit the situation with all their resources. Although not mentioned in the letter, the part of the French front to be attacked was the sector between Reims and the Aisne–Oise canal (where Joffre had intended to make one of his subsidiary attacks). The difference between the two plans was not so much one of strategy but of emphasis. Joffre had hoped to 'destroy the enemy's capacity for resistance' as a first step to a breakthrough, whereas Nivelle's goal was 'the destruction of the principal mass of the enemy's armies in the Western Theatre'. Not only was the brunt of the offensive to be borne by the French Army, with the British taking on a secondary role; Nivelle also wanted Haig to take over about twenty miles of the French front (between Bouchavesnes and the Amiens–Roye road) in order to release French divisions to make up the reserve of twenty-seven. Nivelle thought that, if the offensive succeeded, the Belgian coast would fall into Allied hands as a consequence of the German retreat, and thus a Flanders offensive would not be necessary. Haig agreed in principle with Nivelle's plan, although he was only prepared to take over eight miles of the French front (to the Amiens–St Quentin road), with completion early in February; a further take-over would depend on new British divisions being sent to France. He considered that the date of the offensive could not be before 1 May if his maximum strength was to be deployed. He was not happy that the clearance of the Belgian coast should be left dependent on the success of the proposed offensive. He wanted a firm commitment to that end should the offensive fail, as he made clear to Nivelle:

> But it must be distinctly understood between us that if I am not satisfied that this larger plan, as events develop, promises the degree of success necessary to clear the Belgian coast, then I not only cannot continue the battle but I will look to you to fulfil the undertaking you have given me verbally to relieve on the defensive front the troops I require for my northern offensive.[2]

The Nivelle plan had been discussed at a meeting of the British War Cabinet on 26 December, but a week later, at a conference in Rome of representatives of the governments and military commands of Britain, France and Italy, Lloyd George had pressed strongly for an attack on the Austrian front, mainly by Italian troops but supported by Franco-British artillery. His proposal was, in effect, side-tracked by merely being referred to the military advisers of the three governments to study, but in the event, as Lloyd George expected, it was shelved. His frustration was expressed in his *War Memoirs*:

> When we came to the main purpose for which the Conference had been summoned – a real and not a sham co-ordination of strategy – the Conference reached no final decision and the military staffs were left in possession of the field. There were many reasons for that . . . The professional deems it a point of honour to stand by his brethren against all outsiders, including the facts.[3]

He now realized that the Western Front would remain the dominant theatre of operations and that he would have to consider the Nivelle plan as being the only strategy on offer. Nivelle had wanted to meet Lloyd George when the latter was passing through Paris on his way home from Rome, but instead he was invited to a conference in London on 15 January in order that his plan could be discussed with the members of the War Cabinet. Haig was also invited, and he had an interview with Lloyd George shortly before the conference commenced which appears to have been rather strained. A portent of events to come was contained in Haig's diary:

> After I had explained the general plan for the offensive which is in accordance with General Nivelle's proposals and wishes expressed to me, the P.M. proceeded to compare the successes obtained by the French during the past summer with what the British had achieved. His general conclusions were that the French Army was better all round, and was able to gain success at less cost of life. That much of our losses on the Somme was wasted, and that the country would not stand any more of that sort of thing. That to win, we must attack a soft front, and we could not find that on the Western Front. I listened patiently for some time, and then told him briefly how the British had to attack and had to keep on attacking in order to withdraw pressure from the French front at Verdun, whereas the French attack on the Somme was quite unexpected by the Germans . . .[4]

The conference was attended by Lloyd George, Haig (recently appointed Field Marshal), Robertson, Balfour (Foreign Secretary), Nivelle and staff and the French Ambassador. Like Lloyd George, the War Cabinet was equally impressed with Nivelle, who had an English mother and a fluent command of the language. He was able to put over his ideas lucidly and logically (in contrast to Haig, who tended to be inarticulate). He maintained that he was not a believer in prolonged battles of attrition such as the Somme. His method was one short, decisive rupture, achieved within forty-eight hours, followed by the destruction of the enemy's reserves in open fighting. Lloyd George's fears of yet another costly offensive were thereby dispelled. Nivelle's eloquence, when coupled with his performance at Verdun, had persuaded him that at last he had found a soldier who had the key to unlock the door of the Western Front. It was finally agreed that two more divisions would be sent to France; that, accordingly, the British would relieve the French up to the Amiens–Roye road; and that the offensive would be launched not later than 1 April. Nivelle, however, did not commit himself to the actual date. Winston Churchill summed up the results of the conference:

> So far all had been harmonious, but the Prime Minister in the process of being converted from his previous opposition to the offensive had evolved a further design. He was already set upon his great and simple conception of a united command. Like the War Cabinet he was attracted by the personality of General Nivelle and disposed to back him. . . It was believed that better war direction could be obtained from the French. It was also believed – and in this case with far more justification – that one controlling hand ought to prevail on the whole of the Western Front . . . So Nivelle returned to Chantilly carrying the virtual promise that Haig and the British Army should be subordinated to his directions. These important additional developments were not at this stage imparted by the Prime Minister or the War Cabinet to either Robertson or Haig.[5]

Two other factors now obtruded. The winter of 1916/17 was one of great severity – certainly by far the worst of the war. Frosts throughout January froze the canals, preventing all movement, and the intermittent thaws damaged the thinly metalled roads. This, coupled with an overstrained French railway system, brought about a transport crisis, and Haig wrote to Nivelle on 24 January, warning him that unless the situation improved it might mean revising his (Haig's) plans. He met Nivelle on 29 January to discuss the transport crisis and also the British operational plan for the attack in the Bapaume–Arras sector. Nivelle was not entirely happy with the plan, which included a subsidiary attack on Vimy Ridge, but agreement was reached on the measures necessary to lessen the railway congestion; these would raise tonnages to 200,000 per week. This was 50,000 tons less than the amount Haig considered necessary to support his offensive, but an impression was growing in French minds that Haig was using the transport crisis to defer his attack. The transport crisis continued, however, and Haig complained to Robertson, suggesting that it would be advisable to hold another conference of the heads of the two governments and the two commanders-in-chief. Haig, however, met Nivelle on 16 February and it was agreed that the former would not attack until his requirements had been met.

This discussion appeared to obviate the need for a conference; nevertheless, one took place at Calais on 26 February involving the French and British Prime Ministers, Haig, Nivelle, Robertson and General Lyautey (the French War Minister), ostensibly to discuss the transport problem. This, however, was delegated to the transport advisers to settle, and the real reason for the conference then became apparent. The French, with Lloyd George's support, had produced what Haig termed a 'System of Command' which effectively placed the British Army under French authority, thereby reducing Haig to the status of a French army group commander. This remarkable episode in British political and military history has been well documented elsewhere. In the short term, however, it had little military effect. After Haig and Robertson had resolved on being tried by court martial rather than, as Haig put it, 'betraying the Army by agreeing to its being placed under the French', a compromise was reached by which he would only conform to Nivelle's instructions for the duration of the proposed offensive, but with a right of appeal to the British Government. In the longer term, however, the repercussions bordered on the calamitous. Lloyd George's relations with Haig had been soured by the Somme offensive. He had been appalled at the extent of British losses for so little gain and he now distrusted him and Robertson, regarding the latter as Haig's mouthpiece in London rather than an impartial military adviser. Haig, in turn, had always tended to be suspicious of Lloyd George, but the Calais Conference hardened this wariness into a mistrust which was later to have serious consequences.

Meanwhile, unsuspected by the Allies, moves were being prepared by the German High Command that were to have a profound effect upon Allied plans. In October 1916 Royal Flying Corps observers had seen that the enemy was constructing new trenches at Quéant, twelve miles south-east of Arras, and in November British Intelligence received a report from an escaped Russian prisoner that concrete dug-outs were being constructed near St Quentin – over thirty miles to the east in a direct line from Quéant. No special significance was attached to these reports, but further observation was frustrated by the weather and the activities of German aircraft (which, at that time, were superior to those of the RFC and were causing severe losses in its pilots and observers). It was not until the end of February that the Allies became aware that the enemy had built a massive defensive system, about seventy miles in length, extending from near Arras to St Quentin, which the British came to call the Hindenburg Line. To the Germans, however, it was the Siegfried Stellung, and not a line as such, but a series of concrete gun emplacements arranged chequer-wise, backed by strongly built trenches and dug-outs and scattered over a depth of three or four miles. Moreover a switch line was being constructed from Quéant to Drocourt, joining up with a defensive system covering Lens.

Although it was believed that the German Army had suffered heavy losses at Verdun and the Somme, there was no accurate knowledge as to the extent. Ludendorff wrote in his war memoirs that

> ... the enemy's great superiority in men and material would be even more painfully felt in 1917 than in 1916. They had to face the danger that 'Somme fighting' would soon break out at various points ... and that even our troops would not be able to withstand such attacks indefinitely ...

He had come to the unpalatable conclusion that the German Army could not win a decisive battle on the Western Front. He believed that the sensible course was a strategic withdrawal to the Hindenburg Line, and there stand on the defensive until either the Russians were defeated or the British were forced to make peace as a result of unrestricted submarine warfare. The withdrawal would straighten out a potentially dangerous salient, shorten his front by twenty-five miles and save thirteen or fourteen divisions. It was given impetus by British pressure on the Ancre in January, and the German Emperor signed the order on 4 February.

> The decision to retreat was not reached without a painful struggle [wrote Ludendorff]. It implied a confession of weakness bound to raise the morale of the enemy and lower our own. But it was necessary for military reasons – we had no choice.

By the middle of March the German Army had completed its withdrawal to the Hindenburg Line, but the Allies were slow in following up, mainly because

Field Marshal Sir Douglas Haig and his army commanders, Cambrai, 11 November 1918.
(IWM)

Far left, top: A Vickers machine-gun team
wearing the early gas mask hood.
Far left, bottom: A platoon of the East
Lancashire Regiment wearing the new 'box'
respirator.
Above left: General Sir Edmund Allenby.
Above: General Ferdinand Foch.
Left: General Joseph Joffre.

Right: General Sir William Robertson, Chief of the Imperial General Staff.
Below: The Somme, 1916: British infantry 'going over the top'.

Right: The 1st Battalion the
Lancashire Fusiliers on the
Somme.
Below: The Somme: the ruins of
Guillemont village.

Left, upper: A disabled Mark IV tank. Passchendaele, 1917.
Left, lower: A British 18pdr field gun covering a canal crossing.
Right: Field Marshal Paul von Hindenburg and, on his left, General Erich von Ludendorff.
Below: The ruins of the Passchendaele battlefield: a British artillery ammunition column on the Menin road, October 1918.

Top: Neuve Chapelle: a German strongpoint at Layes Brook.
Above: A German pill-box on Hill 60, Ypres.

of the devastation wreaked by the enemy, particularly on the roads, and the severe difficulties this created for bringing up artillery to support the infantry:

> The pursuit of the Germans was rendered exceedingly slow and arduous by the unspeakable destruction which met our advancing columns at every step. Cross-roads had been mined and vast craters forced all wheeled traffic to deviate on to the sodden fields adjoining. Trees had been felled across the roads and added to the impediments to the advance of our artillery. Everywhere the Germans had committed wanton destruction – young fruit trees were ringed, crops were burnt wholesale, and every sort of livestock had been driven before them in their retreat. The aspect of the villages was most peculiar. At a distance they appeared to be untouched, and the red roofs of the cottages showed nothing unusual. On a closer approach, however, they were found to be ruined and the walls knocked down so that the roofs had subsided intact to the ground. Furniture, too heavy to be moved, had shared in this destruction, and its débris was lying shattered among the heaps of brick and stone. Yet further abominations had been invented, and a serious of ingenious 'booby-traps' were discovered in the shape of common articles such as shovels and helmets. They were left lying about in places where they were likely to be picked up by our troops, and being connected with bombs and even large mines caused explosions when they were touched.[6]

The effect of the German withdrawal was that the great salient of nearly 100 miles between Arras and Soissons had ceased to exist, and the positions to which the enemy had retreated were relatively safe from any concentrated attack. As a result, the Nivelle plan for the Franco-British offensive against the salient, with a surprise attack by the French between Soissons and Reims, had been substan-tially dislocated; moreover, the enemy had become aware, through documents in the possession of captured French troops, that Nivelle's main thrust would be in the latter sector.

On 6 March Nivelle issued a directive to Haig in which he recognized that the German withdrawal constituted a new fact, but he thought that the direction of the Allied attacks would outflank it. Surprisingly, he even considered that the withdrawal might be to the Allies' advantage and he decided 'not to modify in any fundamental way the general plan of operations already settled'. He admitted, however, that the operations could not be carried out as originally planned, and he would re-examine the position. But, in the event, his plans were not modified, and this led to dissension among his subordinates and, ultimately, the French War Cabinet. Nivelle, however, remained obdurate: he considered that complete victory was certain and offered to resign if the War Cabinet had lost confidence in him.

Painlevé, who had replaced General Lyautey as War Minister, was in an acute dilemma. To dismiss Nivelle would bring about a political crisis, even the downfall of the Government, and there was no contingency plan to replace the offensive if it were abandoned – and there was the fact that the British

Government had been won over. On the other hand, Painlevé had no confidence in Nivelle, and the breaking off of relations between Germany and the United States on 3 February, with all the signs pointing to eventual hostilities between the two powers, was a factor in favour of deferment until an American army could take the field. (The United States formally declared war on 6 April.)

A French Council of War was convened on 4 April in Paris, at which Nivelle was supremely, if not arrogantly, confident. He did not think that the Americans could come in sufficient numbers for a long time, while the revolution which had taken place in Russia in March would mean that little could be expected of them in future and he raised the spectre of a Russian collapse and the transfer of German divisions to the west. He had no doubts about the success of his offensive, which should take place as soon as possible. After further debate Nivelle was given the Council's assent to the offensive. So the stage was set and the politicians made their exits, leaving the soldiers to act out the drama. The British would attack at Arras on 8 April (subsequently changed to the 9th), with only a minor role for the French group of armies alongside them. The main French thrust would follow a week later in Champagne.

The Plan

The city of Arras lies in a gentle hollow on the River Scarpe at a point where the uplands of Picardy begin to descend to the plain of Douai. To the east, spurs of low hills reach towards the plain, and to the north lies the dominating feature of Vimy Ridge, rising gently from the west but descending steeply to the plain in the east.

For several hundred years the city had experienced a chequered history of conflict. In the Middle Ages its possession had been disputed by either European kings or Burgundian dukes, but it finally became part of France in the middle of the seventeenth century. The French Army had held the city in 1914 and 1915, but it came within the British sector in 1916 when more front was taken over from the French. It had been heavily shelled by the Germans when the French had been in occupation, but since then it had enjoyed a period of comparative peace, to the extent that some of the inhabitants had returned. Underneath the city were (and are) large cellars and, as in Paris, enormous sewers. Apart from these, there also existed a network of caves in the south-eastern suburbs. These caves had originally been the quarries from which the chalk had been excavated to build the city, and it had been an inspired decision by the British to connect up the cellars to the sewers and from there to drive tunnels to the caves. Two tunnels were bored emerging at the front line, although as a result of the German withdrawal only one of these now reached the front. The cellars and caves were capable of accommodating over 24,000 men (about three divisions): they were lit by electricity and provided with a tramway, piped water from an underground pumping station and even a hospital. Their greatest value was that they could be used to pass men underground unobserved and in safety to the front line in the eastern suburbs little more than mile from the city centre.

To the east of the city, and following his usual practice, the enemy occupied the hills and, of exceptional advantage to him, almost the whole of the summit of Vimy Ridge to the north. The ridge had seen some particularly bloody fighting in 1915 when the French had struggled in vain to take it. The sector had been taken over by the British in March 1916, transforming what had become a quiet sector ever since the previous September into one of constant activity, both above and below ground. There was intense tunnelling by both sides and firing of mines, but a strong German counter-attack in May had gained some ground despite British counter-attacks. When the Canadian Corps took over the sector in November they were able to utilize twelve subways some 25 feet below the ground which had been excavated earlier by British tunnelling companies. These extended from the support to the front trenches and, as at Arras, were provided with piped water, electric light and a narrow gauge railway.

The situation brought about by the German withdrawal, and the decision reached at the Calais Conference to relieve the French up to the Amiens–Roye road, resulted in a substantial change to Haig's original plan. A combination of these factors severely curtailed the support originally to be provided by the Fourth and Fifth Armies and, in consequence, increased the Third Army's burden. The latter's attack, originally to take place between Ficheux and the Scarpe river, was extended south of the river and its strength enlarged from ten to eighteen divisions. Its objective was to capture 'the German defensive line [that is, the Hindenburg Line] which runs from Arras towards St Quentin by turning it and attacking it in flank and rear, continuing to operate in the direction of Cambrai'. The role of the First Army (commanded by General Sir Henry Horne) was to capture Vimy Ridge, and this remained unchanged, but it too was strengthened by the addition of three divisions in the hope that any success could be exploited by pushing forward to Douai. At a later date the Fifth Army was to assault the Hindenburg Line at Bullecourt.

The plans for the Third Army attack submitted by its commander, General Sir Edmund Allenby, originally included a proposal for an intense bombardment lasting only forty-eight hours, but this was vetoed by Haig on the grounds that the wear and tear on guns and personnel would be too great and there was no guarantee that the wire would be effectively cut. The artillery plan had, therefore, to be revised (but not without controversy between artillery specialists) and was now to extend over four days. The total number of guns to be employed (including those for the First Army attack on Vimy Ridge) was almost double the number employed for the preliminary bombardment leading up to the Somme attack on 1 July, but this was for a shorter frontage of twelve miles compared with eighteen on the Somme. Significantly, the number of heavy guns was 963 compared with 455. The British front line extended from Croisilles in the south to Givenchy-en-Gohelle in the north and involved (from right to left) the VII, VI and XVII Corps of the Third Army and, for the assault on Vimy Ridge, the Canadian Corps of the First Army. Forty tanks were allocated to the Third Army and eight to the Canadian Corps, but these were the thinly armoured Mark I and II versions, vulnerable to armour-piercing bullets. Two divisions of cavalry would be on hand to exploit any success.

The preliminary bombardment opened on 4 April, and throughout the days leading up to zero hour on the 9th it was practically continuous in daylight but intermittent during the hours of darkness. The Germans were aware of the probability of an attack in the Arras area, but it was not expected until later in the month. Some preparations had been made to meet it, but the bombardment, purposefully directed against the defences and artillery positions, caused acute problems. The effect on communications and artillery was particularly severe: the relief of front line troops became either extremely hazardous or impossible, food was short and supplies of artillery ammunition could be brought up only with great difficulty, with the result that counter-battery fire during the bombardment and on the day of assault was largely ineffective.

The Assault

The objective of the three corps, VII, VI and XVII, comprising Allenby's Third Army was to breach the four heavily wired defensive lines (Black, Blue, Brown and Green) and finally reach the Drocourt–Quéant line, about eight miles from their front, thus opening the way for cavalry exploitation and an advance on Cambrai. VII and VI Corps were to attack south of the Scarpe and XVII to the north. Zero hour was 5.30 a.m. for VI and XVII Corps but later in the day for VII Corps on the extreme right (facing the formidable obstacle of the Hindenburg Line) in the hope that the attacks of the other two corps would ease its task. The Third Army order was explicit about the timing of the assault: the Black line (the German front line) was to be gained at zero hour plus 36 minutes, the Blue (the German second line) at zero plus 2 hours 44 minutes to 3 hours, the Brown (Wancourt–Feuchy) at zero plus 10 hours and the Green (Fampoux–Monchy) at zero plus 12 hours (i.e. 5.30 p.m.).

The weather, which had been cold and clear on Easter Sunday, deteriorated in the early hours of the morning of Easter Monday and by 5.30 a.m. the snow began to fall, driven against the enemy's front by a strong north-westerly wind. Just before zero hour the bombardment ceased:

Only a few seconds to go, then suddenly a complete silence, an absolute cessation of the intense roar, a stillness punctuated and emphasised by the barking of trench mortars up an down the lines; every gun had stopped firing. That sudden silence was more terrifying than the most reverberating explosion. It had the effect of making men feel that they were losing their balance on the edge of the abyss . . . It did not last long. At 5.30 to the second the earth shook as the mines exploded with a muffled roar and every gun on the fifteen-mile front of attack and beyond it opened fire with a clamour such as had probably never been heard in the world . . . The air screamed as it was torn by a thousand shells. Miles up the great projectiles hummed their mighty drone. Lower down through each layer of air the shells flew according to their kind, until, quite above the lines of men closing in behind the barrage, the missiles of the light mortars and the bullets of machine-guns hissed . . . Within three minutes of the time it took our men to form up behind the barrage, a new kind of illumination was added to the fantastic scene. For miles upon miles, all along the German lines hundreds of flares went up. Red, white, orange, the distress signals shot high, falling back in sprays of multicoloured rain. The German infantry was begging for support. The British were upon them.[7]

South of the Scarpe, the attack of VII and VI Corps experienced a mixture of spectacular success and comparative failure. The main objective of VI Corps (the 3rd, 12th, 15th and 37th Divisions) was the Brown line (Wancourt–Feuchy line), about 3,500 yards parallel to its front. Sixteen tanks were allocated to deal with strongpoints around the village of Tilloy les Mofflaines and the powerful defences of the railway triangle, two sides of the latter being built on high embankments and strongly defended by machine guns. The 3rd and 12th Divisions swept through the enemy defences almost without hindrance. The 3rd Division was held up for a time by resistance from the village of Tilloy which was finally subdued by a tank, and the 12th Division had a problem capturing its part of Observation Ridge, where resistance was strong; elsewhere, however, the enemy infantry freely surrendered. Two battalions swarming down the reverse slope of Observation Ridge into Battery Valley came upon a German artillery position, and although some guns had been abandoned they immediately came under fire from the remainder. Undeterred, the infantry pressed on, capturing thirty-one guns in the process. By the evening both divisions were dug in before the Brown line but unable to go further because of uncut wire. The 15th Division achieved the greatest success of all. Although held up for a time by the railway triangle defences, they swept over the northern end of Observation Ridge and down the reverse slope into Battery Valley, where, like the neighbouring 12th Division, they came under fire from enemy batteries. Although suffering heavily from point-blank fire, they too would not be denied: after capturing thirty-six guns they pushed forward, taking Feuchy village, and by 5.30 p.m. had captured the northern end of the Brown line. The role of the 37th Division was to leap-frog through the three other divisions and breach the Green line (stretching from the Scarpe marshes to the River Cojuel) and in the process take Monchy and Guémappe. Coming under machine-gun fire from the Brown line, the division was halted by uncut wire and with the approach of nightfall was too far south to capitalize on the 15th Division's success.

VII Corps, on the extreme right, had the more difficult task. As referred to earlier, its front faced the Hindenburg Line and its assault was to be delayed until the result of the attack of its neighbouring corps (VI) was known. On the right of VII Corps the 21st Division and a brigade of the 30th Division did not attack until 4.15 p.m., but in the face of heavy machine-gun fire these units had only partial success in securing a trench fronting the Hindenburg Line. On the left of the Corps' front, the 56th Division, attacking at 7.45 a.m., succeeded in capturing Neuville Vitasse but was held up before the Hindenburg Line. The remaining division, the 14th, was more fortunate. It overran the strongly defended redoubt known as The Harp and, with the assistance of three tanks, breached the northern end of the Hindenburg Line, eventually halting 600 yards from the Brown line.

North of the Scarpe, the three divisions of XVII Corps (the 9th, 34th and 51st) had as their objective the Brown line (or Point du Jour line) extending from the river to Farbus Wood, the boundary with the Canadian Corps of the First Army. A reserve division, the 4th, was to pass through the 9th Division on the right of the attack, penetrate the Green line and capture the village of Fampoux. Eight tanks were allocated to the corps. The 9th Division scored an unparalleled success in capturing its objective, the Brown line, taking the village of Athies and many prisoners in the process. Indeed, it could have gone further to Fampoux, a 4th Division objective, but there had been some delay in passing this division through. Nevertheless, by the evening Fampoux had been taken and, as the Official History records,

> This marked the longest advance made that day and the longest made in a single day by any belligerent on the Western Front since trench warfare had set in; it was a distance of 3½ miles.

The 34th Division in the centre of the attack was not quite so successful. Its objective was the Brown line, and the Green line just beyond it, which two brigades managed to reach, but the remaining brigade was held up on the Blue line. Once again many prisoners were taken. The 51st Division's objective was also the Brown line, but it suffered heavy casualties, particularly in officers, in carrying the Black line, and some battalions lost direction veering too much to their right. The attack eventually came to a standstill between the Blue and Brown lines, some units mistakenly believing that the trenches they had taken were in fact their objective.

The success of the first day was not, however, to be confined to the Third Army. Further north the objective of the Canadian Corps of the First Army was the hitherto impregnable fortress of Vimy Ridge. From the west the Ridge does not, as might be supposed, present a commanding feature of the kind involving a laborious climb. In 1917 it was seen as 'merely a long, low, ashen-grey ridge. So unmilitary and unformidable did it appear from a distance . . .'[8] There is a gentle slope until the summit is reached, and then the dramatic view of the Douai plain appears as the ridge falls abruptly away to the east. It was on the western slope, however, that the enemy line had originally been established, but the French, at great cost to themselves, had driven back the Germans. Nevertheless, they still held the upper slopes and the crest in positions which they thought to be unassailable.

The attack was planned in two stages. The four divisions of the Canadian Corps (commanded by Lieutenant-General Sir Julian Byng), together with a brigade of the British 5th Division, would deliver the main thrust on a four-mile front extending from Ecurie to Givenchy. The capture of this sector was considered vital in order to form a protective flank for the simultaneous Third Army attack to the south. Given success, the northern end of the ridge, with a prominent feature known as 'The Pimple', would be assaulted, as would Bois en Hache on the southern extremity of the Notre Dame de Lorette Ridge (a continuation, in effect, of Vimy Ridge but separated by the valley of the Souchez river). The area to be attacked represented a triangle with the apex pointing north-westwards, the Canadians on the western arm and the summit of the ridge, the objective, on the eastern . Thus at the base of the triangle the advance would have to cover about 4,000 yards of ground, in contrast to the attack at the apex where the distance narrowed to 700 yards. The enemy's line was strongly defended, heavily wired, studded with concrete machine-gun emplacements and honeycombed with deep dug-outs. Surprisingly, despite his commanding view of the preparations being made, the enemy had made little attempt to interfere with them, no doubt believing that this was to be yet another assault which would founder on the defences.

The preliminary bombardment was also in two stages. Opening up on 20 March at half strength in order to delude the enemy as to its ultimate threat, it developed to its full fury on 4 April, thus coinciding with the opening of the Third Army's bombardment:

> The British artillery had expended in the preliminary bombardment thirty times the amount of heavy-artillery ammunition employed by the French two years before, and more than double, proportionally to the extent of the front, the quantity of all natures employed prior to the Battle of the Somme on the 1st July 1916. An eye-witness has remarked that, whereas the ground on the Somme battlefield

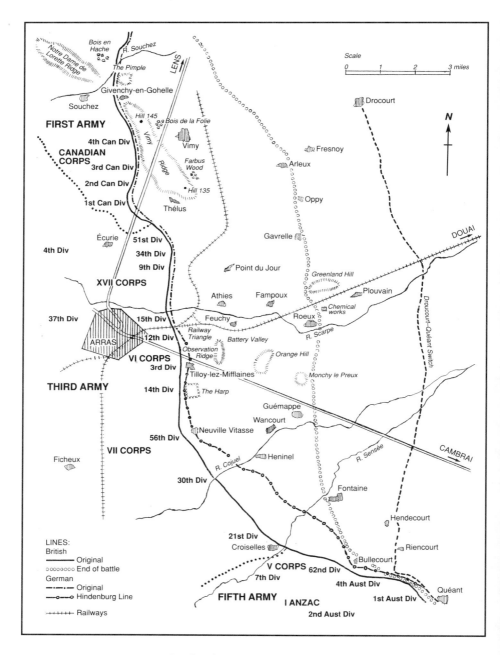

Battle of Arras, April/May 1917

appeared to suffer from smallpox, wide stretches of the Vimy Ridge seemed to be afflicted with confluent smallpox.[9]

At 5.30 a.m., after a hurricane bombardment of only three minutes on the enemy's front trenches, the Canadians advanced in driving sleet across No Man's Land. The 1st and 2nd Canadian Divisions, on the widest part of the triangle, had the furthest to go and, although suffering losses from machine-gun fire, managed to cross three successive lines of enemy trenches. They had attained all their intermediate objectives by about 7 a.m. and were poised to assault the village of Thélus and Hill 135 beyond. Some two hours later two fresh brigades, Canadian and British, spearheaded the advance of the two divisions on the village and the hill. They took the ruins of the village without opposition and, advancing behind a creeping barrage against sporadic resistance, they gained the ridge, but they had reached the limit of advance covered by their own heavy guns:

> Presently they had their reward. Standing on the crest of the ridge, they gazed down on the level plain of Douai, the first Allied soldiers to do so since the far-off days of 1915, when for a few hours the French held the northern extremity of the heights It was an extraordinary sight, a glimpse of another world. Behind them lay an expanse of churned-up mud and desolation completely commanded from where they stood. Even the duckboards at the bottom of some of the communication trenches were clearly visible. Below and beyond them on the German side lay a peaceful countryside with villages that appeared from a distance to be untouched by war. The men were wildly enthusiastic and their sense of victory was enhanced by finding battery after battery abandoned on the edge of the woods that fringed the eastern slopes of the ridge.[10]

On the centre left the 3rd Division gained an immediate success. Surprising some of the enemy still in their dug-outs, the attackers reached their objective of the Bois de la Folie on the summit of the ridge, but more determined resistance was met in the wood itself and, with casualties beginning to mount, the Canadians set about consolidating their gains and beating off counter-attacks. The 4th Division on the extreme left of the attack had the most difficult task. Its objective was Hill 145, the highest point on the ridge, only 700 yards from the Canadian front and strongly defended. Obtaining surprise was of paramount importance, but unfortunately, apart from the right flank of the attack where this was gained, the centre met determined resistance from a strongpoint where the wire was uncut. (According to the Official History, the strongpoint had been left untouched by the artillery because the infantry believed that it would be of use after capture.) This proved to be a tragic error, and the Canadians, suffering severe casualties, could make no headway until early evening when a support battalion arrived. The left flank attack had only 200 yards to go before the summit was reached, and although some progress was made the advance was seriously delayed by enfilade fire from The Pimple and was forced to halt below the summit.

There is no doubt that the result of the first day represented a momentous victory. Although success along the Third Army front had not been uniform, particularly south of the Scarpe where the results, despite early promise, had not been as favourable as those north of the river, all the enemy's front positions had nevertheless been taken and his third line penetrated on a front of nearly three miles. The assault of the Canadian Corps on Vimy Ridge had been an almost total triumph, with only the summit of Hill 145 eluding its grasp. Although the handling of the infantry assault had made great strides since the Somme, the greatest contribution had come from the artillery: not only had the number of guns almost doubled since the opening of the Somme offensive, the ammunition had been of a much better quality and the official adoption of the creeping barrage, only patchily introduced on the Somme, had been of considerable assistance to the infantry advancing behind its protective curtain. This, together with the methodical bombardment of enemy batteries, communications and wire entanglements, made the opening of the Arras offensive primarily an artillery battle. However, the performance of tanks (used once again in driblets) fuelled the doubts of those at GHQ who were opposed to them: of the forty-eight thinly armoured Mark Is and IIs allocated to the two armies, only twenty-six saw any action, and although they proved to be useful in knocking out strongpoints, the mud and cratered ground meant that many broke down or ditched before even reaching the front. All the eight tanks allocated to the assault on Vimy Ridge failed for this reason. The cavalry, once again, took no part in the action: their one opportunity was the exploitation of the success of the 9th Division's advance, but they were too far back to be of any use.

The German High Command was 'seriously perturbed by the surprisingly great success on the first day of the attack'. Thousands of prisoners had been taken and nearly seventy guns. It is reasonably certain that the defenders suffered more heavily than the attackers, but 9 April was to prove to be the high point of the offensive: the enemy's reserves were gathering and the impetus of the advance would begin to falter.

After the success of the first day, progress on the following day represented something of an anti-climax. The main thrust was to be south of the Scarpe, with the object of capturing the remainder of the Brown line still in enemy hands, and then pressing forward to the Green line, capturing the important hilltop village of Monchy en route. The extreme right of the VII Corps attack facing the daunting obstacle of the Hindenburg Line met fierce resistance and even a counter-attack, forcing a withdrawal from the position reached the previous day. The centre fared a little better and succeeded in occupying a section of the Brown line. On the left, VI Corps seized its part of the Brown line and advanced towards Monchy and Guémappe, but artillery fire in enfilade from Greenland Hill north of the Scarpe, and machine-gun fire from Monchy itself, brought the advance to a halt. North of the Scarpe, XVII Corps had only a subsidiary role: it already occupied a small section of the Green line near Fampoux, and its orders were to capture the remainder. The right of its attack, where the deepest penetration had been made the previous day, was to exploit this success by pushing forward beyond Fampoux, and the 2nd Cavalry Division was ordered to take Greenland Hill, some 2,000 yards north-east of Fampoux. In the event, apart from capturing a small portion of the Brown line on the left of the attack, the right made no progress beyond Fampoux owing to the lack of artillery support.

During the night of the 9th and the early hours of the 10th, the Canadians fought on to capture Hill 145 on Vimy Ridge. The hill was strongly held and resolutely defended, but the courage and persistence of the Canadians, despite severe losses, eventually overcame the defence by late afternoon.

By the next day, the 11th, the momentum of the advance was perceptibly slowing. It was as though the attacks of the first two days had forced a door ajar but the gap was now slowly closing under pressure from the gathering German reserves. One more success was to be gained, albeit at a grievous cost, but this was to be overshadowed by the failure of an attack which, in its conception, had all the hallmarks of the ill-planned and wasteful assaults of the two previous years.

The tasks planned for the 11th were nothing if not ambitious. The Third Army was to assault the Green line and then press on eastwards to the Drocourt–Quéant switch line. South of the Arras–Cambrai road the Fifth Army would complement this advance by attacking the Hindenburg Line, thus allowing exploitation by the Cavalry Corps of the Third Army attack. Ten tanks were to be employed, four by VII Corps and six by VI Corps. The attacks both north and south of the Scarpe failed to make much progress, but a real achievement was the capture of the strongpoint of Monchy, important because of the commanding view that the hilltop offered over the battlefield. Its capture was also memorable for being the first time that infantry, tanks and cavalry were all involved in a single operation, although the cavalry in a role that was hardly envisaged for them. The capture, however, was not gained lightly. The task was given to the 37th and 15th Divisions, supported by six tanks. Zero hour was fixed for 5 a.m., but orders were late in getting through and, in consequence, there was a two-hour postponement. News of the postponement was too late to reach the tanks and the infantry, who had already set off in the dark and the driving snow towards the village. The tanks (only three of which now remained, two already having broken down and one ditched) reached the village first, but the infantry struggling in their wake incurred fearful casualties before they too arrived in the village. Then, to the infantry's surprise, came the cavalry:

> During a lull in the snowstorm an excited shout was raised that our cavalry were coming up! Sure enough, away behind us, moving quickly in extended order down the slope of Orange Hill, was line upon line of mounted men covering the whole extent of the hillside as far as we could see. It was a thrilling moment for us infantrymen, who had never dreamt that we should see a real cavalry charge, which was evidently what was intended.
>
> In their advance the lines of horsemen passed over us rapidly, although from our holes in the ground it was rather a 'worm's-eye' view we got of the splendid spectacle of so many mounted men in action.
>
> It may have been a fine sight, but it was a wicked waste of men and horses, for the enemy immediately opened on them a hurricane of every missile he had.[11]

It was not intended that the cavalry should capture the village, but reconnoitre to the east of it once it had been taken by the infantry. However, moving forward and coming under fire, they were forced to shelter there. It proved to be a very precarious shelter because the enemy then brought down a heavy bombardment, causing havoc in the narrow street, particularly to the horses. The position was critical: all the tanks had now been put out of action, and the surviving infantry were pathetically few in numbers and exhausted. But the defence held. Unless the cavalry had taken on an infantry role, it is likely that a counter-attack would have succeeded. Reinforcements arrived by the evening, but the scene in the village was one of devastation, graphically described in the Official History:

> Monchy le Preux, almost undamaged a few days before and with the majority of houses intact when the attack was launched that morning, was now a ruined charnel-house, its street choked with dead horses piled amid the rubble. By next morning, however, its death and desolation were cloaked in a pall of white.

The achievement at Monchy was, however, marred by the failure of the Fifth Army's assault on the Hindenburg Line position at Bullecourt. The main burden of the offensive had so far fallen on the First and Third Armies but, according to the Official History, the suggestion that the Fifth Army should assist had come from its commander, General Sir Hubert Gough. The Fifth Army had been preoccupied during the early months of 1917 in following up the German withdrawal to the Hindenburg Line. This had been an arduous task, not only because of the wasteland left by the enemy but also because of the difficulties in bringing up artillery and supplies across the ruins of the Somme battlefields. Its strength reduced by, in particular, the transfer of a significant number of heavy artillery batteries to the other two armies, it was not in a position to make more than a token assault on the immensely strong Hindenburg Line. Nevertheless, the decision was made to attack a section of the line on a frontage of 3,500 yards around the village of Bullecourt, some nine miles south-east of Arras. The villages of Riencourt and Hendecourt were to be the further objectives. If successful it would allow the 4th Cavalry Division to pass through the breach and join with the other cavalry divisions advancing from Arras. Two corps were to be involved, I ANZAC (Australian & New Zealand Army Corps) and V Corps, together with ten tanks divided equally with two in reserve. The attack was to be synchronized with the Third Army's assault on the Brown line on the 9th, but owing to traffic conditions the artillery had been late in arriving and the preliminary bombardment was not begun until the 5th. Three days later it was apparent that it had been largely ineffective in creating adequate gaps in the wire entanglements and the operation had to be postponed.

When news reached Gough of the success of the attacks further north he was then faced with a delay which he found to be unacceptable. His impatience now led him into a fatal error. A suggestion was made by a junior tank officer that, instead of using tanks in driblets (the original proposal for the attack), all twelve should operate together in a surprise attack on a 1,000-yard frontage, the artillery silent until the line had been breached. The use of tanks en masse had always been advocated by senior tank officers, and although twelve was hardly an overwhelming force, here, on the face of it, was the first opportunity to show what tanks could achieve in their proper role. Gough seized on the proposal and decided, despite the misgivings of ANZAC, to put it into effect the next day. The attack would be on a frontage of 1,500 yards, the tanks preceding the 4th Australian Division, the only infantry now involved. (This was yet another example of a dependence on a single strategy, with no contingency plan if it failed.) The tanks to be used were the original thinly armoured Mark Is, where experience had shown their reliability to be suspect; moreover, there would be no time for the Australians to familiarize themselves with their collaboration. Zero hour was fixed for 4.30 a.m. on the 10th, that is, nearly two hours before dawn, at which time the Australians were already lying out in No Man's Land awaiting the tanks. The tanks were four miles from the front, and in moving up at night to avoid observation they were virtually blinded by a snowstorm on the way and in consequence did not arrive. The operation, perforce, had to be postponed, and it was fortunate that the lines of infantry already in No Man's Land were able to be withdrawn without serious loss. The failure, however, only served to fuel ANZAC's doubts. It might be thought that it would have been prudent to have called off the operation: the battlefield was deep in snow and against its whiteness the advancing tanks and infantry would present easy targets for the enemy.

The operation was repeated the following day, but what ensued after the tanks had begun their advance was little short of a catastrophe. Of the eleven tanks now involved, one having already broken down, nine were soon put out of action, although one managed to reach Bullecourt before being destroyed. Thus the Australians had to advance without their assistance and, what is more, without a covering artillery bombardment:

> When zero hour came, and the first wave went off, it very soon overtook the tanks, which were mostly floundering round close in front. Some of them even fired on our own men . . . As it was fatal to hesitate and wait for the tanks, the line advanced alone. As soon as it came in sight of the Huns the massacre commenced, the enemy lining his parapet and shooting our boys like rabbits. Lots of them reached the wire, but as it had not been cut, they had to run along it until they found an opening. This turning to a flank caused them to bunch together and they fell in heaps on the wire and in front of it. The wonder is that any reached the trench. But reach it they did and took the enemy's front line . . .[12]

It is probable that few, if any, infantry could have emulated the Australians in their determined assault in such dreadful conditions, but now, weak in numbers, they were unable to go further in daylight over open ground to the objectives of Riencourt and Bullecourt. Erroneous reports as to the progress of the battle had led ANZAC and Army headquarters to believe not only that Bullecourt had been entered but also that tanks were pressing on to Riencourt and Hendecourt. Accordingly, Gough ordered the cavalry to go forward and the 62nd Division of V Corps to occupy Bullecourt – both hopeless tasks. The reality was that the Australians, having suffered terrible casualties, were marooned in the Hindenburg Line trenches and increasingly subjected to counter-attacks. Denied artillery support because of the confusion surrounding the extent of the advance, and without reinforcements of men and ammunition owing to the intense fire put down by machine guns, the Australians were gradually driven from their captured trenches. The casualties were appalling, the 4th Australian Brigade losing three-quarters of its strength. The Australians, who had been doubtful about the operation from the outset, were very bitter, blaming the tanks for its failure – an understandable reaction.

Unfortunately the arrangements for drowning the noise of the night-time advance of the tanks by continuous machine-gun fire had been inadequate and the key factor of surprise was lost. Suffering under a hail of armour-piercing bullets and shell-fire, the tanks were given an impossible task, although it is conceivable that they might have had more chance of success if a heavy bombardment of the Hindenburg trenches had preceded their advance. Although nine of the eleven operational tanks had been put out of action, the remaining two were captured, which ultimately proved to be a blessing in disguise: the Germans noted the thin armour and the ease with which it could be penetrated by armour-piercing bullets. If they thought, however, that they now had the measure of tanks, this was to be dispelled when the more heavily armoured Mark IVs made their appearance later in the year. Bullecourt was a tragic fiasco and the blame lies elsewhere than in the performance of tanks, and it is difficult to quarrel with the judgment given in the Australian Official History:

> Gough's general conception of assisting the Third Army by a stroke at the enemy's exposed flank and rear was indeed sound, provided a practical means of delivering the stroke could be discovered. But with almost boyish eagerness to deliver a death blow, the Army Commander broke at every stage through rules recognized even by platoon commanders.[18]

After three days of continuous fighting the divisions in the First and Third Armies were reaching exhaustion. It was realized that the sweeping gains of the previous days were unlikely to be achieved in future attacks, but there was no lessening in the resolve to persevere. Indeed, Haig had no choice: he was committed to his role, albeit a subsidiary one, in co-operating with Nivelle's offensive, the first stage of which opened on the 13th with the attack by the French 11th Army on St Quentin. This attack was also subsidiary to the main thrust on the Aisne, but the French met determined resistance and, after suffering severe casualties, the attack had to be broken off because of the lack of heavy artillery. The Aisne offensive, which had been postponed three times, was now fixed for the 16th.

Four reserve British divisions had arrived on the 12th to replace an equal number in VII and VI Corps, but the Third Army had still to bear the main burden of operations. The weather remained bitterly cold, with frequent snow-falls, and the conditions in the trenches deep in mud were frightful, as were those on the roads. Some progress was made by VII Corps in capturing the villages of Heninel and Wancourt, but an attempt to seize Roeux, north of the Scarpe, was rebuffed with heavy losses. The offensive was now developing into the pattern of piecemeal operations so familiar from the later stages of the Somme battle. A German soldier's view of the situation was contained in a letter home:

> You know that the situation here was anything but rosy when we arrived. The English had broken through to a distance of 5 [*sic*] miles in one push. There was a thin line of infantry in front of us, and the English were just where our heavy guns used to be. All that had been saved in the rear of our section was five heavy howitzers and a few field guns. This was the state of things when we took hold. The enemy had tanks, cavalry, and thick swarms of infantry, while we were entirely dependent on rifles and machine guns; but we were perfectly cool from the start. 'If those chaps were worth anything at all – if they were Germans – they'd have broken through long ago!' we all thought. Day and night, with a calmness and determination which is characteristic only of Germans, our reinforcements arrived. After two or three days we had collected such a lot of guns that no English

attack had any success. Wonderful to relate, our morale remained perfectly good in spite of the intense bombardment and its ensuing casualties.[14]

On 16 April Haig decided to mount a further attack on the 20th involving all three armies, but this had to be scaled down because the plan involved yet more preliminary operations which the army commanders did not favour because of the likely casualties. The attack was postponed until the 23rd, and once again the Third Army was to deliver the main thrust. Meanwhile the French opened their great offensive on the Aisne on the 16th, the outcome of which was ultimately to have the gravest results for the French Army. The Germans, in possession of the French plans through captured documents, were ready. Their defence was constructed on the new doctrine of lightly held forward positions with strong reserves in the rear poised for counter-attack. The French made some progress and by the 20th had taken 20,000 prisoners, but they had not achieved a breakthrough. Their casualties had been very heavy, their morale had been shattered and, most of all, their confidence in the over-optimistic plans of their commander had been destroyed.

The British offensive opened on the 23rd over a nine-mile front straddling the Scarpe. Some initial headway was made. North of the Scarpe the village of Gavrelle was captured, and there was bitter and confused fighting around Roeux and the Chemical Works. South of the Scarpe the village of Guémappe was taken, but all along the line of assault the enemy delivered several vigorous counter-attacks, which were repulsed with artillery fire. The attack was resumed the following day, with further progress east of Monchy and towards the troublesome strongpoint on Greenland Hill.

By this time Haig had become aware that the French offensive had not achieved the promised breakthrough, although Nivelle told him on the 24th that he was still determined to go on. Nevertheless, the French Government was becoming increasingly unhappy with Nivelle. Haig saw Painlevé, the French Minister of War, in Paris on the 26th and was assured

> . . . that whatever happened, the French Government and Army would loyally discharge their duties towards the British Army; that there would be no change of plan; and that the offensive would be maintained.

Disturbingly, however, there was mention of replacing Nivelle by Pétain. On the same day that Haig was in Paris, Robertson wrote to him stressing the anxiety of the War Cabinet in London over French intentions:

> We have reached a critical stage of the war. You and I have always agreed that the Western Front is the main front, and therefore to us everything that happens there is of main importance and consequently we need to do the right thing there. It seems to me that at present the right thing to do is to keep on fighting . . . The situation

at sea is very serious indeed. It has never been as bad as at present . . . There may soon be a serious shortage of food in this country, and this has to be taken in consideration in regard to all theatres of war. For us to stop fighting now would seem to be a confession of failure, and would allow the enemy to do as he likes . . .[15]

Robertson's letter underlined the need for the assault in Flanders which, if successful, would have the bonus of denying to the enemy the submarine base at Zeebrugge, but Haig was uncertain how long the French would continue their offensive and whether Nivelle would be replaced. He realized that the original objective of Cambrai was now unattainable, but until he had definite news that the French had broken off their offensive he decided to continue the battle in the hope that it would assist the French and also enable him to 'move steadily forward up to a good defensive line'.

His plan was for a combined assault by all three armies early in May but, as a precursor to this, secondary attacks were to be made against four strongpoints, Oppy and Arleux (First Army) and Roeux and Greenland Hill (Third Army), on 28 April. In the event the results were not very encouraging. The Third Army initially gained some ground against strong resistance, but it was mostly lost again in counter-attacks. Roeux was entered for a time but could not be held, and once again the key feature of Greenland Hill proved to be beyond reach. The only success was the capture of Arleux by the Canadians. The main assault fixed for 3 May was in essence a general advance towards the Drocourt–Quéant switch line. The Fifth Army was to try again to seize Riencourt and Hendecourt beyond Bullecourt and the Hindenburg Line, the Third Army was to push forward on a line from Fontaine in the south to Plouvain in the north and the Canadians of the First Army were to capture Fresnoy and Oppy south-west of Drocourt.

From the outset things began to go awry. There was disagreement among the three army commanders as to the hour of the assault: both Allenby and Horne wanted it at first light, but Gough, on Australian advice, opted for darkness. With a compromise hour fixed for 3.45 a.m., and sunrise not until 5.30 a.m., it was inevitable that the attack would have to take place in the dark, although a factor overlooked was that an almost full moon would be setting behind the assaulting infantry. If this disunity was unfortunate, the events that followed can only be described as lamentable. At zero hour the infantry of the three corps of the Third Army left their jumping-off trenches, only to be met immediately by an intense artillery bombardment not only of high explosive but also, in some sectors, of gas. Some preliminary objectives were reached, but these could not be held because of determined counter-attacks. The darkness, however, was the real enemy. The infantry lost direction, two brigades prematurely retired because of misleading information and such was the confusion that one battalion became so disorientated that it attacked the British front line:

The British barrage was good, but the enemy was evidently expecting the attack as his counter-barrage was quick and his machine-gun fire devastating in volume and accuracy ... It seems clear that zero hour was too early. In the darkness it was impossible for the troops to see visual signals of command, and the delay caused by having to pass messages down the line owing to the din of the bombardment resulted in the attacking waves moving off zig-zag in shape with officers at the advanced points. In such a formation they became an easy target for the enemy machine guns. Some greater success might, moreover, have been achieved had the creeping barrage moved forward more quickly, which would have been quite possible in view of the comparatively unbroken state of the ground.[16]

The return from this substantial investment by the Third Army was a mere 500 yards of ground.

The Fifth Army's assault fared little better. The village of Bullecourt – by now in ruins but honeycombed with cellars sheltering machine-gunners – had first to be subdued before Riencourt and Hendecourt, the original objectives on 11 April, could be reached. The operation on 3 May was carried out by the 2nd Australian Division and the 62nd Division of V Corps. The latter division was allocated ten tanks, but the Australians, still bitter about the failure of tanks in the April assault, refused their assistance. Once again the Australians had to force their way through the Hindenburg Line to the north of Bullecourt, and, attacking with two brigades at 3.45 a.m., they met strong resistance. Only one brigade succeeded in entering the Hindenburg Line, where it was precariously established in a small section of the front and support trenches.

The 62nd could make little progress against Bullecourt or the section of the Hindenburg Line to the west of the village. One battalion actually succeeded in entering the village, as did three tanks, but the lack of headway elsewhere meant that no support could be provided. The 7th Division of V Corps was launched in a night attack in a renewed attempt to capture the village, but although some ground was gained this was ultimately lost through a counter-attack.

North of the Scarpe the First Army commenced its assault on Fresnoy and Oppy. The two divisions of XIII Corps, the 31st and the 2nd, initially made some headway, but the former suffered heavily from an artillery bombardment before zero hour and this, coupled with darkness and ultimately counter-attacks, resulted in the loss of the ground gained earlier. The 2nd Division was so reduced in strength that it could only find four battalions for the attack. It, too, sustained severe losses from artillery fire before the assault, but it managed to hold a position protecting the left flank of the Canadians attacking Fresnoy, who ultimately captured the village, adding further to their laurels. This, in the words of the Official Historian, became 'the relieving feature of a day which many who witnessed it consider the blackest day of the war'. But even worse was to come at Bullecourt over the next fourteen days.

With the knowledge that Nivelle's offensive had not achieved its objectives and that he was likely to be replaced by Pétain, the British Government was becoming increasingly concerned about French intentions for the future. The indications were that they might do no more than conduct an 'aggressive defence' and sit back and wait until the Americans arrived. A conference was held in Paris on 4 and 5 May attended by the French and British prime ministers and their military advisers. The French denied that they intended to pursue a defensive policy and agreed to continue offensive actions, although it appeared that the British would have to bear an increasing burden of operations on the Western Front with the French 'supporting them in vigorous attacks and taking over a portion of the British front'. This would mean that Haig could at last realize his offensive in Flanders. Thus Haig's commitment to Nivelle was now at an end and he was under no obligation to mount a new offensive at Arras, where, in any case, operations were being scaled down. During the Paris conference Nivelle, Pétain, Robertson and Haig met and it was agreed that a breakthrough to distant objectives was no longer feasible: it was 'now a question of wearing down and exhausting the enemy's resistance'. It was also agreed that this could be achieved by 'relentlessly attacking with limited objectives, while making the fullest use of our artillery'.

Although the Nivelle offensive had fallen far short of its promise, it had not yet been closed down and major attacks by four French armies were planned for 4 and 5 May. As one of the principal reasons for the Paris conference had been to encourage the French to act offensively, Haig decided to continue the struggle for Bullecourt. With hindsight, it would have been better, perhaps, if the Australians had failed to penetrate the Hindenburg Line: the Arras battle had virtually come to an end after the disaster of 3 May, but a decision had to be made whether to abandon the position reached by the Australians. While Bullecourt remained unsubdued they were lodged in a dangerous salient with the enemy menacing them on three sides. As the Third Army's assault had failed, there was no tactical advantage to be gained in capturing Bullecourt, only the grim prospect of a battle of attrition. Haig had already made up his mind that the main British effort should be in Flanders, but he was unwilling finally to close down the battle. Over the next three days the Australians managed to extend their position, but they were increasingly subjected to counter-attacks. The 7th Division succeeded in obtaining a foothold in the south-east corner of Bullecourt on the 7th, joining with the Australians, who had successfully developed their left.

The operations over the next week were mainly confined to relieving the Australians and endeavours to capture the remainder of the village – in which latter the 7th Division almost succeeded. On the 15th, however, the Germans mounted their strongest counter-attack yet and regained most of the village. The 7th Division still clung on to the eastern portion, but it had suffered dreadful losses over the previous days and it was worn out. Two days later, however, a brigade of the relieving 58th Division stormed into the village after a hurricane bombardment and finally captured the whole.

For fourteen days some of the most savage fighting of the war had taken place around the ruins of a small village and over a stretch of ground slightly under a mile in width, but although Bullecourt had been taken at the end, the original objectives of Riencourt and Hendecourt remained in German hands. The casualties had been severe, the Australians suffering 7,400 and V Corps 6,800, with enemy losses unknown but probably substantially less:

> By the end the dead of both sides lay in clumps all over the battlefield, and in the bottom or under the parapets of trenches many hundreds had been hastily covered with a little earth. One witness, after speaking of the nauseating stench, expresses his 'astonishment' that any human beings could hold and fight under these conditions. He adds that he never saw a battlefield, Ypres in 1917 not excepted, where the living and the unburied dead had remained in such close proximity for so long.[17]

The Battle of Arras had almost run its course, but a series of local engagements of a see-saw nature now took place. The Third Army, in a brilliant operation, finally took Rouex and the Chemical Works, but Fresnoy, captured earlier by the Canadian Corps, was lost after a heavy counter-attack. By 24 May the series of offensives making up the battle had come to an end.

* * *

The role of the British Army at Arras was once again in compliance with the plans of its French ally. Loos had been fought over ground which the British thought to be entirely unfavourable, and the Somme and Arras battles had been undertaken when Haig would have preferred action in Flanders. This was particularly so by April 1917, when he was coming under great pressure from the War Cabinet in London to deny the naval bases at Ostend and Zeebrugge to the enemy. Moreover, the British Army's task had been reduced to a subsidiary role and Haig himself had been forced by political manoeuvring to be subordinated to Nivelle. Haig had never envisaged a breakthrough at Arras: his part in Nivelle's strategy had been to keep the enemy occupied and prevent the transfer of reserves to stem Nivelle's main thrust in Champagne. He had hoped, however, if his offensive went well, to reach Cambrai; certainly the results of the first day of the battle gave high promise that this hope might eventually be fulfilled.

Despite the meticulous planning and preparation for the battle, the outstanding success on the first day owed something to good fortune. The preliminary bombardment had been based on the expectation that the enemy's defensive arrangements would be those with which the British had long been familiar – a strongly held front zone which would be resolutely defended and for which, if lost, no effort would be spared in its recapture. Ludendorff's appraisal of the Somme battle had, however, led him to believe that a rigid first line of defence was vulnerable to a determined assault, particularly when preceded by an artillery bombardment which he realized would only become heavier as the war progressed. Instead he planned a front zone of heavily fortified strongpoints with counter-attack divisions poised about a mile or so in the rear, ready to re-take ground lost. It was fortunate for the British that this revised defensive plan had barely been introduced at Arras by the German 6th Army commander (Falkenhausen), and the forward area was held in strength with the usual instruction that it should be defended at whatever cost. Thus the preliminary bombardment had a devastating effect on enemy infantry and Falkenhausen, believing that the British would not attack until later in the month, had kept his reserves up to a day's march from the front.

These blunders played a significant part in the British success on the first day. Had the new defence strategy been in operation it is highly probable that British penetration would have been much less and achieved at a far higher cost. The success served to strengthen the view that the enemy's front could be ruptured provided the preliminary bombardment was as heavy and as purposefully directed as it had been over the days before 9 April. Moreover, despite the success of the hurricane bombardment at Neuve Chapelle, the lessons learned at Loos and the Somme had provided ample confirmation that to destroy enemy fortifications the preliminary bombardment should be as long and as heavy as the availability of artillery and ammunition permitted. The supply and quality of shells had been much improved since the Somme, and for the Arras offensive the number of heavy guns had more than doubled. Thus a future offensive would see an increasing preponderance of artillery, particularly heavy guns. But the drawbacks of heavy bombardments had yet to be discovered.

The deepest penetration on the first day was 3½ miles – an unprecedented advance and a considerable achievement, giving a heartening and much needed boost to morale. But success produced its own problems as the impetus was slowed on meeting stiffening resistance. On the face of it, the ideal solution would have been a pause while the artillery was brought up to deliver a preliminary bombardment on the same scale as that preceding the first day's assault. This, however, would have been barely feasible for a number of reasons. The delay, even if conditions had been perfect, would have given the enemy time to bring up his reserves, concentrate fresh artillery on the new British positions and deliver the inevitable counter-attacks. As it was, there would have been an unacceptable delay in bringing the artillery and its ammunition forward over cratered ground and the cluttered roads, the latter already damaged not only by the severe frosts of the winter but also by constant traffic. There was, indeed, a short pause between 16 and 23 April, enabling some artillery to be brought up, and a preliminary bombardment opened on the 21st. But enemy artillery, so successfully put out of action previously, had been replaced and was difficult to locate. With no possibility of surprise, the tired British divisions attacking on the 23rd met fresh German reserves and made some progress, but the achievement of the first day could not be repeated.

Thus a pattern appears to emerge from British assaults on the Western Front: first the detailed planning and preparation over the months before the offensive, on a scale inhibiting any question of surprise (except for the date); then the preliminary bombardment over several days, followed by the infantry assault, resulting in the rupture of a section of the enemy's front; then the exploitation, eventually to be slowed by stiffening enemy resistance and ultimately brought to a halt by counter-attacks as his reserves are thrown in; then the inevitable pause as the artillery is brought up for a further bombardment of new enemy positions, followed once again by the assault and, if a breach be achieved, the impetus diminishing as further enemy reserves are brought in. How, then, could a decisive breakthrough be achieved if the enemy, despite attacks elsewhere on his front, could always produce reserves to stem the tide of the advance? One solution would be to continue attacks until a point in time arrives when the enemy's reserves are so depleted that a strong attack finally achieves the breakthrough. This is the 'wearing down process' (a euphemism for attrition) by which it is hoped that the defender's losses will be greater than those of the attacker. Should the converse apply, then the wearing down process will have to be terminated, unless of course – and this is a cynical view – it is known that the attacker's reserves of manpower will outlast those of the defender:

> This process of wearing down the enemy is a crude and costly form of generalship, only to be adopted when no other method can be applied, but it may be the only possible method against a skilful and mobile enemy who enjoys the advantage of interior lines. When adopted it becomes a question of reducing the losses of attack, and of increasing the losses of the enemy by tactical skill in the employment of the most suitable weapons.[18]

The continuation of the assault against Bullecourt was indeed a 'crude and costly form of generalship'. It is not implied that Haig's advocacy of wearing down was motivated by the cynical view; rather that far too optimistic reports from GHQ Intelligence of a deterioration in the German Army's morale and the near-famine conditions on the German home front had persuaded him that this policy would, sooner rather than later, bring about the enemy's collapse.

Before the end of May there was indeed a disastrous collapse in morale, but not in the German Army. On 19 May reinforcements destined for a French infantry regiment in the line mutinied. The following day another regiment due for the front refused to march, and the disobedience spread quickly until by the middle of June no less than half French Army was in a state of insurrection. There were a number of reasons for this, the most important being that the Army felt that it had been cruelly deceived by the extravagant claims made by Nivelle . A breakthrough had been promised, and many may have hoped that this would be the turning point of the war. Although French losses had been very heavy, they had taken over 20,000 prisoners, significant tactical gains had been made and German losses had been almost as severe. But there had been no breakthrough, and, coming as it did after the most appalling losses suffered by the French Army since 1914, this crushing disappointment, fuelled by long-felt grievances over poor medical facilities and a lack of leave, proved to be the breaking point. Nivelle was removed from his command and sent to North Africa, and he was replaced by Pétain, whose onerous task it became to restore morale. For the time being the French Army could not be relied upon to take on an offensive role. It was fortunate that the Germans remained ignorant of the mutinies.

To sum up, the cost in human terms of the Nivelle offensive had been over a quarter of a million casualties. The total casualties in the months of April and May for the three British armies involved were approximately 159,000, involving a daily casualty rate of just over 4,000 – a rate, despite battles yet to come, only exceeded by that at the Battle of Loos. Although German casualties are not known, there is reason to believe that they were fewer than those suffered by the British, particularly so in May when over 40 per cent of the total casualties were incurred in wearing down the enemy. The British had succeeded in preventing German reserves from being diverted to the front where Nivelle's main thrust had taken place, but this was of no avail because the thrust had failed. It had reduced the French Army to despair and insurrection and it had caused the British Army, at a disproportionate cost, to endure a prolongation of the offensive without hope of material gain. The only redeeming feature was the capture of Vimy Ridge – an operation that Nivelle had tried to discourage but one which was insisted on by Haig and was prove to be of the greatest value in 1918.

Notes to Chapter 5

1. Blake, Robert, (ed.), *The Private Papers of Douglas Haig 1914–1919*, Eyre & Spottiswoode (London, 1952)
2. *Ibid.*
3. Lloyd George, D., *War Memoirs*, Odhams (London, 1938)

4. Blake, *op. cit.*

5. Churchill, Winston S., *The World Crisis 1911–1918*, Odhams (London, 1938)

6. Grimwade, F. C., *The War History of the 4th Battalion The London Regiment (Royal Fusiliers)* , Regimental HQ (London, 1922)

7. Spears, Brigadier-General E. L., *Prelude to Victory*, Jonathan Cape (London, 1939)

8. *Ibid.*

9. Falls, Captain Cyril, (comp.), *Official History of the War: Military Operations, France and Belgium 1917*, Vol. I, Macmillan & Co. (London, 1940)

10. Spears, *op. cit.*

11. Cuddeford, D. W. J., *And All for What?*, Heath Cranton (London, 1933)

12. Rule, E. J., (14th Bn AIF), *Jacka's Mob*, Angus & Robertson (Sydney, 1933)

13. Bean, C. E. W., *The Official History of Australia in the War of 1914–1918*, Angus & Robertson (Sydney, 1921)

14. Included in Schenkel, Karl, *German Students' War Letters*, Methuen (London, 1929)

15. Blake, *op. cit.*

16. Grimwade, *op. cit.*

17. Falls, *op. cit.*

18. Maurice, Major-General Sir F., *British Strategy*, Constable (London, 1929)

6

The Third Battle of Ypres (Passchendaele)

THE ANCIENT Belgian town of Ypres (Flemish: Ieper) lies at the western end of the Flanders plain about twenty-five miles from the North Sea and connected to it by the canalized River Yser. The plain, protected from the sea by a line of sand dunes, is mostly at or below sea level, drained by a complex network of ditches and canals and traversed by a number of small streams. To the east and south of the town, roughly in the shape of a crescent, lie the Flanders Ridges barely 100 feet above sea level: approached from the west on a gentle slope, scarcely noticeable to a motorist, they hardly present a forbidding appearance, but from their summits all Ypres lies before them.

The town's past is inextricably bound up with the turbulent and complex history of the Low Countries. In the twelfth and thirteenth centuries the towns of Ypres, Bruges and Ghent dominated Flanders, although there was often jealousy among them, resulting in friction and even warfare. It was during this period that Ypres reached the height of its prosperity, with a population of about 80,000 chiefly engaged on the weaving of wool imported from England, but towards the end of the fourteenth century Ypres was besieged by the English (with assistance from Ghent), and although the town held out, the inhabitants were on the verge of starvation and the weavers sought safety elsewhere. It was from then that the prosperity of the town began to decline, and by the late sixteenth century its population had fallen to 5,000. What was lost commercially, however, was replaced by the doubtful benefit of its recognition by the various occupying powers of its strategic value. Over the succeeding centuries Flanders passed in turn to the House of Burgundy, then to Spain, then to France and finally to Holland, until the revolution of 1830 brought about the independent state of Belgium eight years later. Each power either fortified the town or dismantled the defences according to military need, but after Belgian independence its remaining defences were mostly removed and by 1914 it had shrunk to a small provincial town. But it still retained substantial relics of its past: the fine and imposing Cloth Hall, completed in 1304; its cathedral, dating from the twelfth century; and the remnants of the seventeenth century ramparts, designed by the French engineer Vauban. Ultimately the last were to provide an enduring shelter for the British Army when most of the town had been destroyed.

The earlier battles of Ypres had been defensive affairs against German attacks. The first, delivered by the German 4th Army in the autumn of 1914, fell against the cordon of French and British troops around the town, including Haig's newly arrived I Corps protecting the town itself. The attack failed, but only just. The second, in April 1915, saw the first use of poison gas[1] on the Western Front, causing panic and severe casualties among the French Algerian troops holding the north-west portion of the salient. In the confusion the Germans advanced two miles and then halted, mainly because they distrusted their own primitive gas masks, but also because they met resistance from Canadian troops. There were further gas attacks over the following days and more ground was gained. Although the French promised a strong counter-attack to regain the lost ground, nothing ultimately came of this and the British, now overlooked by the ridges, were forced to make a withdrawal of some two miles into a much reduced salient. For the next two years a position of deadlock was reached in the Ypres area. No major offensive was mounted by either side, but it was always an unquiet sector, with frequent attacks of a local nature, always bitterly contested, and German shelling gradually reduced the town to ruins.

On 1 January 1915 the First Lord of the Admiralty wrote to Kitchener:

> The Admiralty are of the opinion that it would be possible, under cover of warships, to land a large force at Zeebrugge in conjunction with any genuine forward movement along the seashore to Ostend.[2]

This had arisen because of fears that the enemy was developing a submarine base at Zeebrugge with the consequent threat to communications between England and France. The French were informed of this proposal, but Joffre would not be sidetracked from his plan for his attacks in Champagne and Artois and nothing came of the scheme. It was to surface again, however, when Vice-Admiral Bacon met Haig in December 1915. The latter recorded in his diary:

> We discussed the co-operation of the fleet with my Army. He said that the front from Zeebrugge to Ostend was of vital importance to England because the Germans command the east end of the Channel from there and threaten England. We arranged to work out plans together but the time of execution must depend on General Joffre's plan for the general offensive in the Spring.[3]

It was not until almost a year later, however, that the Government's concern over submarine activity emerged in an instruction to Robertson to consider the problem and report on the action to be taken. This instruction was contained in a draft letter from Asquith to Robertson following a discussion of the War Committee on 20 November 1916, and on 1 December Robertson wrote to Joffre:

> My Government has been viewing with some anxiety the increase of German naval activity on the coast of Belgium, which clearly has for its object the interruption of

communications between Great Britain and France . . . It is obvious that the maintenance of sea communication between Great Britain and France is vital to the successful conduct of the War on the Western Front, and in these circumstances my Government desire that the occupation of Ostend and Zeebrugge should form one of the objectives of the campaign next year.[4]

Joffre was replaced by Nivelle at the end of December, and Haig became committed to the Arras battle, but the need to clear the Belgian coast was by no means forgotten. At the London conference in January 1917 to discuss the Nivelle plan the agreement included the proviso that, if the operations proved to be unsuccessful, the battle would be broken off 'in order to allow the British Armies to engage in other operations on a front further north, in co-operation with the Belgian Army and the French Nieuport Group'.[5]

The failure of the Nivelle offensive and British concern over future French intentions brought about the Paris Conference on 4 May 1917, attended by French and British political and military leaders. The previous evening Haig recorded in his diary:

At 9.30 p.m. I saw the Prime Minister with Gen. Robertson. The former is afraid that the French Government is not going to act offensively! He is here, he says, to press whatever plan Robertson and I decide. Rather a changed attitude for him to adopt since the Calais Conference.[6]

The morning was given over to discussions between the military representatives, Pétain (now Chief of the French General Staff), Nivelle, Haig and Robertson. The last produced a statement of intent which included the following:

It is no longer a question of aiming at breaking through the enemy's front and aiming at distant objectives. It is now a question of wearing down and exhausting the enemy's resistance . . . In order to wear him down we are agreed that it is absolutely necessary to fight with all our resources with the object of destroying the enemy's divisions . . . We are all of [the] opinion that the object can be obtained by relentlessly attacking with limited objectives, while making the fullest use of our artillery. By this means we hope to gain our ends with the minimum loss possible.

Having unanimously agreed to the above principles, we consider that the methods to be adopted to put them into practice, and the time and place of the various attacks, are matters which must be left to the responsible Generals . . .[7]

The statement was considered in the afternoon by the full Conference. The proposal to mount attacks with 'limited objectives' was endorsed, and Lloyd George stressed that, as the British were prepared to deploy their full strength in future attacks, it was vital that the French do likewise. He was assured that they would, and the discussion ended on a note of complete accord. But Lloyd George was to return to Robertson's statement to the Conference in his *War Memoirs*:

It will be noted that Sir William Robertson, at the Conference and after, accepted unreservedly the Pétain policy of 'making the fullest use of our artillery' – that meant the Pétain scheme of saving your own men and wasting the enemy by heavy bombardment. The C.I.G.S. stated categorically that 'it is no longer a question of aiming at breaking through the enemy front and aiming at distant objectives'. He thus by clear implication ruled out the project of an offensive on a large scale to rupture the German lines in Flanders and clear the Belgian coast. That certainly could not be described as a limited offensive, with no distant objectives.[8]

Haig's plans for an offensive in the Ypres sector had existed since January 1916, but he had decided that an attack along the Belgian coast combined with a seaborne landing would be too difficult. In October 1914 the Belgians had let in the sea to flood the lower Yser, leaving only a narrow coastal strip of about two miles of sand dunes. Although the flooded areas could be drained off, a month of dry weather would be necessary to make the ground firm enough for operations. Haig's preferred alternative was an assault north-eastwards from the Ypres salient by the Second and Fourth Armies, and, depending on progress, this would be followed later by an attack along the coast and a seaborne landing at Ostend. The German assault at Verdun in February, however, meant a drastic change to these plans and the Fourth Army became committed to the Somme offensive, leaving the Second Army to propose a modified plan. During the earlier consideration of the wider plan, the Second Army commander, General Sir Herbert Plumer, had proposed that the capture of the Messines–Wytschaete ridge due south of Ypres was an essential preliminary to the main assault and Haig had agreed. The demands of the Somme, however, precluded any possibility of the Messines operation, as did Haig's commitment to the Nivelle offensive, and the plans were shelved – although not to gather dust.

Shortly before the Paris conference Haig submitted a memorandum to the War Cabinet. Apart from dealing with the situation at Arras where the battle was still in progress, he referred to the 'urgent need to clear the Belgian coast this summer' and set out the conditions which he thought necessary to give the operation a reasonable chance of success. He concluded:

> . . . even if a full measure is not gained, we shall be attacking the enemy on a front where he cannot refuse to fight, and where, therefore, our purpose of wearing him down can be given effect to . . .[9]

One of the conditions thought necessary by Haig was contained in a letter to Nivelle dated 5 May in which he stressed the vital need to deny the use of the Belgian ports to the enemy, observing that

> The forces at my disposal are insufficient to enable me to undertake the operations necessary for the purpose in view. I therefore hope that you may be able to relieve the troops on a portion of my front.[10]

After the Paris conference on 4 May Haig considered that he was now free to develop his plans for the Ypres offensive and on the 7th, at a conference with his Army commanders, he gave his views on future operations:

> . . . the objective of the French and British will now be to wear down and exhaust the enemy's resistance by systematically attacking him by surprise. When this end has been achieved the main blow will be struck by the British forces operating from the Ypres front, with the eventual object of securing the Belgian coast and connecting with the Dutch frontier.[11]

The first operation would be the attack on the Messines–Wytschaete ridge in early June, followed some weeks later by the 'Northern Operation' to secure the Belgian coast.

Meanwhile, however, events of the gravest nature were occurring in the French Army. A portent of this, according to the Official History, was Pétain's report to the Paris Conference that on the Western Front 'the confidence of the Army in its chiefs and in the Government was undermined'. It was not revealed, however, that insurrection had already begun – it was rapidly to spread in the next few days – but no inkling of this reached Haig or the War Office in London. This, clearly, was a time of great anxiety for the French Government, and an indication of the turmoil existing in French political and military circles came when the British chief liaison officer at French Army headquarters, Lieutenant-General Sir Henry Wilson, met Pétain (shortly to replace Nivelle) on 10 May. It appeared that Pétain 'was opposed to Haig's plans of attack. He is opposed to big attacks, and favours small fronts and great depths . . .' Moreover, Pétain told Wilson that 'he disagreed with every single thing agreed to' at the Paris Conference.[12]

A meeting had been fixed at Amiens for 15 May at which Haig was to meet Nivelle, but this was postponed because of the latter's imminent replacement by Pétain. On 12 May Robertson telegraphed to Haig:

> Prime Minister desires me to remind you of War Cabinet's intentions to support your policy as was in fact done by him at the Paris Conference, but on express condition that the French also play their full part as agreed upon at our Conference with Nivelle and Pétain. He is anxious that you should clearly realize this in your discussion with Nivelle, because Cabinet could never agree to our incurring heavy losses with comparatively small gains, which would obviously be the result unless French co-operate wholeheartedly.[13]

On the 16th Pétain, now having formally replaced Nivelle, agreed to meet Haig at Amiens two days later. Before the meeting Haig responded to Robertson's telegram. He intended to wind down the Arras offensive and complete his preparations for clearing the Belgian coast in the summer. He envisaged a two-stage operation. The preparations for the first stage, the assault on the Messines–

Wytschaete Ridge, were well advanced, and the second would 'take place several weeks later, and will not be carried out unless the situation is sufficiently favourable when the time for it comes.'[14] He did not feel that his arrangements committed him to undue risks and could 'be modified to meet any developments in the situation'. At the Amiens meeting, Haig, according to his diary, asked Pétain, 'Did the French intend to play their full part as promised at the Paris Conference? Could I rely on his wholehearted co-operation?' Pétain assured Haig that 'the French Army would fight and would support the British in every possible way.'[15] The outcome of the meeting was reported to Robertson in London and thence to the War Cabinet. Haig now believed that the fact that he had obtained Pétain's promise that the French would 'co-operate wholeheart-edly' would satisfy the War Cabinet and the way would now be clear to proceed with his plans. Events yet to come, however, would reveal that Pétain would be unable to live up to his promise, that the War Cabinet would become severely critical of Haig's plans and that the seeds of mistrust between Lloyd George and Haig, already sown earlier in the year, would develop into a growth of such malignancy as not only permanently to impair their relationship but also to have a serious impact on the future direction of the war.

Amid all these doubts and uncertainties the preparations for the assault on the Messines–Wytschaete ridge went ahead and were completed by 19 May. The ridge is the southern extremity of the Flanders Ridges and curves round to dominate Ypres from the south. The German position on the ridge formed a massive salient extending from St Yves in the south to Mount Sorrel in the north, a distance of nearly ten miles. The position was occupied according to the Ludendorff defence doctrine – a lightly held forward position, studded with strongpoints and nests of machine guns, with strong counter-attack formations in the rear prepared to retake any lost ground. The surprise factor in the assault, however, would be the detonation of nineteen mines placed beneath the enemy front line. The work of tunnelling the mines had begun as early as August 1915 and, in all, twenty-four mines were completed, although five were not fired. The mines were tunnelled at depths of between 50 and 100 feet, with some galleries extending a mile or more under the ridge, and were positioned along the whole length of the front although twelve were clustered around the apex of the salient. The total weight of explosive was over 800,000lb – nearly 400 tons. The arduous and dangerous work of installing the mines was a unique feat of wartime mining engineering and was largely unsuspected by the enemy. The artillery plan was to destroy the strongpoints and machine-gun nests in the preliminary bombard-ment while, at the same time, harassing enemy communications; once the assaulting infantry had moved forward, they would advance under the protec-tion of a creeping barrage designed to fall on the counter-attacking formations.

During May the Second Army's artillery was gradually reinforced by artillery from the Arras sector and the First Army, resulting in a total of 2,266 guns and howitzers (compared with 1,537 for the opening of the Somme offensive and on a front of attack over four miles longer). The preliminary bombardment began on 21 May and continued intermittently until the 31st; it then expanded to its full capacity and continued until 7 June, the day of assault.

The plan of operation was an attack by three corps (II ANZAC, IX and X) of Plumer's Second Army, making a total of twelve divisions; in addition there would be 72 of the new Mark IV tanks[16] to assist in knocking out strongpoints. The attack had a limited objective – a maximum depth of advance of two miles, gaining the ridge in the process, and ultimately eliminating the salient. Zero hour was timed for 3.10 a.m. on 7 June – about ninety minutes before dawn:

> Deep silence reigned everywhere. Dawn was just breaking. The nightingales in Rossignol Wood were still finishing their night's song, when suddenly hell was let loose, and the greatest earthquake ever felt in Northern Europe, accompanied by the mightiest crash ever heard by mortal man, broke on the still summer morn. Immediately from the whole enemy's system rose his coloured lights – the signal to his artillery that the battle had begun. Three of the mines were on the immediate front of the battalion, and although all ranks knew what was to happen, the stupendous effect was almost more than human nerves could stand. Three great columns appeared out of the earth and rose slowly, majestically almost . . . Higher and higher the columns rose, and gradually the most beautiful colour-effect was observed. Orange, blue, green and yellow flames seemed to emerge from the brown columns, and then slowly bursting into shapelessness, the mass commenced to lurch. For minutes, literally, the falling debris, earth and stones, rained down, and it was almost impossible to move . . .[17]

All nineteen mines were fired successfully – the shock waves were felt as far away as the south of England – then a massive barrage was brought down on enemy positions and artillery batteries. Progress by the advancing infantry was at first made difficult by the churned up state of the ground and the almost impenetrable fog following the detonations and the bombardment,

> . . . for none could see five yards in the early dawn of mist and indescribable dust . . . Gradually some order came out of chaos . . . slowly the fog lifted and the troops could see their objectives and some idea of direction.[18]

The fearful impact of the mines and the artillery barrage virtually decimated the troops holding the forward positions; those who survived were so unnerved that they surrendered as soon as the British infantry appeared: 'They made many attempts to embrace us; I have never seen men so demoralised,' wrote an officer in ANZAC. Plumer's plan had envisaged three distinct forward movements. The first objective was gained in 35 minutes, by 5 a.m. the second objective had been reached and by 9 a m , although a contracted salient still existed, the British now occupied the whole of the ridge and waited for the inevitable counter-attack. However, for the present there were no indications that one was in preparation:

> Apart from the shell bursts of the protective barrage, the scene, to quote the words of an Australian officer, was more like a picnic than a battle. Behind was a ploughed-up wilderness of shell-holes and battered trenches, with a litter of tangled wire, broken rifles and abandoned equipment; it reached back as far as a clean-cut line in the original No Man's Land, beyond which grass still grew. In front, however, was a green countryside, with woods of leaf-covered trees, and the gentle sloping grassland was intersected by tree-lined hedgerows . The lower half of this eastern slope, where lurked most of the German batteries, was out of sight owing to its convexity, but in the distance could be seen the towns, woods and water meadows for many miles along the Lys valley. The panorama slumbered under a bright sun which already gave promise of an exceptionally hot day.[19]

By midday, however, definite signs of the movement of counter-attack formations were observed, and an attack launched at 2 p.m. was quickly dispersed by artillery and machine-gun fire. The next and final phase of the first day's attack was planned to be the establishment of a line to the east of Oosttaverne. Zero hour for the advance was fixed for 3.10 p.m. (after a delay of two hours to enable artillery to be brought up), and, with the barrage preceding them, the infantry surged forward to the Oosttaverne Line, which by now had been reinforced. The Australians, attacking the southern end of the line, met strong opposition from pill-boxes and, although their casualties were severe, succeeded in penetrating the defences. Further north the resistance was much lighter and by late afternoon virtually the entire Oosttaverne Line was in British hands. But there was a gap in the centre south of Wambeke which, owing to a tragic misunderstanding, led to the Australians' coming under fire from their own artillery, resulting in their withdrawal from the southern portion of the line. Over the following days Plumer concentrated on pushing forward his right flank: by the 12th the enemy had withdrawn from the portions of the Oosttaverne Line he still retained and by the 14th had retired to the Warneton Line.

The results represented an undoubted victory for British arms. All their objectives had been achieved, over 7,000 prisoners had been taken at a cost of nearly 25,000 casualties (over half incurred in ANZAC), and although the extent of German losses is uncertain it is probable that they exceeded British losses by a significant amount. The plans for the assault, long in gestation, had been meticulously prepared. The nature of the attack had come as a surprise to the Germans, for although they knew that mining activity had taken place they had no conception of the scale, nor indeed did they anticipate such a superiority in artillery. One German view was that they should have evacuated the ridge before the attack, and that had this taken place 'the German Army would thereby have been spared one of the worst tragedies of the war'. One ominous portent of things to come, however, was that, for the first time, the infantry were confronted by German pill-boxes. They were to become only too familiar with them in the bitter fighting of the summer and autumn of 1917.

The success at Messines was like a brief shaft of sunlight piercing the prevailing darkness, but its momentary illumination only served to emphasize the depth of the returning gloom. The mutinies in the French Army were approaching a critical stage, and General Wilson warned the War Cabinet on 8 June that 'the French would not stick it much longer'. The situation in Russia was also one of acute uncertainty. The revolution begun in March had led to the overthrow of the Tsar, and although the new regime had undertaken to continue the fight against Germany, there was talk of making peace, raising the spectre of the transfer of German divisions to the west.

On 8 June the War Cabinet decided to set up a small War Policy Committee consisting of the Prime Minister, Lord Curzon, Lord Milner and General Smuts, with Sir Maurice Hankey as its secretary. As its title suggests, its task was to review war policy as a whole and 'to conduct its investigations without interfering with the daily meetings of the War Cabinet, where day-to-day decisions had to be taken over a vast field'. It was becoming clear, however, that Robertson was uneasy about Haig's projected Flanders offensive. He met Haig in France on the 9th, and Haig's diary records:

> I had a long talk with Robertson. He wished me to realise the difficult situation in which the country would be if I carried out large and costly attacks without full co-operation by the French. When Autumn came round, Britain would then be without an Army! On the other hand it is possible that Austria would make peace if harassed enough. Would it not be a good plan, therefore, to support Italy with guns? I did not agree. Altogether I thought Robertson's views unsound. I told him that I thought that the German was now nearly at his last resources, and that there was only <u>one sound</u> plan to follow, viz., <u>without delay</u> to
> 1. Send to France every possible man
> 2. " " " " " aeroplane
> 3. " " " " " gun. [Haig's emphases][20]

On 12 June Haig submitted to the War Cabinet a 'Memorandum on the Present Situation and Future Plans' in which he referred to the successful completion of the assault on the Messines–Wytschaete Ridge and its 'considerable importance in facilitating preparation for a further advance and improving our defensive position around Ypres'. He referred to the portions of the line taken over by the French, and reported that Pétain was 'arranging for offensive operations on other portions of the front, on a sufficient scale to prevent withdrawal of German forces to oppose my advance . . .'; accordingly, he was pushing on with his preparations for 'the Northern Operations'. He then referred

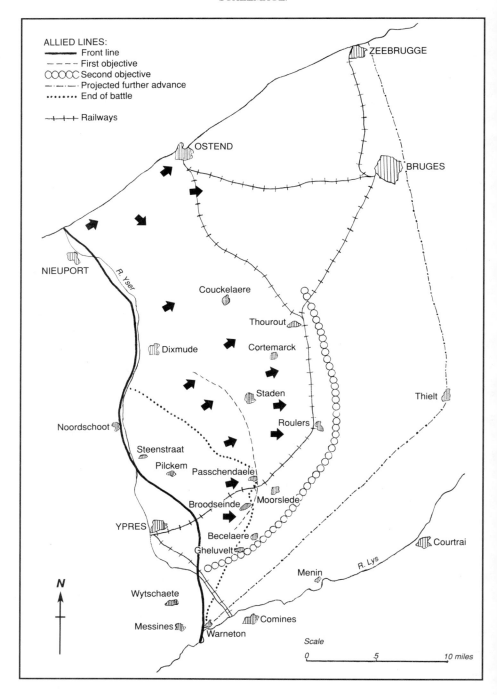

The Flanders Offensive Plan

to the critical state of German morale, both on the home front and in the Army, and in support of this he attached an appendix prepared by Brigadier-General Charteris, his Head of Intelligence at GHQ. The appendix detailed the serious condition of German resources, both military and economic, and the deterioration in German morale. It concluded:

> From all these definite facts, it is a fair indication that, given a continuance of circumstances as they stand at the present and given a continuation of the effort of the Allies, then Germany may well be forced to conclude peace on our terms before the end of the year.[21]

Haig's case rested heavily on the predictions made in the appendix, but Robertson was concerned about the optimism expressed, particularly as the Director of Military Intelligence at the War Office (Brigadier-General Macdonogh, who had been Charteris's predecessor at GHQ) did not agree with the conclusions reached. Robertson immediately telegraphed Haig:

> Your appreciation of June 12th arrives very opportunely and I entirely agree with your views and will support them to the utmost of my power. But I cannot possibly agree with some of the statements in the appendix . . . I hope, therefore, you will agree appendix not being circulated to the War Cabinet . . . It would be very regrettable at this juncture if different estimates of enemy resources were presented to the War Cabinet as it would tend to destroy value of your sound appreciation.[22]

In a follow-up letter on the same day, Robertson advised Haig to argue that his plan was the best plan, and

> . . . then leave them to reject your advice and mine. They dare not do that. Further, on this occasion they will be up against the French.[23]

Haig agreed to omit the appendix, and on 17 June he submitted a detailed statement of his views on the advantages to be gained by clearing the Belgian coast; it was this statement which was considered by the War Policy Committee at meetings commencing on 19 June and extending over the 21st and 22nd. What the Committee had to consider was not a tactical battle with limited objectives but a strategic one with an ultimate depth of advance of over sixty miles. Haig's plan was (i) to capture the ports of Ostend and Zeebrugge by a coastal advance of twenty-five miles and (ii) to advance up to thirty miles and cut the railways serving those ports. Success in (i) and (ii) would have the effect of pushing German forces up the Dutch frontier, which, in the event of their breaching Dutch neutrality, could mean the co-operation of the Dutch Army in driving the Germans out of Belgium entirely. An attack by the French towards Mezières–Valenciennes could ultimately mean the enemy's withdrawing entirely from the line Lille–Champagne. The battle was in no sense planned as a breakthrough, but an advance by stages with each dependent on the success of the previous one. The advance could be discontinued if further effort were not justified.

Not surprisingly, Haig's plans were subjected to an intense and far-ranging investigation by the Committee, which was now joined by Bonar Law, leader of the Conservative Party. Doubts were expressed as to whether the Allies possessed enough strength, both in men and armaments; whether the French could be relied on to play their part; whether the depth of the advance was attainable, with the example of the Somme in mind when only seven miles was achieved; and whether, as it seemed to the members of the Committee, the British Army would be pitted against the main strength of the German Army. To all these fundamental questions Haig and Robertson between them contrived to give plausible replies. Haig's diary entry for 19 June set the atmosphere:

> The members of the War Cabinet asked me numerous questions, all tending to show that each of them was more pessimistic than the other. The Prime Minister seemed to believe the decisive moment of the war would be 1918. Until then we ought to husband our forces and do little or nothing, except support Italy with guns and gunners . . . I strongly asserted that Germany was nearer her end than they seemed to think, that now was the favourable moment for pressing her and that everything possible should be done to take advantage of it by concentrating on the Western Front all available resources. I stated that Germany was within six months of the total exhaustion of her available manpower, _if the fighting continues at its present intensity_. To do this more men and guns are necessary. [Haig's emphasis][24]

The discussion was resumed the following day, when both Haig and Robertson argued strongly against the Prime Minister's alternative of an attack against Austria from the Italian Front (Austria had already made peace overtures). The debate returned to Flanders and the First Sea Lord, Admiral Sir John Jellicoe, was brought in to give his views. To the astonishment of those present, he claimed that unless the Germans were cleared out of Zeebrugge the war could not be continued in 1918 for lack of shipping. In his _War Memoirs_, Lloyd George recorded: 'This startling and reckless declaration I challenged indignantly, but The First Sea Lord adhered to it'.[25] The Committee met again the next day, when the Prime Minister summed up his arguments against the Flanders offensive and put forward two alternatives. He recognized 'that the responsibility for advising in regard to military operations must remain with the military advisers' and that 'it would be too great a responsibility for the War Policy Committee to take the strategy of the War out of the hands of the military'. Nevertheless, he entreated Haig and Robertson 'to carefully weigh his misgivings' and, if their views remained unchanged, 'then, subject to the condition they had themselves suggested as to breaking off the attack if it did not work out in accordance with expectation, we would not interfere and prevent the attempt'. His misgivings covered much the same ground as the doubts expressed at the first meeting, and he concluded by saying that none of his colleagues, 'whether they were in favour of or opposed to the adoption of Sir Douglas Haig's plan, were sanguine of success'. He then turned to the alternatives. The first was wearing down the enemy by 'a punch here and there'; when this was added to

> ... the privations of the Germans, the prospect of a big reinforcement from America and a regeneration of the Russian Army, the enemy, feeling that time was against him, might be considerably damaged and discouraged by such a course.

The second was an attack on the Austrian front. It was known that Austria was anxious to be out of the war. If Austria could be forced out, Bulgaria and Turkey would automatically have to go too. This would mean that 'the whole of the forces now locked up in Salonika, Mesopotamia and Egypt would be set free for operations on the Western Front'. The Prime Minister concluded by saying that, if the military advisers cautioned against his suggestions, he would, nevertheless, support them, but he believed 'that one course would lead to victory and the other course to a hopeless and costly struggle bringing us no nearer victory'.[26]

Thus concluded one of the most fateful meetings of the war, with nothing settled, only a decision deferred until Haig and Robertson had responded to the Prime Minister's misgivings. Over the following two days they each prepared their responses. Haig remained convinced that his plan was the best alternative, and Robertson, after ranging over the points made by Lloyd George, concluded that the offensive in Flanders was the only alternative and to abandon it and attempt to seek a decision in Italy was unsound. The final meeting of the Committee took place on the 25th, when the replies from Haig and Robertson were considered. The ground covered at the earlier meetings was gone over again, but Robertson, when put under pressure to confirm that he shared Haig's views of success, would not be drawn further than to quote from Haig's Memorandum of 12 June:

> ... if our resources are concentrated in France to the fullest extent the British Armies are capable and can be relied on to effect great results this summer – results which will make final victory more assured and which may even bring it within reach this year.

He added, however, that the chances were good if France and Russia 'pulled their weight'. The meeting concluded with the decision to allow Haig to continue with his preparations, and that pressure would be put on the French Government to 'use all their available forces in co-operation with Sir Douglas Haig'.

After four meetings the Committee and its military advisers had failed to find common ground. Neither Haig nor Robertson had budged from their respective positions and the Committee now found itself in an acute dilemma. For the Committee to have rejected the military advisers' counsel and forced on them the alternative of an attack against Austria would undoubtedly have brought about Robertson's resignation and possibly Haig's. Lord Hankey, in *The Supreme Command 1914–1918*, summed up the situation (in a slightly different context):

> They might criticize the operations proposed by their naval or military advisers; they might force them to justify their proposals by convincing arguments or insist on the examination of alternative suggestions; they might point out that their plans would make too great a drain on the total resources of the Allies; they might make such dispositions as they thought best for the exercise of the Supreme Command in the field, even to the point of putting the Commander-in-Chief of one army temporarily or permanently under the command of another; they might dismiss an admiral or general in whom they no longer felt confidence; in the interests of the war as a whole, when the naval or military advisers of the various nations took different views, one or other might become parties to a joint decision against the advice of their respective generals – but rarely on any purely naval or military issue of a major character did the civilians attempt, either individually or collectively, to override a consensus of agreed naval or military opinion. Moreover, all of them kept a sharp eye on public opinion . . .[27]

To attempt to draw together all the complex strands of the events leading up to the Flanders offensive results in a number of imponderables. Despite Robertson's opposition to Lloyd George's alternative of an attack against Austria, he had, as referred to earlier, made the suggestion to Haig on 9 June that Austria might make peace 'if harassed enough' – a suggestion which found no favour with Haig. It would seem evident that he was worried about Haig's optimism over the decline in German morale, hence his advice to omit the Charteris appendix. As John Terraine has pointed out,

> One extremely serious aspect . . . was that the evidently very different views of the condition of Germany held by Haig (based on Charteris) and Robertson (based on Macdonogh) were never properly discussed and resolved, because of their fear that any apparent crack in their united front would be exploited by Lloyd George for his own purposes.[28]

One possible reason for this 'united front' has been advanced:

> As long as Haig's policy of the offensive prevailed, the Cabinet could scarcely authorise any substantial reduction in his strength, but it seemed likely that, if the offensive was abandoned, Lloyd George would insist upon diverting a considerable force from France to Italy. Haig, therefore, was not faced with a simple choice of an offensive or defensive policy. If he remained on the defensive it seemed probable that he would have to do so with his armies seriously weakened – and weakened, moreover, for a purpose of which he strongly disapproved. He naturally became more determined than ever not to abandon the Flanders offensive . . .[29]

Admiral Jellicoe's dramatic warning that the war could not be continued in 1918 unless Zeebrugge was cleared was greeted with disbelief by those present, but its effect was to add support to the Flanders offensive. It is true that by June 1917 the losses in merchant shipping due to enemy action were very disturbing. Losses of Allied and neutral vessels rose from 298,000 gross tons in January to 849,000 by April, a significant proportion of them caused by submarine action, particularly since Germany had announced unrestricted submarine warfare in February. These losses were by no means attributable to the twelve small submarines based on Zeebrugge, but Jellicoe seemed equally concerned about the three squadrons of destroyers based there and the threat that these also represented to naval patrols and cross-channel traffic. There was a tragic irony in the fact that, at the end of April, the trial of a convoy system for merchant shipping was adopted by a hitherto reluctant Admiralty. It proved to be successful, and from July the losses gradually began to fall.

Part of the statement agreed by the military representatives at the Paris Conference in May was that

> It is no longer a question of aiming at breaking through the enemy's front and aiming at distant objectives. It is now a question of wearing down and exhausting the enemy's resistance . . . We are all of opinion that our objective can be obtained by relentlessly attacking with limited objectives . . .

The Messines operation was a perfect example of this intention. Haig's plan undeniably aimed at distant objectives, but Robertson maintained that it was not in conflict with the Paris agreement because the intention was to wear the enemy down and then exploit the situation. He acknowledged that the ultimate objective was the Belgian coast, but it was not intended that this would be pursued if it involved disproportionate cost. The inference that can be drawn from the exploitation of a wearing-down attack was the step by step approach advocated by Haig. This, on the face of it, appeared to possess inherent safeguards in that, having gained one step, the next would not be attempted unless dictated by results. It is clear that the primary decision to take the next step would be a military rather than a political one, but where it would appear that there was an element of doubt as to the wisdom of taking the step – for example, an unacceptable casualty rate, unacceptable not only because of its impact on manpower resources but measured against a shortfall in achievement – then should it still remain a military decision? The underlying implications of this were not debated at the meetings of the War Policy Committee, but they would loom large in the months to come.

Perhaps the greatest of the imponderables was how far, and how aggressively, the French would co-operate. Ever since the outbreak of insurrection in their Army, the French had been sending confusing signals as to the extent of their support for the Flanders offensive. Pétain had assured Haig at the Amiens Conference on 18 May 'that the French Army would fight and would support the British in every possible way'. In confirmation of this, he had referred to four attacks already in preparation, but these attacks were later scaled down to two, Craonne on 10 June and Verdun on 15 July. By early June, however, even the former had been cancelled. The critical meeting would appear to have been that between the French Chief of Staff and Haig on 2 June:

> The 'Major-General' of the French Army arrived about 6.30 p.m. and stayed to dinner. His name is General Debeney. He brought a letter from General Pétain saying that he had commissioned him to put the whole situation of the French Army before me and conceal nothing. The French Army is in a bad state of discipline.[30]

At the meeting Haig was told that six French divisions would be at his disposal in the Yser sector and would come under his orders. But from then until the opening of the Flanders offensive on 31 July the question of French intentions elsewhere on the Western Front remained in doubt. The War Cabinet was aware that there had been problems of indiscipline in the French Army, and throughout all its meetings with Haig and Robertson its anxiety over French co-operation ran in counterpoint to the theme of Haig's optimism. During the discussions Haig had expressed confidence that the French would do more than just hold the line, but he did not mention the discussion with Debeney on 2 June. He may have felt that the situation in the French Army was so secret that it could not even be revealed to the War Cabinet or, ever an optimist, he may have believed that French morale would have recovered by the time he mounted his offensive, or, if not, then it would keep German pressure off the French. Another reason might have been that, since the Committee's agreement to his plans depended on French co-operation, any doubt he expressed would mean the cancellation of his offensive and the adoption of the alternative, the attack against Austria.

On 18 July the decision to give Haig the go-ahead was made at a dinner party given by Lloyd George to members of the War Policy Committee, but with the proviso that if the results proved indecisive, then it would be stopped and replaced by an attack on the Italian Front:

> The decision to allow Haig to undertake the Flanders offensive was taken by Lloyd George and by most of his colleagues with reluctance and misgiving. No one believed that a strategical result could be achieved, and all shrank from the terrible losses which they knew it must involve. But the consensus of naval and military opinion was so overwhelming that the War Cabinet could not take the responsibility of rejecting the advice thrust upon them with so much cogency. It is true that they adopted the Italian plan as a reserve plan in case the Flanders attack failed or degenerated into a mere slogging match. They went so far as to order that staff

officers should be sent to Italy, railway timetables worked out, and that ammunition dumps should be built up for an eventual force of heavy guns. With this in view the progress of the Flanders attack was to be kept under constant review by the War Cabinet.[31]

The authority to undertake the offensive was conveyed to Haig by Robertson on 21 July. Haig was nettled by the tone, particularly the implication that the decision as to when the offensive should be stopped might be taken other than by himself. This, he felt, displayed a lack of confidence in him, and in his reply he requested to be told whether he had the 'full support of the Government or not'. On the 25th Robertson telegraphed Haig with a message of confidence from the War Cabinet and the assurance that 'you may depend upon their wholehearted support', and that 'they will obtain your views before arriving at any decision as to the cessation of operations'.

Plans and Preparations

Ever since the War Policy Committee meetings in June, Haig had been completing his preparations, and on 5 July he wrote to his army commanders, outlining his plans for the offensive. These were prefaced by optimistic references to the resumption of Russian operations on the Eastern Front, which he thought would come as a 'very heavy blow' to the enemy. He also thought that confidence in the invincibility of the German armies had been so shaken 'that it cannot survive many fresh defeats', and that German faith in the submarine campaign 'must soon be abandoned entirely' – a curious statement, bearing in mind that the clearance of the Belgian coast owing to the submarine menace had been the justification for his offensive.

In summary, his plans were for the Fifth Army to capture the Passchendaele–Staden ridge and its extension to Dixmude, and then, in co-operation with the French and Belgians, to push north-eastwards to a line Thourout–Couckelaere. Simultaneously with the latter advance, the Fourth Army, with naval support, would attack around Nieuport and on the coast to the east of the town. Thereafter both armies would push on towards Bruges. After the capture of the Passchendaele–Staden ridge, 'opportunities for the employment of Cavalry in masses are likely to offer'. The role of the Second Army was to cover the right flank of the Fifth Army and be prepared to press forward between Warneton and Menin, or even further to Menin itself if all went well. After sounding a cautionary note that progress may require modifications, 'especially in view of the comparatively short period of fine weather which we can count on', he thought, nevertheless, that the results 'may exceed general expectations, and we must be prepared for the possibility of great developments and ready to take full advantage of them'.[32]

The main assault had been entrusted to General Gough, as Fifth Army commander, rather than to General Plumer commanding the Second Army; Gough had not been in the Ypres sector since October 1914, whereas Plumer had known the area intimately for the last two years. Plumer, a cautious and methodical general, had conducted a brilliant operation at Messines, but Haig considered him to be imbued with the 'bite and hold' doctrine, and his choice fell on Gough, a cavalryman and, at 47, the youngest general in the British Army. The inference drawn from the choice of Gough, with his reputation as a 'thruster', was that Haig was hoping for a breakthrough. As will be seen later, the decision to use Gough was to bring controversy in its wake.

During June and July the Fifth Army's strength was built up to four corps (II, XIX, XVIII and XIV), comprising sixteen divisions with two in reserve. Apart from its own artillery, batteries of heavy and field pieces were drawn from the other Armies (except the Fourth), and by early July there were 752 heavy howitzers and 1,422 field guns and howitzers. In addition to this formidable array of artillery, 216 tanks had been allocated. To the north of the Fifth Army's left flank there was the French 1st Army, comprising six divisions commanded by General Anthoine, and six Belgian divisions, under the command of King Albert; on the coast was the XV Corps of Rawlinson's Fourth Army, augmented by five divisions drawn from the other Armies. Thus, poised for the attack, were 24 British and French divisions; the six Belgian divisions, however, were only to be committed when conditions were judged to be favourable.

Although the main effort was to be in the Ypres sector, the other Armies not involved had been instructed by Haig to conduct wearing-out operations which, it was hoped, might have the benefit of deluding the enemy as to where the main blow was to fall. Accordingly, the First and Second Armies planned attacks towards Lille and Lens respectively. The First Army's assault, delivered on 28 June, was successful in gaining some ground, but the Second Army's attack had to be scaled down because of its eventual commitment to the main offensive: only local attacks were carried out in June and July, but these met strong resistance and further operations were postponed. There was, however, a serious reverse to the plans for the coastwise assault when on 10 July the enemy launched a surprise attack on the British position north of the Yser river. The attack was preceded by a heavy artillery bombardment and ultimately the 1st and 32nd Divisions were forced back across the river, having suffered over 3,000 casualties. Haig, however, was not unduly worried by this set-back: '... we shall be able to overcome his guns and then to blow him out of his position as effectively as he blew us out of ours, and over a wider area.'[33]

The original date for the main offensive had been fixed for the 25th, but by early July both the British and French Army commanders were asking for postponements: Gough wanted an extra five days to allow for the arrival of the remainder of his heavy artillery, and Anthoine was concerned that the dull weather had prevented adequate observation of enemy gun positions and asked for an extension of three days. Haig had earlier agreed to a postponement until the 28th and was loath to agree to any further delay, principally because he was concerned about the weather. Nevertheless, he reluctantly agreed to a postponement until the 31st. The preliminary bombardment had begun on the 16th, growing to its full force by the 28th:

> Contrary to the teachings of the great military commanders of the past, it was accepted as an axiom at this stage of the war that the achievement of the element of surprise in the delivery of an attack was out of the question. The stereotyped method of advertising the part of the line on which the impending assault would fall by a lengthy preliminary bombardment reached its climax at Ypres in 1917. From the middle of June to the end of July, the process of packing the base of the historic Salient with guns went on without cessation. Abandoning all hope of secrecy, the higher command crammed guns behind every hedge and wall, and into every field and street. In any case, every possible battery position in that small area was already well known to the enemy. They had been occupied by a succession of British batteries during the past two and a half years, and the German artillery had had ample opportunity of verifying and re-verifying their exact line and range. A large number of siege batteries had been told off to engage the hostile artillery, which, owing to the open nature of British preparations, had been concentrated in almost equal numbers by the opposing army. There developed, in consequence, throughout the month of July an artillery duel which exceeded, in magnitude and intensity, anything that had ever before been experienced on any front.[34]

For roughly the same length of front, the number of artillery pieces was over double the total employed in the Somme battle, with a corresponding increase in ammunition expended. There was a considerable emphasis on counter-battery work, but this was hampered by the enemy artillery's being positioned out of sight on the reverse slopes of the Flanders ridges. Their location was largely dependent on aerial observation, which the enemy was determined to deny, and for most of July the Royal Flying Corps was involved in fierce battles over Flanders. The limitations imposed by the weather, however, together with frequent movements of batteries by the enemy, meant that their neutralization was not as successful as that achieved at Arras or Messines. But counter-battery work was not confined to the British, and enemy artillery was active not only in seeking out battery positions but also in harassing communications. As Haig wrote in his Fourth Dispatch,

> On no previous occasion, not excepting the attack on the Messines–Wytschaete Ridge, had the whole of the ground from which we had to attack been so completely exposed to the enemy's observation. Even after the enemy had been driven from the

Messines–Wytschaete Ridge, he still possessed excellent direct observation over the salient from the east and south-east, as well as from Pilckem Ridge to the north. Nothing existed at Ypres to correspond with the vast caves and cellars which proved of such value in the days prior to the Arras battle, and the provision of shelter for the troops presented a very serious problem.[35]

To add to the problem, the Germans were now using shells charged with the new mustard gas – a liquid gas, disabling rather than fatal, causing intense burning and severe vomiting, and persisting in the soil for days or even weeks.

Undeceived by the feint attacks against Lens and Lille, the Germans were well aware of the purpose of British activity at Ypres and were confident that their preparations could prevent an advance making any significant progress. As at Messines, their front line was not held in strength. Ever since Arras the convention of a definitive front line with its support and reserve trenches had ceased to exist. Instead, there would be a thinly held forward zone scattered with strongpoints, and at Ypres these were pill-boxes constructed from reinforced concrete and designed to give direct and flanking fire. Further back, the ruins of farmhouses had been converted into miniature fortresses. In the event of these obstacles being overrun, counter-attack formations waited in the rear, and behind them lay a second line with yet more reserves poised for counter-attack; there was even a third line of reserves in support. Thus the advancing infantry had a series of hurdles to surmount, and the further their penetration the greater would be the resistance.

As already mentioned, the British artillery had experienced problems in seeking out and destroying enemy battery positions, but the task of locating strongpoints was even greater because they were all but invisible from the air; even then the pill-boxes were proof against anything other than a direct hit by the heaviest shell. The preparations for the battle included the construction of a model of the area on a two-acre site and the attacking brigades were rehearsed in their role, including the tactics involved in silencing fire from pill-boxes – but the British were unaware how numerous these had become. The three nights before the day of assault saw intense activity behind the Fifth Army front as infantry, tanks and two divisions of cavalry moved up to their assembly positions. Its strength reduced to twelve divisions owing to the transfer of eight to the Fifth Army, the Second Army had as its role to protect the right flank of the Fifth Army's attack and to make a limited advance towards the Warneton line.

The Assault: 31 July

Zero hour was 3.50 a.m., and, under a lowering sky giving promise of rain, the infantry of both Armies left their trenches and moved forward into No Man's Land under the protection of a creeping barrage. On the extreme right, the

Second Army's attack was successful in capturing the villages of La Basse Ville and Hollebeke and pushing its front forward up to 1,000 yards, but further progress depended on the outcome of the Fifth Army's assault.

The four corps of Gough's Fifth Army (from right to left, II, XIX, XVIII and XIV) employed nine divisions for the initial assault in what was to be known as the Battle of Pilckem Ridge. South of the Ridge and the line of the Ypres–Roulers railway, II Corps attacked astride the Menin Road. The Official History records that II Corps 'had, it was generally recognized, the hardest task of the day'. It had to capture the strongly held Gheluvelt plateau, and, as will be seen later in this account, its failure to do so was ultimately to bring recrimination upon Gough's head and fuel a controversy that still endures. In contrast to the open ground to be crossed by the neighbouring corps north of the railway, II Corps' initial problem was to force a passage through three woods, Shrewsbury Forest, Sanctuary Wood and Chateau Wood. The woods, at this stage in the war, were now ruins of fallen tree-trunks and pitted with shell-holes. Progress was made where open ground existed, but strongpoints in Shrewsbury Forest defied attempts by the 24th Division, on the extreme right, to push forward. The centre of the attack (30th Division) had to pass through Sanctuary Wood, but progress in the wreckage of the wood was so slow that the barrage, timed to a quicker pace, had moved on. (The Official History notes that on 29 July the divisional commander had asked for the creeping barrage to be reduced from 25 yards a minute to 20 in his sector. The reply received the next day was that it was too late to make the alteration.)

Nevertheless, the infantry struggled on, incurring heavy casualties from fire from strongpoints, and were eventually brought to a halt some 200 yards from their objective. To make matters worse, enemy artillery opened a heavy bombardment on both woods, causing further casualties. On the left of the corps attack, two brigades of the 8th Division had to battle their way through Château Wood and managed to overrun their first objective, Bellewaarde Ridge, by 6 a.m. In pushing on to its second objective, the right brigade encountered frontal and flanking machine-gun fire and had to withdraw to the Westhoek Ridge. At 10.10 a.m. an attempt was made by the reserve brigade to gain the third objective, but this failed. The tanks allocated to II Corps had an impossible task. Out of the 48 tanks provided, only 19 reached the front line, the remainder either ditching or suffering mechanical problems. The woods were impassable, and in attempts to bypass them they came under fire from anti-tank guns. Nevertheless, they were able to render some assistance to the infantry, particularly in silencing nests of machine guns, but by the end of the day only one vehicle had survived.

North of the Ypres–Roulers railway the position was somewhat brighter. Advancing over open ground, the seven assaulting divisions of XIX, XVIII and

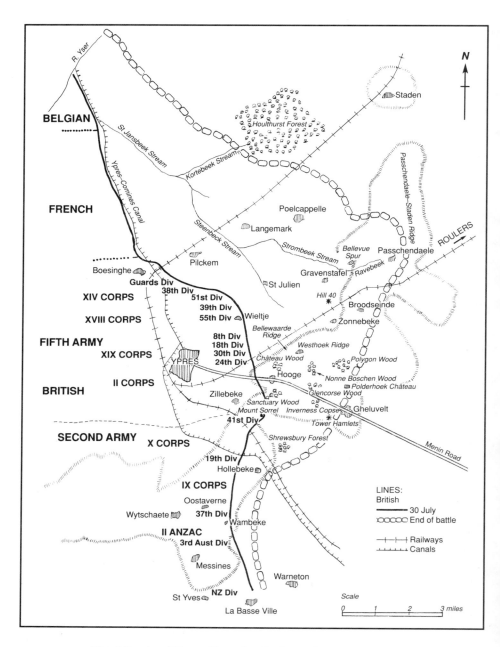

Third Battle of Ypres (Passchendaele), July–November 1917

XIV Corps rapidly overran the enemy's forward positions and had reached their second objective along the Steenbeek stream by 9 a.m. According to the Official History,

> ... the main offensive by the two southern corps, the II and XIX, was to be resumed within a few hours, as soon as the northern defensive flank had been formed, and events seemed to justify such an aggressive course ...

At 10.10 a.m. the barrage recommenced, but II Corps infantry could make little progress in the face of heavy machine-gun fire north of the railway. The divisions of XIX Corps continued their successful advance, although it was evident that the defence was stiffening. Meeting intense machine-gun fire and even fire from artillery over open sights, they, despite severe casualties, managed with the assistance of some battalions from the neighbouring XVIII Corps to cross the Zonnebeke–Langemark road and reach their third objective. Thus by 1 p.m. a salient had been established on the front of XIX and XVIII Corps, some two and half miles wide and a mile deep at its apex.

This penetration was now the signal for the German counter-attack formations to move up from behind the Broodseinde–Passchendaele ridge, but, unfortunately, the movement was not observed. Their advance was heralded at 2 p.m. by a heavy artillery bombardment on the salient earlier created by XIX and XVIII Corps, followed by strong attacks along the whole of its length. The strength of the counter-attack was such that the position on the left of the salient in front of St Julien could not be held, forcing a withdrawal and causing a falling back from all positions held in the salient. It was also unfortunate that the British artillery was uncertain as to the positions reached by the infantry earlier in the day, and in consequence no artillery support could be provided to break up the enemy counter-attack. Counter-attacks also fell on the north of the front held by XIV Corps and on the left of XVIII Corps, but they were dispersed by artillery and machine-gun fire and the position along the obstacle of the Steenbeek stream held. A counter-attack was also launched on the Second Army position, but this too was dispersed by artillery fire. By nightfall the left of the Fifth Army held on to its third objective, but on the right II Corps, which had had the hardest task of all, barely held its second.

The Fifth Army attack had been comparatively successful. Haig wrote in his diary, 'This was a fine day's work'. For the first time for two years the enemy was denied observation over Ypres, a penetration at its deepest of about two miles had been achieved and over 6,000 prisoners had been taken, albeit at a cost of nearly 30,000 casualties. German casualties for 31 July cannot be established, but the losses incurred in counter-attacks must have been severe. Gough had hoped that the fourth objective would have been reached by the end of the day, but the rain, that ominous harbinger of things to come, developed from a drizzle in the afternoon to a torrent by early evening.

Gough held a conference with his corps commanders in the evening to decide on further action. He had earlier met Haig, who recorded in his diary:

> As regards future operations, I told Gough to continue to carry out the original plan; to consolidate ground gained, and to improve his position as he may deem necessary, for facilitating the next advance; the next advance will be made as soon as possible, <u>but only after adequate bombardment and after dominating the hostile Artillery</u>. [Haig's emphasis][36]

The immediate priority, however, was the capture of the Gheluvelt plateau before any general advance could be made. This was planned for 2 August but had to be postponed, mainly owing to the need to bring up fresh divisions. Further postponements were to occur, however, and not for purely military reasons. The rain that had fallen on the first day was but a precursor of what was to become the wettest August in Flanders for twenty years. The situation was graphically described in Haig's Fourth Dispatch, although written nearly five months after the event:

> The weather had been threatening throughout the day, and had rendered the work of our aeroplanes very difficult from the commencement of the battle. During the afternoon, while fighting was still in progress, rain began, and fell steadily all night. Thereafter for four days, the rain continued without cessation, and for several days afterwards the weather remained stormy and unsettled. The low-lying, clayey soil, torn by shells and sodden with rain, turned to a succession of vast muddy pools. The valleys of the choked and overflowing streams were speedily transformed into long stretches of bog, impassable except by a few well-defined tracks, which became marks for the enemy's artillery. To leave these tracks was to risk death by drowning, and in the course of the subsequent fighting on several occasions both men and pack animals were lost in this way.[37]

The operation against the Gheluvelt plateau was eventually fixed for the 10th, after a twenty-four-hour postponement due to rain. The plateau astride the Ypres–Menin road was the principal feature in the German defence and its importance had been recognized ever since planning for the offensive had begun; indeed, the occupation of the Messines–Wytschaete ridge had been seen by Plumer as an essential step in the capture of the plateau. In the centre of the arc of the Flanders ridges, 'German artillery, concealed in its woods and on its slopes, dominated the low ground on either side, and could enfilade such a movement [that is, across the Steenbeek] with observed fire.'[38] Evidence of German relief that the II Corps attack had failed is provided by Crown Prince Rupprecht's diary: '…the results of the day's fighting [31 July] were all the more satisfactory because the counter-attack divisions of Group Wytschaete behind Gheluvelt plateau had scarcely been used.'[39]

In support of the advance, many artillery batteries had moved up on 31 July into new positions, but German counter-battery fire was heavy and unremitting:

> ... I received orders to move the guns further forward under the lee of what had once been Sanctuary Wood ... And the weather worsened and it rained and rained, and the whole area became a great morass and ammunition could no longer be brought up in a wagon but had to be carried, eight rounds at a time, on a led pack-horse. All night and all day the German artillery pounded the gun lines and quite early on we had two guns damaged by shell fire, one badly. We had had no time to dig gun pits and, even if we had had time, we could not have done it in the flooded and boggy ground in which we stood. The best we could do for ourselves was to make a little scrape about one foot deep and try to get what shelter we could in that when it was our turn to sleep. I remember waking up in the morning and feeling the water squelching between my shoulder blades. Many of our men had ague from the damp and could hardly talk for the chattering of their teeth or keep their hands still ... [40]

On 10 August II Corps opened its assault on the Gheluvelt plateau. The objectives were Inverness Copse and Glencorse Wood on the right and Westhoek village on the left. At first, apart from south of the Menin road, the advance went well, but enemy counter-attacks, and an artillery barrage falling behind the attackers to prevent reserves moving up in support, brought it to a halt. Only on the left of the attack was any progress made towards the objective, but the attempt on the plateau failed.

It was becoming evident that the Fifth Army's offensive was running into serious problems. The heavy and sustained rain, combined with the intensive shelling, had produced appalling ground conditions, creating a glutinous obstacle to rapid progress, while the enemy's artillery was far from being dominated and was able to pour a relentless fire on both infantry and artillery positions.

The divisions that had taken part in the offensive since the first day were now not only severely depleted in strength but also physically exhausted, and for the next assault, fixed for the 14th, the eight reserve divisions were employed. After two postponements, the second due to heavy rain on the 14th, the attack took place at dawn on the 16th in what was to be known as the Battle of Langemark. Once again II Corps had the most arduous task, and the objective of the two divisions (the 56th and the 8th) was to penetrate the German third line from Polygon Wood to the Ypres–Roulers railway, but the 56th Division on the right had in its path Inverness Copse and Glencorse Wood. The 56th suffered almost at once from heavy artillery and machine-gun fire and only a few survivors managed to reach the objective, the westerly edge of Polygon Wood. The attacking brigades of the 8th Division reached their objective but were driven out of it by a heavy artillery barrage and a counter-attack. By the afternoon the two brigades of the 56th Division, precariously placed on the outskirts of Polygon

Wood, were counter-attacked and they too were forced back to their starting line. Total casualties in the two divisions were over 4,000.

The two divisions of XIX Corps, the 16th (Irish) and the 36th (Ulster), had a similar objective, that is, the penetration of the German third line. Until 4 August they had been in Corps reserve, but since then, while in the line, they had been subjected to constant artillery fire to the extent of suffering over 3,000 casualties, and by the 16th they were seriously under strength:

> The story of the attack, alas! is not a long one. The German barrage came down swiftly, but, as it was for the most part on the assembly trenches and behind them, it had small effect on the leading waves. But the enemy machine guns all along the front opened fire almost simultaneously with our barrage. The concrete pill-boxes, containing in some cases half a dozen separate compartments, seemed to be entirely unaffected by the pounding of many weeks. Moreover, strong wire entanglements running down obliquely [from the front] were encountered. The lanes cut by artillery fire were covered by machine guns. The ground was a veritable quagmire. The 'mopping up' system was found to be impossible. The concrete works had to be fought for; they could not be passed by and left to 'moppers-up' in rear. The inevitable result was that men quickly lost the barrage. The strength of the attacking force had become inadequate to its frontage of one thousand five hundred yards. The foremost wave must have consisted of less than three hundred men, probably reduced to a third within half a minute. Not unfitting was the description of a sergeant who took part in the attack: 'it looked more like a big raiding party than anything else'.[41]

Both divisions were set a task beyond their capabilities. Despite attempts by isolated units of the 16th Division to reach their objective, the attack was a failure in the face of a heavy artillery barrage followed by the inevitable counter-attack. The remnants were eventually forced to withdraw to their starting line, and although Fifth Army headquarters ordered a fresh advance to secure a line approximately half way to the original objective, it had to be abandoned because the troops were exhausted (Gough later complained of their performance to Haig, although he was later to accept that he had been unjust to do so):

> The two Irish divisions were broken to bits, and their brigadiers called it murder. They were violent in their denunciation of the Fifth Army for having put their men into the attack after those thirteen days of heavy shelling, and, after the battle, they complained that they were cast aside like old shoes, no care being taken for the comfort of men who had survived. No motor-lorries were sent to meet them and bring them down, but they had to tramp back, exhausted and dazed. The remnants of the 16th Division, the poor despairing remnants, were sent, without rest or baths, straight into the line again, down south. I found a general opinion among officers and men, not only of the Irish division, under the command of the Fifth Army, that they had been victims of atrocious Staff work, tragic in its consequences. From what I saw of some of the Fifth Army staff-officers I was of the same opinion.

Some of these young gentlemen, and some of the elderly officers, were arrogant and supercilious, without revealing any symptoms of intelligence. If they had wisdom it was deeply camouflaged by an air of inefficiency.[42]

Only on the left of the attack was anything approaching success achieved. The four divisions of XVIII and XIV Corps (from right to left, the 48th, 11th, 20th and 29th), attacking in a north-easterly direction, reached their objective on the left and overran the village of Langemark, but they were less successful on the right, although the whole of St Julien was now in their hands. The French 1st Army reached its objective just short of the Kortebeek and St Jansbeek streams.

Shortly after the battle Gough saw Haig and told him that, under present conditions, there was no possibility of success and that the attack should be abandoned. Haig's response was that there was no alternative. If Russia should sue for peace it would mean the transfer of a large number of German divisions to the Western Front – or the Italian Front. This, coupled with the doubt as to whether the French Army could withstand a powerful attack, meant that to prevent a German victory the British Army would continue to bear the main burden of maintaining pressure on the Western Front.

Further attacks of a limited nature took place over the next few days, including another attempt by II Corps, supported by tanks, on 22 August to make progress towards the Gheluvelt plateau by capturing Inverness Copse. Although a position was established in the copse, it was ultimately lost three days later following a determined counter-attack.

Gough now believed that he could make little progress unless Plumer's Second Army was thrown in so as to offset the impact of enemy artillery fire on his front. (It had been estimated that out of a total 558 enemy guns on the Fifth Army's front, over 40 per cent were positioned in the Gheluvelt area.) This suggestion was put to GHQ, and there followed a meeting involving Lieutenant-General Sir L. Kiggell (Haig's Chief of Staff; Haig himself was in London), Gough and Plumer. Initially Plumer was not happy with the suggestion, believing that he would simply be exchanging one salient for another. Nevertheless, on Haig's return it was decided that the Second Army should take over the frontage of II Corps early in September and make a series of attacks with limited objectives, the initial task being the capture of the southern portion of the Passchendaele Ridge from Broodseinde southwards to Hollebeke. Plumer asked for three weeks in which to make his preparations, and in the meantime the Fifth Army's operations were to be restricted to gaining a line between Inverness Copse and Glencorse and Nonne Boschen Woods.

Thus the main responsibility for the offensive had passed from Gough to Plumer, and the high hopes that Haig had placed on the outcome of the Fifth Army's offensive had been dashed. Lloyd George viewed the results with gloom:

As the futile massacres of August piled up the ghastly hetacombs on the Ypres Front without achieving any appreciable result, I repeatedly approached Sir William Robertson to remind him of the condition attached to the Cabinet's assent to the operation. It was to be abandoned as soon as it became evident that its aims were unattainable this year and our intention was to be concentrated on an Italian offensive. He was immovable. He attributed the slowness of our progress to the exceptional rains. As soon as the weather improved we should sweep forward . . . But Robertson still believed in the possibility of great things after we had worn down the enemy's strength. According to him everything pointed to the growing exhaustion of the German Army. Why give in when we might be near a real triumph for our arms?[43]

Haig, too, remained confident. In his report to the War Cabinet of 21 August he 'regarded the prospects of clearing the coast before the winter sets in as still very hopeful' and observed that 'the right course to pursue is undoubtedly to press the enemy in Flanders without intermission and to the full extent of our powers'.[44] Lloyd George, not surprisingly, did not share Haig's optimism, and Haig attended a War Cabinet meeting on 4 September not only to review the situation but also to consider Foch's suggestion of sending one hundred heavy guns from the French 1st Army to Italy. Despite being pressed by Lloyd George, Haig was unwilling to discontinue the Flanders offensive or to support the Italians in their offensive against the Austrians. He believed that such a course would pass the initiative to the enemy to strike wherever the Allied defence was weakest. By a majority decision, the War Cabinet agreed that the Flanders offensive should continue, and the transfer of guns was delegated to Haig to discuss with the French.

On 29 August Plumer submitted his plan for the capture of the Gheluvelt plateau to GHQ. It was a methodical scheme embodying the 'limited objectives' approach which Haig had originally rejected as being too cautious; it also included Plumer's response to the GHQ memorandum on methods to be adopted to meet the enemy's new defence in depth strategy. Two corps, X and I ANZAC, plus the 19th Division of IX Corps on the extreme right, were to be employed (with II ANZAC in reserve) in an attack involving four clearly defined steps and a pause of six days between each in order to bring up artillery and supplies. The delay of three weeks needed by Plumer was to enable supplies to be brought up and to prepare the ground, bury telephone cables, lay light railways and tracks across the swamps, rest his infantry, dump ammunition, collect a massive amount of artillery and position new gun emplacements. For the assault on his front Plumer eventually had 1,300 guns and howitzers at his disposal, of which nearly half were heavy and medium, and, for the preliminary bombardment and day of battle, a total of 3½ million rounds of ammunition. This was slightly more than for the Messines assault, but twice as much compared with the Somme, and with a greater preponderance of heavy and medium pieces. The Second Army's assault was to be simultaneous with that of the Fifth, whose objective was the enemy position stretching from west of Zonnebeke to east of Langemark. Given a successful outcome of the assault on Gheluvelt, the Fifth Army's advance, particularly its right flank, would be protected from artillery fire in enfilade.

The spell of fine weather that had begun early in September was to last for three weeks. The battlefield began to dry out, except in the valley bottoms, and now, with all vestiges of greenery gone, resembled a brown desert – a desert, however, littered with the debris of battle and deeply cratered by the shelling of the previous month. The opening day of the battle was fixed for 20 September, and the preliminary bombardment began in earnest on the 13th, increasing in power and destructiveness up until the day preceding the day of battle. The artillery plan was most methodical and purposeful, being a combination of bombardments and creeping barrages, the former designed to destroy enemy batteries, communication aids and strongpoints, using both high explosive and gas shell, and the latter sweeping the approaches to the enemy's forward areas and battery positions, as a gardener would hose a flower bed, to interfere with the bringing up of ammunition and supplies. The enemy's forward positions were not a continuous line of entrenchments but a chequerwork of pill-boxes and fortified shell-holes, and the plan was

> ... to teach the enemy to lie at the bottom of his shell-holes or dug-outs whenever barrages are going on. After one barrage has passed over him he must always expect others. In doing this, cause as many casualties as possible to reduce his morale. This will be effected by working a succession of deep creeping barrages of every nature of gun and howitzer over the whole area to a depth of 2,000 yards beyond the last objective.[45]

The Germans had hoped that the lull had meant that the Flanders offensive was at an end. Indeed, General von Kuhl, Chief of Staff to Crown Prince Rupprecht, recorded, 'My inmost conviction that the battle in Flanders is at an end is more and more strengthened', but three days before the battle opened German 4th Army headquarters were certain that another offensive was about to be mounted. By the 18th the assaulting formations of the Second and Fifth Armies had moved up towards the front:

> At dusk on the 19th the approach march began. Well-signposted tracks had been made for each brigade, mostly across country, so as to leave the roads clear for the nightly stream of wheeled traffic. On nearing the line, white tapes, laid after dusk, guided battalions and companies to their destinations. After a fine sunny day a drizzle set in at nightfall, increasing to steady rain by 11 p.m. The troops were soon wet through; and the tracks, where not duck-boarded, became slippery and difficult. Soon after midnight, however, the rain ceased, leaving a clear starlit sky.[46]

Gough was worried about the rain and suggested to Plumer that the attack should be postponed, but the latter, on meteorological advice, decided that it should go forward.

At 5.40 a.m. the Battle of the Menin Road Ridge began, and the four attacking divisions (the 41st, 23rd, 1st and 2nd Australian) of the Second Army involved in the main assault advanced behind the protection of 'an artillery barrage of an extent and weight beyond all precedent.'[47] Aided by a ground mist, the infantry, following within a hundred yards or so behind the barrage, pounced upon the outposts and strongpoints and rapidly crushed any resistance. Indeed, there was generally little opposition: the barrage had literally stunned the enemy and many surrendered. Only south of the Menin road, on the far right of the attack, was there any hitch in the advance: the barrage was lost owing to fire from machine guns protecting the approach to Tower Hamlets spur – a fiercely defended strongpoint of pill-boxes – and the attack on the spur had to be abandoned because of heavy losses. Nevertheless, north of the Menin road the Australians achieved all their objectives and set about consolidating their gains to await the counter-attack.

The three corps of the Fifth Army (V, XVIII and XIV), comprising five attacking divisions, advanced in parallel with the Second Army. Artillery support, however, was not on the same scale as that provided for the Second Army, but otherwise the barrage plan was the same. Once the attack had begun it became apparent that the preliminary bombardment had not had quite the same impact: resistance all along the front, particularly from strongpoints and machine-gun emplacements, made progress difficult, but the training given earlier in the tactics of silencing fire from pill-boxes and in mopping-up procedures ultimately proved successful. All the objectives were achieved except in the centre of the attack, where a heavy enemy barrage at zero hour had caused disruption, and on the extreme left immediately south of the Ypres–Staden railway. By noon the third (and final) objective had been gained by both Armies, and the expectation was that the enemy would now mount counter-attacks. (Local counter-attacks had already been repulsed by artillery and machine-gun fire.) The plan was to consolidate the defence by utilizing enemy strongpoints (even though pill-box entrances faced east) and shell-holes. Fortunately the weather was fine, and the gathering of enemy counter-attack formations was quickly spotted from the air. It was anticipated that his main thrust would be at the Gheluvelt plateau:

> Visibility during the late afternoon became exceptionally good. Looking back from the battle area every detail of the gaunt ruin of the Old Cloth Hall within the ramparts of Ypres could be seen lit up by the setting sun. Clearer still to ground observers, with the sun at their backs, was the detail in front; no movement on

Gheluvelt plateau and on the long western slopes of the Broodseinde–Passchendaele ridge could escape the eye. Under such conditions, with every disadvantage, were the enemy counter attacks launched.[48]

By early evening the enemy reserves began their counter-attacks, but the advancing waves of infantry melted away under the devastating fire from a combination of artillery, machine guns and small arms, and the attacks came to nothing:

> This day's battle cracked the kernel of the German defence of the Salient. It showed a limited advance, and the total of 3,000 prisoners had been often exceeded in a day's fighting; but every inch of the ground won was vital. We had carried the southern pillar on which the security of the Passchendaele ridge depended. Few struggles in the campaign were more desperate, or carried out on a more gruesome battlefield. The maze of quagmires, splintered woods, ruined husks of 'pill-boxes', water-filled shell-holes and foul creeks which made up the land on both sides of the Menin road was a sight which to the recollection of most men seemed like a fevered nightmare. It was the classic soil on which during the First Battle of Ypres the 1st and 2nd Divisions had stayed the German rush for the Channel. Then it had been a broken but still recognizable and featured countryside; now the elements seemed to have blended with each other to make of it a limbo outside mortal experience and almost beyond human imagining. Only on some of the tortured hills of Verdun could a parallel be found. The battle of the 20th September was a proof of what heights of endurance the British soldier may attain to. It was an example, too, of how thought and patience may achieve success in spite of every disadvantage of weather, terrain, and enemy strength.[49]

After a pause of six days, Plumer's next step was an attack with the limited objective of capturing the remainder of Polygon Wood and the south-western edge of Zonnebeke village. The flanks of this, the main assault, would be covered on the right by an attack astride the Menin Road and on the left by a push forward by the Fifth Army north of Zillebeke. Once again this was to be an attack on a wide front, but the Fifth Army would be preparing for the eventual assault on Passchendaele – the last obstacle in clearing the ridge and paving the way for an advance north-eastwards towards the coast.

The weather still remained fine and dry and the preliminary bombardment planned for the next assault, fixed for 25 September, was on the same pattern as that for the previous attack. The difficulties remained, however, in bringing up the artillery over the cratered ground and constructing gun platforms:

> So clayey and soft was the soil here that we had to lay down gun platforms of a special kind. It would not have been sufficient to place, as usual, strong planks on the ground; we had first to sink fascines in it, throw road metal on the intervening spaces, and on this surface rest a double-deck platform, well nailed together, of beech slabs. Similarly for trail supports, we had to drive in a quarter-circle of seven foot stakes, in which we wove some more fascines.[50]

In the early hours of the day before the battle the enemy mounted a surprise attack, preceded by a heavy artillery bombardment, on the sector between the Menin road and Polygon Wood:

> With such energy was the attack pressed that the whole of our line was thrown back. It was impossible to know the position of our own troops and in how far the German attack had penetrated. Commanders of all formations from those of Brigades, even down to Platoons, were out of touch with their commands and with their flanks. The enemy, possessed of the advantage of ground, seems to have been in no such dilemma, for the bombardment lifted, and, as it seemed, with an even greater ferocity smote our communications and every approach to the beleaguered line. British batteries, which in the rear kept up a hurricane fire, from their deep formation, possessed of no new information, although themselves under the heaviest shell-fire, brought down the barrage line with the object of stemming any further infiltration. But although the German attack had overrun the Divisional [33rd] right, and had made a deep impression on its left, two Companies, some of the 1st Middlesex, the other of 93rd Highlanders, held their ground.[51]

The counter-attack, indicative of how seriously the enemy viewed the position reached by the British in the Gheluvelt area, brought about a change to the plan for the following day's attack. Zero hour, however, remained unaltered, and at 5.50 a.m. on the 26th the 5th and 4th Australian Divisions advanced behind the barrage and within three hours had captured Polygon Wood without serious loss. The situation on their left was almost as favourable. The assault had been carried out by two divisions (the 3rd and the 59th) of V Corps (Fifth Army). The village of Zonnebeke was taken, but the north-easterly edge had eventually to be given up in the face of a strong counter-attack; further north all the objectives were gained, but Hill 40, covering the north of Zonnebeke and the railway, was a nest of machine guns and, with strong enemy reinforcements arriving down the line of the Roulers railway, the 3rd Division was pinned down on the western slope of the hill. Only on the right flank was progress disappointing, owing mainly to the enemy counter-attack on the previous day. The 33rd Division had borne the brunt of the attack and the disruption had caused a modification of its objective. Its advance had started badly. A heavy bombardment fell on the assembled infantry, and the delay caused them to lose the protection of their own barrage, but, after fierce hand-to-hand fighting, the ground lost the previous day was regained. On the far right the 39th Division, despite initial success, failed in its attempt to occupy the Tower Hamlets spur. Enemy counter-attacks materialized by mid-afternoon, but they were all dispersed, mainly by artillery fire.

Once again Plumer's careful planning had achieved an almost complete success, and there was growing confidence that the new German defence strategy had been mastered. The German High Command also recognized that this needed revision, and Ludendorff admitted that 'the enemy [had] managed to adapt himself to our method of employing counter-attack divisions'. This revision took the form of a partial reversion to previous practice by manning forward areas more strongly, thus slowing down the British advance, and delaying counter-attacks for a day in order to make artillery preparations. The consequence of this, however, was inevitably more casualties among troops in the forward areas from artillery.

Haig was greatly encouraged by the events of the day. It appeared to him that, given a continuation of the fine weather, the bastions of Broodseinde and Passchendaele were ripe to fall in subsequent attacks, the ridge would be his and the way would be clear to push 'masses of cavalry' through into open country to cut railway communications between Roulers and the Belgian ports. The mood in London, however, was unenthusiastic. Robertson wrote to Haig on the 27th:

> Certain people here think it would be exceedingly difficult to bring about a decision on the West Front [*sic*] if the German troops there are materially reinforced (from the Russian Front), and therefore they are incessantly looking for means of detaching some of the hostile Powers. To detach them they maintain that more punishment is first required, and that naturally takes away from our concentration in the West.
>
> My views are known to you. They have always been 'defensive' in all theatres but the West. But the difficulty is to prove the wisdom of this now that Russia is out. I confess I stick to it more because I see nothing better, and because my instinct prompts me to stick to it, than because of any good argument by which I can support it.[52]

Undeterred by Robertson's somewhat half-hearted attitude, Haig met Plumer and Gough on the 28th to discuss future objectives. These were the capture of Broodseinde and the remainder of the Gheluvelt plateau in an assault planned for the first week in October, to be followed on the 10th by an attack on the Passchendaele ridge. Both Plumer and Gough had doubts about further exploitation: they would have preferred step-by-step operations. Their views were aired at a further meeting on 2 October, but, according to Haig's diary, their misgivings were apparently dispelled:

> I held a Conference at my house at Cassel at 11 a.m. Kiggell, Davidson and Charteris accompanied me. Generals Plumer and Gough were also present . . . I pointed out how favourable the situation was and how necessary it was to have all necessary means for exploiting any success gained on the 10th, should the situation admit, e.g., if the enemy counter-attacks and is defeated, then reserve Brigades must follow after the enemy and take the Passchendaele ridge at once. Both Gough and Plumer acquiesced in my views, and arranged wholeheartedly to give effect to them when the time came. At first they adhered to the idea of continuing our attacks for limited objectives.
>
> Charteris emphasised the deterioration of German Divisions in numbers, morale and all-round efficiency.[53]

On 28 September II ANZAC had taken over V Corps' sector from the Fifth Army (leaving Gough with only two corps), and four divisions of I and II ANZAC would be used in the assault on Broodseinde ridge and the Gravenstafel spur to the north of Broodseinde village. This would form the spearhead of the attack. The flanks would be supported by, on the left, four Fifth Army divisions, who would advance towards Poelcappelle, and, on the right, two divisions of X Corps (plus a division from the Fifth Army), with the objective of securing the remainder of the Gheluvelt plateau. South of the Menin road a division of IX Corps would provide a protective flank on the far right. Thus twelve divisions would assault on a front of almost eight miles, with an advance varying in depth from 1,000 to 2,000 yards.

Between 29 September and 1 October enemy storm-troops mounted a series of determined counter-attacks between Polygon Wood and Tower Hamlets, but these were all repulsed, with the enemy suffering severe losses. The sole gains were two isolated outposts south-east of Polygon Wood.

The weather had remained fine and dry for much of September, but in the evening of 3 October, as the troops moved up to the line, a south-westerly gale sprang up, accompanied by rain. Zero hour was 6 a.m., but at 5.20 a.m. a heavy German bombardment fell on the waiting infantry of I ANZAC, causing casualties. This was not in anticipation of the Australian attack but heralded a counter-attack timed for 6.10 a.m. (It had been planned for the previous day but postponed because of the losses suffered on 1 October.) At zero hour the British barrage crashed down on the enemy infantry forming up for the assault, and with no time for them to recover the Australians were upon them. After a brief and bloody encounter the enemy retreated in disorder, and after subduing pockets of resistance the Australians reached their final objective shortly after 8 a.m. On their left the 3rd Australian Division and the New Zealand Division were equally successful in their attack on the Gravenstafel spur. On other sectors of the front the Fifth Army divisions, with valuable assistance from tanks, captured part of Poelcappelle village. Only on the far northern and right flanks did the advance fall somewhat short of the objectives set. The attack was a serious set-back for the enemy. Over 5,000 prisoners had been taken and Ludendorff considered that

> The battle on the 4th October was extraordinarily severe, and again we came through it with enormous losses. It was evident that the idea of holding the front line more densely, adopted at my last visit to the front in September, was not the remedy.

The Australian Official History recorded:

> An overwhelming blow had been struck, and both sides knew it. The objective was the most important yet attacked by the Second and Fifth Armies, and

they had again done exactly what they planned to do . . . This was the third blow struck at Ypres in fifteen days with complete success. It drove the Germans from one of the most important positions on the Western Front; notwithstanding their full knowledge that it was coming, they were completely powerless to withstand it . . . coming on top of the achievements of September 20th and 28th, its success was of an entirely different order.[54]

The British were now only a mile and a half from Passchendaele, but the main objectives still lay beyond. It was evident that the only hope of attaining them before the winter set in depended on the continuation of the fine September weather through October. The next step, the capture of the Passchendaele–Staden ridge, was planned for the 10th, and, as foreshadowed at the Cassel Conference on the 2nd, Haig hoped that the time had come to depart from the methodical step-by-step approach and attempt a breakthrough.

Once again the Second Army was to deliver the main assault. Two Australian divisions were to attack on the right (with two in reserve), and the attack on the left was to be delivered by two Fourth Army divisions attached to II ANZAC (again with two in reserve). The Fifth Army would employ five divisions of XVIII and XIV Corps, with two cavalry divisions on hand for the exploitation of a breakthrough. The plan was for a morning attack which, if successful in penetration, would be followed in the afternoon using reserves. Haig's hopes for a continuation of fine weather, however, were to be dashed. Rain had fallen almost continuously since the 4th, and on the 7th Plumer and Gough met Haig and told him 'that though willing to continue, they would welcome a closing down of the campaign'.[55] The prospects for capturing the Belgian ports were now bleak, and the projected coastal attack had been abandoned, but Haig was still unwilling to release his hold on the offensive. He believed that by maintaining pressure in Flanders it would avert attacks on the French Army, only now gradually recovering from the acts of insurrection of the previous months. At the very least he wanted to capture the rest of the Passchendaele ridge in order to give drier ground for the winter and deny the enemy observation over the Steenbeek valley.

On the 8th Haig wrote to Robertson, setting out his argument against taking over more line from the French (he had earlier heard from Robertson that the Government, at a conference with the French on 25 September, had approved 'in principle' such a take-over). He insisted that

. . . since the British Armies alone can be made capable of great offensive effort, it is beyond argument that everything should be done by our Allies as well as ourselves to enable that effort to be made as strong as possible . . .

He entreated the War Cabinet to have more faith in the possibility of success on the Western Front, and 'resolve finally and unreservedly to concentrate our resources on seeking it, and to do so at once . . .' In this Haig was to be disappointed.

The rain ceased on the 8th, giving rise to hopes that a drier spell might be in prospect, but the weather forecast was for more rain. The problems in movement up to the front were now becoming nightmarish:

> The difficulty was to get the assaulting troops up to the jumping-off tapes at all, and in some sort of a condition to make an attack. The chief cause of the great discontent during this period of the Flanders fighting was, in fact, the continuous demands on regimental officers and men to carry out tasks which appeared physically impossible to perform, and which no other army would have faced. It must be emphasised again, too, that in all that vast wilderness hardly tree, hedge or wall or building could be seen. As at the Somme no landmarks existed, nor any scrap of natural cover other than the mud-filled shell-holes. That the attacks ordered were so gallantly made in such conditions stands to the immortal credit of battalions concerned.[56]

Equally affected was the forward movement of artillery batteries to support the next attack. The task of finding stable platforms so that guns would not sink into the mud after firing a few rounds was fraught with great difficulty. Not only had the artillery to be positioned, it had to be supplied with ammunition brought up with immense labour over the slippery duckboard tracks. The artillery was undergoing its greatest ordeal of the war:

> The batteries had no daily life, but rather a daily death, while their experiences – day in, day out – were invariably the same. Morning, noon, and night, the men were splashing about in mud, trying to keep their ammunition clean and their guns serviceable; daily they were shelled, sometimes with long deliberate bombardments, sometimes in hurricane shell-storms which descended on them for forty minutes or so two or three times a day. They were always wet, always cold; they continually saw the guns and ammunition, which they had spent hours in cleaning and preparing, blown to bits in the passing of a second; they helped to bring up more guns, more ammunition, and saw, in the serving of these new guns, their mates blown to pieces, shattered, torn. They grew to believe that relief would never come . . .[57]

Zero hour on the 9th was fixed for 5.20 a.m. The timetable for the assaulting infantry was that they should be in position by midnight, but the march up in the pouring rain was seriously delayed by the dreadful ground conditions: some battalions were not in position even by zero hour. Coupled with a less than effective barrage, the attack, in what was to be known as the Battle of Poelcappelle, began in highly unfavourable circumstances. The main assault was launched by two brigades each of the 49th and 66th Divisions attached to II ANZAC. The former division immediately ran into difficulties crossing the swollen Ravebeek stream, suffering severe casualties from fire from pill-boxes and nests of machine guns in attempts to penetrate undamaged wire entanglements. Untried in battle, the 66th Division, meeting less resistance, fared better and actually reached the Passchendaele ridge, but, lacking support on the flanks, was forced to withdraw. The only gain was in the north, where the French and XIV Corps reached the southern edge of Houlthurst Forest.

Haig considered that the results were 'very successful', but Charteris recorded in his diary:

> I was out all day yesterday at the attack. It was the saddest day of this year. We did fairly well but only fairly well. It was not the enemy but the mud that prevented us from doing better. But there is now no chance of complete success this year. We <u>must</u> still fight on for a few more weeks, but there is no purpose in it now, so far as Flanders is concerned . . .[58]

It is doubtful whether this pessimism – seemingly out of character for Charteris – was communicated to Haig, for the latter had already decided that the next attack should take place on the 12th. This decision had been based on Plumer's report that II ANZAC had reached 'a sufficiently good jumping-off line for the next attack', when he anticipated that Passchendaele would be captured. This was a hopelessly optimistic forecast which did not take account of the strength of the enemy's defences that had defeated the 49th Division, nor, indeed, the continuing difficulties in bringing up artillery and the appalling state of the battlefield:

> Front trenches meant a zig-zag of scattered shell-craters. A particularly large hole protected by a hurdle might be a battalion headquarters, a lesser hole might hold the leader of a company. The difficulty of conveying orders or of allotting objectives in such circumstances needs no emphasis, yet seldom did it receive sufficient allowance in high places. Strictly speaking, the campaigning season was over. In a tongue of waterlogged territory hemmed in by the enemy on two sides and dominated by the concentrated German artillery, the British Army groped and floundered.[59]

It might be questioned whether Haig and his Army commanders were wholly aware of these conditions. The Official History records that Haig

> . . . was kept regularly informed of the condition of the ground by his liaison officers and by the staff officers of the G.O.C. Royal Artillery and of the Engineer-in-Chief; and occasionally members of his own Operations Section flew over the battlefield and their reports did not minimize the bad conditions.

Flying over the battlefield was one thing, but living, moving and fighting on it was quite another, as any battery or company commander would have made abundantly clear. Haig nevertheless remained buoyant. Addressing war correspondents on the 11th, he said that 'It was simply the mud that defeated us on Tuesday. The men did splendidly to get through as they did.' Rain fell on the 10th and 11th, and in the evening of the 11th Gough telephoned Plumer, saying that he thought the attack should be postponed. Plumer, after consulting his corps commanders, told Gough that 'they considered it best for the attack to be carried out'. The Second Army's objective was the Passchendaele ridge, and the 3rd Australian Division and the New Zealand Division were to be employed. The Fifth Army on the northern flank was to push on beyond Poelcappelle. Zero hour was 5.25 a.m. on the 12th, and a woefully thin barrage heralded the advance. The Australians actually reached Passchendaele village but could not establish a position there because the New Zealanders on their left had suffered dreadful losses in attempting to penetrate belts of uncut wire entanglements. The attack was a failure. The Fifth Army made some headway, but its attack was largely peripheral to the assault on Passchendaele. Thus ended the First Battle of Passchendaele, with only insignificant gains achieved at a disproportionate cost – the New Zealand Division alone suffered nearly 3,000 casualties.

The next day Haig held a conference with Plumer and Gough:

> The Army Commanders explained the situation; all agreed that mud and bad weather prevented the troops getting on yesterday. We all agreed that our attack should only be launched when there is a fair prospect of fine weather. When the ground is dry no opposition which the enemy has put up has been able to stop our men. [Haig's emphasis][60]

Despite this set-back Haig was still intent on gaining Passchendaele, not only because of the advantages that the high ground would give him for the winter but also to maintain German concentration on the Flanders area because of a limited French attack planned for later in the month at Malmaison.

On the 18th II ANZAC were relieved by the Canadian Corps. It was hoped that this formidable fighting force, the victors of Vimy Ridge, would add further to its laurels by capturing Passchendaele ridge. The day of the assault was fixed for the 26th, with an advance planned in three stages, an interval of three days after the first attack and four days between the second and third. In the meantime the Fifth Army, in conjunction with the French, was to improve its position around Houlthurst Forest. The rainy weather had relented around the middle of the month, but in the early hours of the 26th it returned. Zero hour was 5.40 a.m., and the Canadians attacked with two divisions. The 3rd and 4th Divisions advanced on each side of the Ravebeek (a tributary of the Strombeek stream flowing into a re-entrant of the ridge) but met enfilade fire from the high ground, in particular from the strongpoint on Bellevue spur, and were forced to withdraw. The following morning, however, after being reinforced, they gained a foothold on the ridge though not in the village itself. South of the Canadians a diversionary attack was made by two divisions of X Corps on Gheluvelt and the Polderhoek Château, but although the village was entered and the ruins of the château captured, neither could be held and the divisions withdrew. Further north, in another diversionary attack, two divisions of the Fifth Army could make no headway:

> ... the mud, knee-deep, checked progress to a crawl of rather less than a yard a minute. The barrage was lost, rifles became quickly clogged and the men fell back, if they could, or were cut off.[61]

The conditions on the ground now almost defied description. Preparatory to the assault on Polderhoek, the march up to the front by a battalion of the Royal Warwickshire Regiment was graphically described by a company commander:

> For the first few miles we moved along a single duck-board track laid down on a vast sea of mud. Movement was difficult and slow, although separate up and down tracks were in use. By the time we had reached the end of the duck-boards night had fallen and guides from the front line met us to lead us as best as they could on solid ground between the maze of water-filled shell-holes. Into these many men fell and got soaked in the foul water, and were fortunate indeed if they were seen and hauled out and saved from almost certain drowning, weighed down as they were by their heavy equipment. Picture the puny efforts of a small fly to cross the pudding basin full of batter and you have some idea of the hopelessness of the man who has missed the track and become bogged in this appalling mud which appeared to have no solid bottom. A party of 'A' company men passing up to the front line found such a man bogged to above the knees. The united efforts of four of them with rifles beneath his armpits, made not the slightest impression, and to dig, even if shovels had been available, would be impossible, for there was no foothold. Duty compelled them to move on up to the line, and when two days later they passed down that way the wretched fellow was still there; but only his head was now visible and he was raving mad.[62]

The weather again relented on the 27th, and on the 30th the Canadian Corps made a limited advance preparatory to the main advance on Passchendaele village, but elsewhere little progress was made. At 6 a.m. on 6 November the Canadians again went forward. Their front only extended to about 2,000 yards, and, following closely behind the barrage, they stormed through the village. Despite Hindenburg's orders that the village must be held at all costs, and that it should be retaken if lost, the Canadians would not be denied. Four days later, in pouring rain, the Canadians and the British 1st Division extended their hold on the ridge by pushing several hundred yards northwards and the Flanders campaign effectively came to an end. There was, indeed, no prospect of a further advance.

On 24 October an Austro-German army of five Austrian and seven German divisions began a devastating bombardment of the Italian position at the little town of Caporetto on the Isonzo river using high explosive and gas (Italian gas masks were largely ineffective) and the Italian armies were soon in full retreat.

On the 26th Haig was instructed to send two divisions to Italy, and these were later followed by another three. Not only did Haig lose five divisions, but on 9 November Plumer left to take over their command.

* * *

Over the long years since the Great War, the Third Battle of Ypres – or, rather, 'Third Ypres' – lingers merely as a title in one of the volumes of the Official History: it became 'Passchendaele' between the wars, and so it has remained. As will be evident, Passchendaele was the culminating battle in a series of seven stretching over nearly four months, but its name seems to encapsulate all that was most dreadful about the battles on the Western Front. To some, however – and perhaps it is nòt too fanciful – its name, or rather the pronunciation of it, has an association with passion in the biblical sense of suffering and martyrdom: indeed, in Germany the fighting in Flanders was regarded as 'the greatest martyrdom of the World War'. Its impact on the British Army was summed up by the war correspondent Philip Gibbs:

> The battles of Flanders ended with the capture of Passchendaele by the Canadians ... and though we had dealt the enemy heavy blows from which he reeled back, the drain upon our man-power was too great for what was to happen next year, and our men were too sorely tried. For the first time the British Army lost its spirit of optimism, and there was a sense of deadly depression among many officers and men with whom I came in touch. They saw no ending of the war, and nothing except continuous slaughter, such as that in Flanders.[63]

Of the five offensives mounted so far by the British on the Western Front, Passchendaele had been the only one with a strategic, rather than a tactical, purpose. Since Haig had been Commander-in-Chief, it had also been the only one fought to his own design, instead of one in which he was obliged to defer to French plans. Even if the Admiralty's need to clear the Belgian coast had not existed, it is very likely that Haig would have embarked on his Flanders offensive. At the outset, the capture of the Flanders ridges would at last have freed Ypres from enemy observation, and then pushing the Germans up to the Dutch frontier would have meant that, short of breaching Dutch neutrality, there could be no withdrawal in depth such as had occurred on the Somme early in 1917: the Germans would have had to stand and fight. This would have resulted in a wearing-out battle which, with Haig's insistent belief in deteriorating German morale, he had confidently expected to win.

Despite Haig's optimism in July on the impact of the resumption of Russian offensives, the British General Staff had believed in April that the crisis brought about by the revolution in the previous month had 'greatly reduced, if not entirely destroyed, Russia's value as an Ally'. Nevertheless, early in July the Russians had opened a powerful offensive against a composite force of German, Austrian and Turkish troops near Brody and another against the Austrians further south. Some initial success had been gained, particularly against the Austrians, but both offensives were soon blunted by German reserves (four divisions transferred from the Western Front), and in the face of a counter-attack the Russians retreated in disorder. A further attack by joint Russian and Romanian forces towards the end of July achieved some success, but the gains were all lost in a German counter-attack. On 1 September the Germans opened a surprise and devastating bombardment on the bridgehead covering the city of Riga and the Russian defence collapsed. Henceforward the Russian Army as an effective ally ceased to exist. In consequence the transfer of many German divisions from the Eastern Front would have meant that Haig's hopes of winning a wearing-out battle would not have been realized.

As earlier referred to, the War Policy Committee had been by no means persuaded that approval should be given to the Flanders offensive, but then came Jellicoe's dramatic statement that, unless the Germans were cleared out of Zeebrugge, the lack of shipping owing to submarine activity would mean that Britain could not continue the war in 1918. Despite general disbelief in this view, it had the effect of adding support to Haig's plans. Winston Churchill, however, considered that

> The U-boat argument was wholly fallacious. A grave responsibility rests upon the Admiralty for misleading Haig and his Staff about the value of Ostend and Zeebrugge to the submarine campaign ... The whole U-boat war was based on the main German naval harbours, and was never dependent upon anything else ... Whatever influence this erroneous argument may have had upon the Haig–Robertson decision to launch a new offensive, it certainly contributed to baffle the objections of the Prime Minister and the War Cabinet ...[64]

According to Stephen Roskill's *Hankey: Man of Secrets*, Hankey 'did much later express the opinion that the Admiralty's statement was "rigged" and that Jellicoe's air of sincerity prevented the Cabinet demurring.'

Haig had assured the Committee that the French Army would support the offensive, but he did not reveal the extent of its weakness. It is possible that this was due to a mixture of motives, of which one might have been his fear that the focus of the war would be shifted to Italy. According to Hankey's diary entry for 8 June, General Wilson had warned the War Cabinet that the French 'would not stick it much longer', which had caused much anxiety. Thus it is open to doubt how far the War Cabinet believed that the French would have actively supported the offensive elsewhere than in Flanders, but ultimately, and belatedly, it gave its assent because it felt powerless to overrule military judgment. In this atmosphere of uncertainties and misgivings the campaign in Flanders had been launched, but what must be deplored is the lack of meaningful communication between Lloyd George and his military advisers and the mistrust engendered by the Calais Conference in February when Lloyd George secretly attempted to subordinate Haig to Nivelle.

Sadly, if uncertainties and misgivings had underlain the Cabinet's approval, then they were to be repeated in the planning and conduct of the opening of the offensive by the Fifth Army. It had failed, and the Official History considered that Gough was the culprit. It is evident that the exceptional rainfall during August was a contributory factor, not only because of the state of the battlefield but also because it severely hindered air observation of enemy artillery positions and troop movements. The preliminary bombardment had deluged the battlefield with nearly five tons of shells for every yard of front, and even if no rain had fallen the destructive impact of such an enormous weight of explosive would in any case have resulted in water-filled craters because of the high water table. The changed German defence strategy had not been fully appreciated, although it had been in operation at Messines in June. Rawlinson, waiting impatiently for the signal for the start of the coastal offensive, recorded in his diary on 8 August:

> A letter arrived from G.H.Q. this morning, pointing out that the new German tactics were to organize defence in depth, and rely chiefly on counter-attack. Should not, they ask, our major tactics be altered to meet them by limiting our objective and reducing the number of troops on the front of the assault? This is what I advocated before the battle of the Somme, and I have always been in favour of it. I am replying in this sense, welcoming the limited objective.[65]

Before Plumer's attack at Messines, Haig had urged that 'in the event of the situation developing in our favour, reserves will be placed at the disposal of General Gough, G.O.C. Fifth Army, in order to enable him to gain that Ridge [i.e., the Passchendaele Ridge]'. Plumer was equally seized with exploiting success and arranged for II and VIII Corps to attack towards the Gheluvelt plateau after a pause of three days to enable guns to be transferred from the Messines sector. Gough, however, was not in favour. He told Haig that he would prefer to make the attack the main constituent of the operation rather than carry out a limited assault with the possibility of placing his infantry in a dangerous salient. According to Gough, Haig agreed to this change.[66]

Henceforth the situation became confused – and, indeed, for present-day analysis, remains so. The GHQ plan had originally envisaged the 'capture of the enemy's front line and most of his second line on the front of Fourth Army [subsequently Fifth Army] on Zero + 2 day or earlier'. But Gough changed the objectives, which had the effect of a more ambitious advance in that Zero day's objective was extended to the third line (a mile beyond) with the possibility of a further advance to the east of the line Langemark through Gravenstafel to Broodseinde – the fourth objective – involving an advance of nearly three miles. These changes were approved by Haig but were afterwards criticized in a memorandum produced by Brigadier-General J. Davidson, Director of Operations at GHQ. He had pressed for the limited advance advocated in the original GHQ plan:

> An advance which is essentially deliberate and sustained may not achieve such important results during the first day of operations, but will in the long run be much more likely to obtain a decision. By a deliberate and sustained advance, I refer to a succession of operations each at two or three days' interval, each having as its object the capture of the enemy's defences, strongpoints, or tactical features, to a depth of not less than 1,500 yards and not more than 3,000 yards.[67]

This memorandum had been given to Gough for his comments. He agreed with broad principles expressed in so far as they advocated 'a continuous succession of organized attacks', but he questioned whether, having attained the first day's objective, there should be a pause of three days:

> It is important to recognize that the results to be looked for from a well-organized attack which has taken weeks and months to prepare are great, much ground can be gained, and prisoners and guns captured during the first day or two. I think therefore it would be wasteful not to reap all the advantages possible resulting from the first attack . . .[68]

This response was considered when Haig, Gough and Plumer met on 28 June. The outcome of the meeting, to quote the Official History, was that Haig,

> . . . after discussing the Davidson memorandum with him [Gough] and General Plumer at Cassel . . . had, with General Plumer's support, allowed the Fifth Army scheme to stand: it seemed perhaps worth trying an all-out attack on the first day.[69]

The upshot was that Haig had decided to disregard the Davidson memorandum and attempt a breakthrough, although he once again impressed on Gough the importance of capturing the Gheluvelt plateau. Indeed, Gough had always been convinced that Haig intended an attempt at a breakthrough, and the nature of his response to the Davidson memorandum was in the belief that it reflected Haig's wishes. Nearly thirty years later, when the volume of the Official History covering Passchendaele was in draft form, Gough wrote to the Official Historian:

> I have a very clear and distinct recollection of Haig's personal explanations to me, and his instructions, when I was appointed to undertake this operation. He quite clearly told me that the plan was to capture Passchendaele Ridge, and to advance as rapidly as possible on Roulers. I was then to advance on Ostend. This was very definitely viewing the battle as an attempt to break through, and, moreover, Haig never altered this opinion till the attack was launched, so far as I know. The G.H.Q. plan failed to amass anything like sufficient forces to carry out so ambitious a task

– 20 to 30 divisions were necessary – and the front of the attack was too narrow and directed at the wrong place. It should have been directed farther south – with its left, say, on Zonnebeke and its right on Messines. It was also a mistake not to entrust the operation to the General (Sir H. Plumer) who had been on that front for more than two years, instead of bringing me over on to a bit of ground with which I had practically no acquaintance.[70]

It is possible that Gough had eyes only for the north-east, with the goal of combining with the Fourth Army in a victorious sweep towards Ostend and Zeebrugge. His fateful omission was not to strengthen his right flank in order to capture the Gheluvelt plateau – an omission he tried too late to repair by calling the August conference. It was then that the main role in the offensive passed to Plumer.

To sum up on this unhappy affair of misunderstandings, it is clear that the planning for the Fifth Army offensive was bedevilled by a mixture of motives and afterthoughts. Haig was undoubtedly in error in choosing Gough for the main assault and, for reasons which remain unclear, in agreeing to his changes to the plan. The rejection by Haig of the step-by-step approach advocated earlier by Rawlinson (when the Fourth Army was to be involved) and Plumer, and his selection of Gough, a 'thruster', clearly demonstrated his desire for an assault uninhibited by the 'limited objective' concept. He had been encouraged by over-optimistic reports of the deterioration in German morale to believe that an all-out attempt at a breakthrough, albeit one involving heavy fighting, would bring about a German collapse in Flanders. It would appear that these views were expressed in the many talks he had with Gough during the planning stages, but then came the Davidson memorandum, which may have stirred up any latent doubts he had about the form the offensive should take. These, however, were apparently dispelled at the conference with Gough and Plumer on 28 June.

It seems, in passing, to be a lamentable state of affairs that so many critical decisions were apparently made verbally, without any written confirmation. Three-quarters of a century have passed since the events in question took place, and all the principals in the drama have long since passed away, some leaving diaries, books or papers through which historians and biographers have searched diligently for illumination. But, for the most part, they were, and are, interpreting the daily thoughts committed to diaries, or the recollections in books or papers where the passing of time may have played the memory false, or where actions and events might have been portrayed as they ought to have been rather than as they were, or where, indeed, material considered sensitive may have been suppressed.

The main responsibility for the offensive had passed to Plumer at the end of August. His employment of the 'limited objectives' concept, including a series of sweeping barrages of great intensity, brought about the successful advances in September and the attack on Broodseinde on 4 October. Plumer's approach, particularly in his use of artillery, was to blunt the impact of counter-attacks. In this he was so successful that the enemy had to resort to a partial return to the former system of manning his front more strongly, with the result that he incurred more casualties in the preliminary bombardments. After Broodseinde, however, the weather worsened, and the tortuous advance in quite dreadful conditions over the mile or so towards the final goal of Passchendaele had only been achieved at a heavy cost in casualties.

The appalling condition of the battlefield throughout much of the campaign that gave Passchendaele its evil reputation was in part caused by the heavy rain, but the major factor in bringing about these conditions had been the artillery. Ever since Neuve Chapelle the lessons learned had been that an essential preliminary to a successful attack must be the heaviest possible bombardment, and in all subsequent battles the artillery preparation had increased in duration and particularly in the employment of heavy guns. However, in some respects this was self-defeating: it eliminated surprise, and at Passchendaele it produced innumerable craters which soon filled with water owing to the high water table and the destruction of the drainage system. The rain only added to the problem. These conditions impeded the advance of the infantry to such an extent that on several occasions the protective barrage was lost. When the infantry eventually reached their objective and consolidated their position prior to the next forward move, the artillery had to be brought up with immense labour over the ruined ground and new gun emplacements established in the swamps with the difficulties already described. Hence, in the final stages of the campaign the artillery barrage had become less effective. Apart from this, the mud tended to stifle the impact of high explosive, and when shells fell in the craters the fountains of water thrown up were reminiscent of a naval battle.

The cratered ground and the mud had also been the cause of the failure of tanks to make a significant contribution. Representations had been made before the battle by the Tank Corps:

We pointed out that the surface soil was of small depth, that below it lay a bed of clay, that much of the ground we were to attack over had at one time or another been reclaimed from the sea, and that, bearing these points in mind, a bombardment would convert it into a bog ... We pleaded eloquently enough, but we might just have appealed to a brick wall ... As ground was our supreme problem, Hotblack, determining to keep a check on its destruction, arranged with the R.F.C. to have daily aeroplane photographs taken of the entire front over which tanks would eventually advance. From these, as the drainage system was more and more destroyed, he worked out the spread of the swamp areas. Then he transferred this information to a large-scale map, which we realistically called the 'Swamp

Map' . . . A copy of each day's Swamp Map was sent to G.H.Q., until we were instructed to discontinue sending them . . .[71]

Over two hundred tanks had been employed in the campaign, but few remained at the end in a serviceable condition: they littered the battlefield, half-submerged in mud, and the Menin road became known as the 'tank graveyard'.

The inevitable questions are, what was achieved and was it worth it? They are difficult, if not impossible, to answer. In theory, Haig's plan was imaginative, but only if it had managed to force the Germans up to the Dutch frontier and if neutrality was breached, bringing the Dutch Army in on the side of the Allies and combining with them to drive the Germans out of Belgium. This, however, depended on the Russians' keeping the Germans occupied on the Eastern Front, which ultimately was not to be. The distinguished historian Correlli Barnett considers that Haig made a cardinal error in not waiting until Allied forces had been built up, and that he persuaded himself that victory could be achieved before the Americans arrived in any combative strength.[72] As has been shown, the importance of the capture of the Belgian ports had been exaggerated. The military historian Liddell Hart came to the conclusion that

> The real source of the offensive, more potent than any of the arguments with which he buttressed his case, seems to have been Haig's optimistic belief that he could defeat the German armies single-handed – in Flanders.[73]

Although it is clear that Flanders was by no means an ideal choice for a battlefield, it is tempting nevertheless to speculate on what the results might have been if the offensive had been mounted at the outset by Plumer rather than Gough, and if August, like September, had been a reasonably dry month – or, again, if the offensive could have been carried out early in the summer, had Haig not been obliged to mount the attack at Arras in support of the ill-fated Nivelle offensive. Getting rid of the 'if's', and using hindsight, it is quite possible that Haig would at least have reached the Belgian ports, but, as it was, the campaign ended in November in a position which should have been reached in early September.

Thus the achievement in terms of ground gained was an advance at its greatest penetration of some five miles, in the process exchanging one salient for another which within five months would have to be given up as a result of the great German offensive in March 1918. But it might be contended that achievement should not simply be measured in terms of ground gained. As autumn progressed, Haig saw the campaign as a means of wearing out the enemy and distracting him from putting pressure on the French. It can only be a matter for conjecture how, at this particular time, the French would have reacted to a powerful German offensive, but they had virtually recovered from the mutinies of the summer and had even mounted two minor offensives of their own. Haig, in his letter to Robertson of 8 October, had stated that, although the French armies were not capable of 'great and sustained offensive effort', they were nevertheless 'staunch in defence'.

This leaves the question of whether wearing out the enemy was the main achievement. Ludendorff, in his *War Memoirs*, wrote that

> The costly August battles...imposed a heavy strain on the Western troops. In spite of all the concrete protection they seemed more or less powerless under the enormous weight of the enemy's artillery. At some points they no longer displayed that firmness which I, in common with the commanders, had hoped for... I myself was put to a terrible strain. The state of affairs in the West appeared to prevent the execution of our plans elsewhere. Our wastage has been so high as to cause grave misgivings and had exceeded all expectations ...[74]

The German Official History recorded:

> The offensive had protected the French against fresh German attacks, and thereby procured them time to reconsolidate their badly shattered troops. It compelled O.H.L. [the German Supreme Command] to exercise the strongest control over and limit the engagement of forces in other theatres of war ... But, above all, the battle had led to an excessive expenditure of German forces. The casualties were so great that they could no longer be covered, and the already reduced battle strength of battalions sank significantly lower.[75]

The controversy that ran as a recurrent theme throughout the campaign even continued into the measurement of the cost of the battle. The Official History gives British casualties at 244,897, and the German official account estimated German losses at 217,000 but calculated British losses at 400,000. The Official Historian took the view that German losses 'were the 400,000 at which they assess the British ...' There are no grounds available to allow an acceptance of this view, but the figure of 217,000 excludes the lightly wounded. To arrive at parity with British calculations, which included the lightly wounded, the Official Historian estimated German casualties at 'about 289,000' but still maintained that there was 'every probability that the Germans lost about 400,000.' Even the 'official' British figure of 244,897 has been challenged in some quarters: Churchill thought that British losses were 400,000 (presumably using the German estimate) and Lloyd George 399,000. Liddell Hart used a figure of 300,000 but thought it would be more. To sum up, it is possible that the Allied and German total came to 600,000, perhaps – but only perhaps – shared equally, but in this welter of melancholy statistics it appears that upwards of 70,000 British and German soldiers were killed, of which the British total was over a half. If this is at all proportionally indicative, it could give some slender clue to the weighting of the casualties to the detriment of the British.

Was it worth it? The question remains. German accounts written after the war confirm that the German Army had suffered a severe blow, affecting its future actions. It is undeniable that it incurred heavy casualties, but opinions or verdicts expressed after an event are either sharpened by objectivity gained by the passing of time or flawed by using the event to vindicate a subsequent failure. Driving a middle course through these two propositions, it emerges that, despite the British successes of September, it is after Broodseinde on 4 October that the offensive should have been brought to an end. The morale of the British Army was high, and, this being so, Haig's temptation to push on is understandable. His decision to do so, regardless of the fact that conditions were by then wholly unfavourable, dissipated morale and also squandered reserves which would have been invaluable in his next battle. On this analysis, the answer is that ultimately the cost, in human terms, was greater than the advantage gained.

* * *

Just over a mile south-west of the village of Passchendaele (now Passendale) is the Tyne Cot military cemetery. With nearly 12,000 graves, it is the largest Commonwealth War Cemetery, and on the panels of the Memorial, covering the period from 16 August 1917 to the end of the war, there are the names of nearly 35,000 British and Dominion troops who have no known grave. In a biography of Plumer, General Sir Charles Harington, his former Chief of Staff, wrote:

I have knelt in the Tynecot Cemetery below Passchendaele on that hallowed ground, the most beautiful and sacred place I know in this world, I have prayed in that cemetery oppressed with fear lest even one of those gallant comrades should have lost his life owing to any fault or neglect of myself and the Second Army staff. It is a fearful responsibility to have been the one who signed and issued all the Second Army orders for those operations. All I can truthfully say is that we did our utmost. We could not have done more. History must give its verdict. I do not for one moment contend that we did not make mistakes, and many of them, and as I read through these old orders before me, I keep recalling the old problems with which we were faced.[76]

Notes to Chapter 6

1. This was chlorine gas, causing death within one or two minutes if inhaled and against which there was no protection other than a wetted handkerchief. The first gas mask for British troops was introduced in June 1915 and the box respirator in August 1916.
2. Churchill, Winston S., *The World Crisis 1911–1918*, Odhams (London, 1938)
3. Blake, Robert, (ed.), *The Private Papers of Douglas Haig 1914–1919*, Eyre & Spottiswoode (London, 1952)
4. Lloyd George, D., *War Memoirs*, Vol. II, Odhams (London, 1938)

5. Falls, Captain Cyril, (comp.), *Official History of the War: Military Operations, France and Belgium 1917*, Vol. I, App. 8, Macmillan & Co. (London, 1940)

6. Blake, *op. cit.* It is possible that Lloyd George was in a chastened mood after his previous espousal of Nivelle.

7. Lloyd George, *op. cit.*

8. *Ibid.*

9. Edmonds, Brigadier-General Sir James, (comp.), *Official History of the War: Military Operations, France and Belgium 1917*, Vol. II, HMSO (London, 1948)

10. Blake, *op. cit.*

11. Edmonds, *op. cit.*

12. Calwell, Major-General Sir C. E., *Field Marshal Sir Henry Wilson*, Cassell (London, 1927)

13. Blake, *op. cit.*

14. *Ibid.*

15. *Ibid.*

16. The Mark IV tank superseded the Mark I and II versions; the Mark III was experimental only. A number of design improvements had been made: it was easier to control and its armour was now of hardened steel, believed to be proof against armour-piercing bullets.

17. Whitton, F. E., *The History of The Prince of Wales's Leinster Regiment: Royal Canadians*, Gale & Polden (Aldershot, 1926)

18. *Ibid.*

19. Edmonds, *op. cit.*

20. Blake, *op. cit.*

21. Edmonds, *op. cit.*, App. XII

22. Blake, *op. cit.*

23. *Ibid.*

24. *Ibid.*

25. Lloyd George, *op. cit.*

26. *Ibid.*

27. Hankey, Lord, *The Supreme Command 1914–1918*, Allen & Unwin (London, 1961)

28. Terraine, John, *The Road to Passchendaele*, Leo Cooper (London, 1977)

29. Blake, *op. cit.*

30. *Ibid.*

31. Hankey, *op. cit.*

32. Quoted by Lloyd George, *op. cit.*

33. Edmonds, *op. cit.*

34. Severn, Mark, *The Gambardiers*, Ernest Benn (London, 1930)

35. Buchan, John, *Nelson's History of the War*, Vol. XX, Nelson (London, 1915–19)

36. Blake, *op. cit.*

37. Buchan, *op. cit.*

38. Edmonds, *op. cit.*

39. *Ibid.*

40. Talbot-Kelly, R. B., *A Subaltern's Odyssey*, William Kimber (London, 1980)

41. Falls, C., *History of the 36th (Ulster) Division*, McCaw, Stevenson & Orr (London, 1922)

42. Gibbs, Philip, *Realities of War*, Heinemann (London, 1920). In December 1917 Haig told Gough that many divisions hoped that they would not be sent to the Fifth Army: 'This feeling I put down to his Staff.' (Blake, *op. cit.*).

43. Lloyd George, *op. cit.*

44. Charteris, Brigadier-General J., *At G.H.Q.*, Cassell (London, 1931)

45. Edmonds, *op. cit.*, App. XXIII

46. Edmonds, *op. cit.*

47. *Ibid.*

48. *Ibid.*

49. Buchan, *op. cit.*

50. Walker, G. G., *The Honourable Artillery Company in the Great War 1914-1919*, Seeley (London, 1930)

51. Hutchison, G. S., Warrior, Hutchinson (London, 1932)

52. Robertson, Field Marshal Sir W., *Soldiers and Statesmen 1914-1918*, Vol. 2, Cassell (London, 1926)

53. Blake, *op. cit.*

54. Bean, C. E. W., *The Official History of Australia in the War of 1914-1918*, Angus & Robertson (Sydney, 1921)

55. Edmonds, *op. cit.*

56. *Ibid.*

57. Stewart, J., and Buchan, J., *The Fifteenth (Scottish) Division, 1914-1919*, Blackwood (London, 1926)

58. Charteris, *op. cit.*

59. Nichols, G. H. F., *The 18th Division in the Great War*, Blackwood (London, 1922)

60. Blake, *op. cit.*

61. Edmonds, *op. cit.*

62. Bill, C. A., *The 15th Battalion The Royal Warwickshire Regiment in the Great War*, Cornish (Birmingham, 1932)

63. Gibbs, *op. cit.*

64. Churchill, *op. cit.*

65. Maurice, Major-General Sir Frederick, *The Life of General Lord Rawlinson of Trent*, Cassell (London, 1928)

66. Gough, General Sir Hubert, *The Fifth Army*, Hodder & Stoughton (London, 1931)

67. Edmonds, *op. cit.*

68. *Ibid.*

69. *Ibid.*

70. *Ibid.* Gough's role in the Passchendaele battle, and the controversial manner in which it is dealt with in the relevant volume of the Official History, is examined in Travers, Tim, *The Killing Ground*, Allen & Unwin (London, 1987)

71. Fuller, J. F. C., *Memoirs of an Unconventional Soldier*, Nicholson & Watson (London, 1936)

72. Barnett, Correlli, *The Swordbearers: Studies in Supreme Command in the First World War*, Hodder & Stoughton (London, 1986)

73. Liddell Hart, A. H., *A History of the World War 1914–1918*, Faber & Faber (London, 1934)
74. Ludendorff, General E., *My War Memoirs*, Hutchinson (London, 1919)
75. Edmonds, *op. cit.*
76. Harington, Sir C. H., *Plumer of Messines*, Murray (London, 1935)

7

Cambrai

The battle which concluded this weary year of deferred hope was the most original and interesting of the war, and ultimately had by far the most important consequences. In the first place it regained the lost art of surprise, and both sides clung desperately to this secret of decision. Secondly, it signalized the correct tactical employment of the new arm, which till now had been so pitiably wasted contrary to the advice of its chief begetter, Swinton.—C. R. M. F. Cruttwell, *A History of the Great War*

CAMBRAI is slightly over twenty miles south-east of Arras on the right bank of the canalized River Scheldt. It had been a prosperous industrial town before the war, notable for the manufacture of fine white linen – hence 'cambric', derived from Kamerijk, the original Flemish name for the town. It was occupied by the Germans in late August 1914 and established as an important centre for communications. It had been Haig's objective during the Arras battle. Several roads and railways converged on the town; one of the latter, vital to the Flanders area, ran northwards to Douai and Lille.

The British front line was about eight miles south-west of the town, but in between was part of the Hindenburg Line constructed on the 'defence in depth' theory adopted in early 1917. Immediately facing the British front, and partly sandwiched between two canals, the unfinished Canal du Nord and the St Quentin Canal, were three defensive systems, an outpost zone, a battle zone and a rearward battle zone. The most formidable feature in the system was the trench fronting the battle zone. This was between ten and twelve feet in width – considered by the Germans to be too wide for tanks – and nearly eight feet deep, chequered with machine-gun posts under reinforced concrete and provided with deep dug-outs. Moreover, it was protected by daunting belts of wire entanglements 100 yards in depth. Strongpoints ranging from fortified farm buildings to whole villages were scattered throughout the three zones . It was therefore an immensely strong position, behind which the enemy felt secure, so much so that it was a rest and recuperation area for battle-worn divisions withdrawn from the fighting in Flanders.

In June 1917 a plan for a large-scale tank raid in the Cambrai area had been suggested by Lieutenant-Colonel J. F. C. Fuller, the chief staff officer to

Brigadier-General H. Elles, the Tank Corps commander. He considered it an ideal area for the employment of tanks – the rolling chalk downlands, similar to the Somme, were comparatively uncratered and well drained – but for the time being nothing came of the suggestion.

Fullers's plan was revised early in August, and the preface to it foretold what was eventually to become reality:

> ... from a tank point of view the third battle of Ypres may be considered dead. To go on using tanks in the present condition will not only lead to good machines and better personnel being thrown away, but also to a loss of morale in the infantry and tank crews through constant failure. From an infantry point of view the third battle of Ypres may be considered comatose. It can only be continued at colossal loss and little gain . . .[1]

The plan was submitted to GHQ on 4 August, but with the Flanders offensive in its early stages it failed to make any real impression. Nevertheless, it was considered the following day at a meeting at Third Army headquarters, when it immediately appealed to the army commander, General Sir Julian Byng, who was already considering an offensive in the area. On the 6th Byng took the plan to GHQ and proposed to Haig that an attack by massed tanks followed by cavalry exploitation north-east of Cambrai should take place on 20 September. Haig was sympathetic to the scheme, but Kiggell, Haig's Chief of Staff, insisted that the demands of the Flanders offensive were paramount. But the proposal remained in being. It was now abundantly clear that Flanders was an unsuitable area for tanks and the Tank Corps proposed that they should be withdrawn, suggesting that they be used for a possible operation in the Lens area. This was approved by GHQ, but after a reconnaissance of the area it was decided that Cambrai was preferable. By the middle of October, however, it was apparent that the Flanders offensive had failed, and there was now a degree of urgency to obtain some sort of success before the arrival of winter.

As these events were unfolding, developments were taking place in the method of delivering the preliminary artillery bombardment. A bombardment on traditional lines would eliminate surprise – and surprise was essential if the tanks were not to be destroyed in their initial advance. With the use of aerial photography, flash-spotting and sound-ranging, coupled with maps produced by field surveying companies, it was now possible to identify the position of enemy batteries. The advantages of these techniques meant that the time-consuming task of preliminary registration (thus alerting the enemy to an impending attack) could be dispensed with, enabling the guns, hitherto remaining silent, to open fire at zero hour.

Byng outlined his plan at a Third Army conference on 26 October. After the tanks had smashed their way through the Hindenburg defences, closely followed by the infantry, the cavalry would pour through the gap to capture Cambrai and Bourlon Wood and push on to secure the passages over the Sensée river. Haig subsequently amended the plan, giving greater emphasis to the capture of Bourlon Wood rather than Cambrai itself. The next step, according to the Official History, 'might consist of an advance towards Douai and Somain, with the bulk of the cavalry moving on Valenciennes and thence eastwards'. Fuller's original conception had been a raid

> ... to destroy enemy personnel and guns, to demoralize him and to disorganise him, and not to capture ground. Moreover the duration of the raid must be short – eight to 12 hours . . .

To his dismay it had now blossomed into a not inconsiderable offensive, and the growing optimism of what the cavalry might achieve had overtones of the distant objectives planned for them at Loos in 1915.

The preliminary assault was to be on a frontage of 10,000 yards and delivered by 378 Mark IV fighting tanks (including 54 in reserve), supported by 98 tanks (including nine fitted with wireless) for supply purposes, wire clearance, bridging and telephone cable laying. Following the tanks would be four infantry divisions of III Corps (commanded by Lieutenant-General Sir William Pulteney) attacking on the centre and far right and two divisions of IV Corps (commanded by Lieutenant-General Sir Charles Woolcombe) attacking on the left centre. The two remaining divisions of IV Corps were positioned on the far left to follow up the initial assault. The attacking force was by no means fresh: five of the eight divisions had been through the Passchendaele campaign, some more than once, but although the Germans had six divisions in the area only two faced the impending assault. When the breach had been made in the enemy's defences, III Corps was to push on over the St Quentin Canal and IV Corps to head north to capture Bourlon Wood. Then would come the opportunity for the Cavalry Corps to exploit the success thus gained. It was to surround and isolate Cambrai and then proceed northwards to the Sensée river. Aside from the main assault, there would be local attacks elsewhere. Byng told GHQ on 8 November:

> With feint attacks in the intermediate portions of the line I hope to show a continuous battle front from opposite Vendhuille to Fontaine les Croisilles, a distance of 30,000 yards.

Training the infantry in co-operation with tanks commenced early in November. The plan was for the advanced guard of tanks to crush the wire entanglements, creating gaps, and then swing left to sweep the front trench with fire. The main body of tanks would now pass through the gaps and drop their fascines (bundles of brushwood) into the front trench and also swing left to rake the support trench. The last tank in each section would then penetrate the wire of the support trench, drop its fascine, cross the trench and push forward. The infantry would follow within 25 to 50 yards of the main body of tanks in two single files, pass through the gaps and clear the trenches of any opposition. Finally, tanks with grapnels would enlarge the gaps by hauling away the flattened wire in order to create passages wide enough to enable the cavalry to be passed through.

These were the tactics designed by Fuller, but, although they were approved by Third Army headquarters, the commander of the 51st (Highland) Division, Major-General G. M. Harper, had other ideas. He had already denounced the proposed use of tanks as a 'fantastic and most unmilitary scheme', and he departed from Fuller's ideas by directing that the advance guard of tanks should move in line abreast, crush the wire, and penetrate as far as possible, leaving the main body of tanks to assist the infantry in clearing up any remaining opposition. The most significant change, however, was his insistence that the infantry should follow not less than 100 yards from the tanks, and not in file but in extended order. These changes were to have a significant impact on operations on his front.

Haig had told Pétain of the plan on 1 November. The latter was eager to take part and offered two cavalry and three infantry divisions, but Haig, who was still doubtful about the offensive capability of the French, was lukewarm: he would rather they took over more line. French troops did arrive at Peronne on 19 November but, in the event, they played no part in the battle.

On 13 November GHQ finally gave its approval to the attack fixed for the 20th. Preparations gathered pace in an atmosphere of great secrecy and urgency, aided by the dull, misty weather typical of late autumn. Nearly 500 tanks had to be assembled, involving feverish activity at workshops in servicing and reconditioning, particularly on those vehicles recovered from the Ypres area. Just over a thousand guns had to be positioned, ammunition dumped, petrol and oil depots established, engineer stores brought up, roads improved, railhead facilities provided, sites for assembling and concealing tanks prospected and billets or shelters for troops selected. The Cavalry Corps began its march up to the concentration areas, but, according to the Official History,

> ... the nearest, that of the 5th Cavalry Division, about Tincourt, [was] ... ten miles from the front line at Villers Plouich, and the farthest, the 3rd, lying round Bray sur Somme, not less than 20 miles away in a direct line.

Between 15 and 18 November the tanks began to arrive, initially by rail, and were then de-trained and moved from the railheads to their places of concealment. Unsuspected by the Germans, all the movements took place at night, the tanks crawling in bottom gear to avoid undue noise. However, during a raid on

19 November the Germans captured six men of the 36th Division, some of whom revealed that a large attack, possibly with tanks, was to be launched in the Havrincourt area on the 20th. The Germans considered this to be unlikely: there had been no preliminary bombardment, and the Hindenburg Line was thought to be impassable for tanks. Nevertheless, a state of alert was ordered in the Havrincourt sector and a division newly arrived from the Eastern Front was added to the enemy's strength.

All was now ready, and on the eve of the battle the commander of the Tank Corps, consciously or unconsciously echoing Nelson's historic signal before the Battle of Trafalgar in 1805, issued a special order to tank commanders:

> 1. Tomorrow the Tank Corps will have the chance for which it has been waiting for many months – to operate on good going in the van of the battle.
> 2. All that hard work and ingenuity can achieve has been done in the way of preparation.
> 3. It remains for unit commanders and for tank crews to complete the work by judgement and pluck in the battle itself.
> 4. In the light of past experience I leave the good name of the Corps with great confidence in their hands.
> 5. I propose leading the attack in the centre division.
>
> Hugh Elles, B.G. [Brigadier-General]
Commanding Tank Corps

At 6.20 a.m. on Tuesday 20 November a thousand guns, hitherto unheralded, opened a devastating fire on enemy defences and artillery positions, and at that moment the first wave of tanks lumbered across No Man's Land. On the centre and right of the main assault three divisions of III Corps, the 12th, 20th and 6th, surged forward behind the advancing tanks and, passing over the outpost defences and the Hindenburg Line in the paths cleared for them by the tanks, captured all their first objectives by 10 a.m. No serious resistance was offered by an enemy who was clearly stunned by the ferocity and weight of the bombardment and the ease with which the formidable armada of tanks had penetrated their defences:

> The immediate onset of the tanks was overwhelming. The German outposts, dazed or annihilated by the sudden deluge of shells, were overrun in an instant. The triple belts of wire were crossed as if they had been beds of nettles, and 350 pathways were sheared through them for the infantry. The defenders of the front trench, scrambling out of dug-outs and shelters to meet the crash and flame of the barrage, saw the leading tanks almost upon them, their appearance made the more grotesque and terrifying by the huge black bundles they carried on their cabs... It is small wonder that the front Hindenburg Line, that fabulous excavation which was to be the bulwark of Germany, gave little trouble. The great fascines were loosed and rolled over the parapet to the trench floor; and down the whole line tanks were dipping

and rearing up and clawing their way across into the almost unravaged country beyond. The defenders of the line were running panic-stricken, casting away arms and equipment.[2]

Each division had employed two of its three brigades in the initial assault and it was now the turn of the reserve brigades to push on to the second objective. This was reached by 11.30 a.m., but, in some cases, only after subduing sporadic but stubborn resistance. Having now breached the Hindenburg support line, capturing Lateau Wood and Couillet Wood and the village of Ribécourt in the process, the way was now open to advance on the third and final objective – the Masnières–Beaurevoir line to the north-east of the villages of Masnières and Marcoing and the last enemy defence system. Once gained, Cambrai would be less than 4,000 yards distant and, with the success already achieved, seemingly within reach.

Pressing on, the 59th Brigade (20th Division) cleared the village of Les Rues Vertes, the enemy withdrawing over the canal to Masnières, leaving the main bridge intact; but, such was the resistance offered, the brigade was unable to force a passage over the canal. After having been delayed on Welsh Ridge by fire from a battery of field guns which they eventually captured, all three brigades of the reserve division (the 29th) of III Corps arrived at the near bank of the canal. Two companies of the 88th Brigade succeeded in crossing the canal, but, meeting heavy and sustained machine-gun fire, they could make no further progress. Shortly before 1 p.m. a tank tried to cross the canal by the main bridge (already partly destroyed), but it collapsed under its weight and the tank became wedged and had to be abandoned. It seemed as though the situation at Masnières was reaching deadlock, but south-east of the town a battalion found its way across the canal by means of a lock gate; it was followed by a squadron of Canadian cavalry (Fort Garry Horse) prepared to ride on to Rumilly. In mid afternoon the 2nd Cavalry Division arrived at Les Rues Vertes, but, according to the Official History,

> The brigade-major of the 88th Brigade, himself a cavalryman, expressed the opinion that it was not practicable for any considerable force of cavalry to pass over the marshy approach or to cross the canal at the lock used by the Canadian squadron; and Major-General Greenly [the division's commander] felt constrained to agree. No officer present seemed to know of the bridge, some 1,600 yards south-east of the main bridge ... This was a wooden structure, hidden from fire and view and quite suitable for cavalry, but no reconnaissance had discovered it ...

The decision was made to recall the squadron of Fort Garry Horse and an opportunity was lost, but on a late November afternoon, with sunset little more than an hour away,

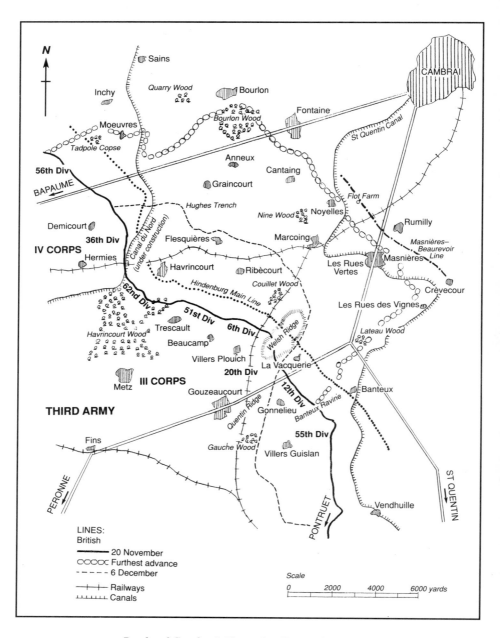

Battle of Cambrai, November/December 1917

Major-General Greenly explained that he made these decisions on the grounds that there was not sufficient daylight left for the cavalry to co-operate, and that, as the infantry had not reached the Masnières–Beaurevoir line, the necessary preliminary to any large-scale cavalry action was lacking.

Further north, fourteen tanks of the 6th Division had arrived by 11.30 a.m. in Marcoing (on the west bank of the canal) followed by units of the 71st Brigade who began house-to-house clearance in the village. Bypassing Marcoing, a further fourteen tanks advanced on Nine Wood (overlooking Noyelles), arriving shortly before noon. Meanwhile the 87th Brigade of the 29th Division had arrived in Marcoing and crossed the canal by means of the railway bridge and a lock. But in attempting to push on they came under enfilade fire from the direction of Rumilly and were brought to a standstill awaiting reinforcements. Two tanks also crossed the canal and moved on to Flot Farm, the brigade's final objective. At 2 p.m. forward units of the 5th Cavalry Division arrived in Marcoing but after crossing the canal came under machine-gun fire and were forced to dismount. Infantry reinforcements arrived at 2.30 p.m. to assist in subduing enemy resistance, holding up the advance towards Rumilly, but, although this was successful, a further delay occurred on the approach to the Masnières–Beaurevoir line. This proved to be too strong an obstacle, and with the onset of dusk any further advance was not possible.

At 3.30 p.m. further units from the 1st Cavalry Division had arrived at Marcoing with the objective of capturing Noyelles, Cantaing and Fontaine and then riding on to Bourlon. Noyelles was entered by the cavalry, the infantry taking possession of the village at 4 p.m., and two squadrons of cavalry rode on to Cantaing but met wire and machine-gun fire and were forced to withdraw.

The attack of III Corps had been a spectacular success, only its third objective eluding it, but all had not been well with the attack by the neighbouring IV Corps. Its third objective had been a line from near Nine Wood passing through Graincourt and crossing the Bapaume–Cambrai road to east of the Canal du Nord, near the village of Moeuvres, whence it would move on Bourlon in collaboration with the cavalry. The preliminary assault was to be delivered by the 51st and 62nd Divisions. The attack of the two brigades of the former division went reasonably smoothly, and with comparatively few casualties they reached their first objective, but in their advance to the second objective they immediately ran into problems. The way ahead lay uphill to the Flesquières ridge, but the infantry of the 152nd Brigade, at the divisional commander's insistence, were too far behind the tanks and following in extended order rather than in file.

The impact of these changes to the tactics recommended by Fuller was that shortly after 9.30 a.m. twenty-six tanks breasted the crest of the ridge and immediately came under fire from artillery concealed on the reverse slope. All were put out of action. Thus the infantry, strung out in extended order rather than following in file along the paths made by tanks, were unable to come to grips with the artillery and, meeting uncut wire, were forced to dig in below the crest of the ridge. The neighbouring brigade, the 153rd, succeeded in crossing the Hindenburg support system, but its leading tanks were similarly put out of action by artillery fire and this brigade also was forced to dig in below the crest. It was particularly unfortunate that the tanks were confronted by enemy batteries specially trained in anti-tank operations. Although the batteries had been attacked by aircraft at 7 a.m., the mist and smoke of battle, aggravated by rain, had prevented further attacks. Moreover, the bombardment of the area by heavy artillery which had ceased at 9.15 a.m. had for some reason been inadequate and the barrage had moved on beyond the village ten minutes later.

The destruction of the tanks gave rise to an unprecedented tribute in Haig's Dispatch to a German artillery officer who, alone, 'had served a field gun single-handed until killed at his gun . . .' Thus grew a legend, since discounted on the grounds that the losses suffered 'could never have been inflicted by one gun or even by one battery'. By late afternoon, however, the guns had been silenced and six tanks entered Flesquières, but even then the capture of the village was not to be achieved. As the tanks moved on, the infantry, following too far behind, immediately came under fire from the enemy still positioned in the village and were forced to withdraw. Nevertheless, the position of the defenders was precarious: the tide of the advance earlier in the day had flowed past the village, leaving it in danger of being enveloped.

The 62nd Division, on the immediate left of the 51st Division, had better fortune, although, as will be seen later, the check to the 51st was to have a serious impact not only on its further progress but ultimately on the offensive as a whole. Both brigades, the 185th and the 187th, had reached their first objective before 9 a.m. but only after quelling stubborn resistance around Havrincourt. Moving forward again against weakening resistance, they achieved their second objective by 10.30 a.m. The reserve brigade, the 186th, passing through the other brigades, then had the objective of capturing the section of the line from Graincourt north-westwards to the Bapaume–Cambrai road and beyond to east of Moeuvres. (This was to be in conjunction with the attack of the 36th Division on their left.) Accompanied by tanks and several squadrons of cavalry, the brigade crossed the Hindenburg support line and reached the outskirts of Graincourt, but six tanks leading the assault were all knocked out by artillery fire. Fortunately the arrival of three further tanks from a different direction silenced the guns and the infantry took possession of the village. However, because of the failure of the 51st Division to take Flesquières, the commander of the 62nd Division realized that any further advance would leave his right flank exposed, and he suggested to the 51st Division that the capture of Graincourt would enable him to attack Flesquières from the rear. For reasons which remain unclear no action was taken, and, accordingly, the commander of the 186th Brigade was instructed not to move beyond Graincourt. Before this order was received, however, he had already decided to push on towards Anneux and the Bapaume–Cambrai road, but the cavalry, meeting machine-gun fire from Anneux, were brought to a halt although the infantry captured some factory buildings on the Cambrai road. Meanwhile

> ... a patrol of three tanks, under Lieutenant Baker, was sent towards Bourlon Wood to see what conditions there were like. [He] returned after an hour or so with the information that the Germans were in full retreat towards Cambrai and Bourlon Wood and Ridge were free to be occupied.[3]

The driver of a tank named *Early Bird* had a somewhat similar story to tell:

> My own [tank] had led the advance through Havrincourt and then hours later on through Graincourt, where I cast longing eyes at the deserted estaminets and food shops as we rolled through. When dusk began to fall at 4.20 p.m. we had skirted the important village of Anneux and were well out on the Bapaume–Cambrai national road. The 'wanderlust' had taken possession of us, and I really believe we would have gone on all through the night had it not been for our dwindling petrol supply. As it was, we continued along this fine poplar-lined roadway until it got really dark at 5 p.m., and on consulting our map found we had reached a point just north-west [*sic* – he meant south-west] of Bourlon Wood . . .[4]

This was another opportunity lost that was to have far-reaching results in the coming days.

The two remaining divisions of IV Corps, the 36th (Ulster) and the 56th (1st London), had only a subsidiary role in that they were to follow up the main assault. The 36th, using a single brigade, stormed the Hindenburg front trenches and by 3.30 p.m. was beyond the Bapaume–Cambrai road, level with the 62nd Division. The 56th Division had merely to establish contact.

By nightfall the first results could be assessed. It had indeed been a remarkable day. Since the advent of trench warfare an advance on the Western Front of between three and four miles on a frontage of over six miles was quite unprecedented. The immensely strong Hindenburg Line had been crossed with comparative ease and with relatively few casualties. Hitherto such a penetration would have required a preliminary bombardment of at least a week, thus alerting the enemy to an impending attack and giving him time to prepare. The chalk subsoil allowed the construction of deep dug-outs and there would have been no guarantee that they could be adequately destroyed, or that sufficient paths could be cut through the barrier of wire entanglements. Casualties would undoubtedly have been heavy. As it was, the artillery bombardment had fallen at zero hour and, in effect, the tanks had acted as a mobile preliminary bombardment and secured that most valuable of battlefield aids, surprise. According to the Official History, British casualties were not much over 4,000; a similar number of prisoners had been taken and several hundred guns of all varieties had been captured or destroyed. Such was the euphoria when the news reached England that church bells were rung in London in celebration. And yet, despite the undoubted success, the achievement was one of hope deferred, bearing an ominous resemblance to the result achieved on the first day at Arras in April. The combination of the difficulties in crossing the St Quentin Canal and beyond to the Masnières–Beaurevoir line had brought the advance on the right flank to a stand, and, in consequence, no gap had been provided for the cavalry. On the left flank the advance on Bourlon ridge upon which Haig had placed such importance had been seriously delayed by the check at Flesquières.

Nevertheless, the impact on the enemy had been severe: two divisions had been as good as destroyed and, according to the Official History, 'eastwards from Masnières to Crèvecour the Masnières–Beaurevoir line was, for several hours, absolutely undefended, presenting a gap of a mile'. The assault had come as an unpleasant surprise to Ludendorff, who had expected attacks elsewhere, particularly in Flanders. But the enemy reserves were gathering. A division newly arrived from the Eastern Front for the purpose of relieving another division was an unexpected bonus. Reinforcements were ordered from the Lens and Loos sectors and three divisions began to entrain from other sectors on the Western Front.

During the evening of the 20th orders were issued by the Third Army for the resumption of operations on the 21st. The advance was to continue. The Masnières–Beaurevoir line was to be gained, Bourlon was to be captured (after a dawn attack to resolve the deadlock at Flesquières) and the Cavalry Corps was to cross the St Quentin Canal in conformity with the original plan.

The joint attempt by the 20th and 29th Divisions of III Corps to capture the Masnières–Beaurevoir line and secure the crossings of the St Quentin Canal for the cavalry at Crèvecour ended in failure. From the outset the attack was beset with problems. The 88th Brigade of the 29th Division had made some progress clearing houses in Masnières in the darkness of early morning but met strong resistance in trying to push on to the Masnières–Beaurevoir line, with the result that it was unable to take part in the main assault timed for 11 a.m. Meanwhile the 59th Brigade of the 20th Division on the right launched a preliminary attack at 6.30 a.m. but was stopped by machine-gun fire on the near canal bank north of Les Rues des Vignes. Time was wasted waiting for tanks to take part, and, unaware of the check to the 88th Brigade, the infantry, after a delay of over two hours, attempted to push on without their assistance but were unable to make much progress in the face of fire from the Masnières–Beaurevoir line. A section of four tanks arrived shortly after 3 p.m. (orders to move had not been received at their rallying place until zero hour), but, because of doubts about the strength of the canal bridges, the tanks did not cross and with approaching darkness the attack was called off. Further north, positioned on the bend of the canal east of Marcoing, the 87th Brigade (29th Division) awaited the arrival of tanks. After an hour's delay, the latter crossed the canal by the railway bridge. A relatively strong force of eighteen tanks was involved, but they

> . . . worked laterally along the German trenches and wire instead of leading the infantry in a frontal assault, a change of tactics which in some cases prevented the infantry following close enough to benefit from the first onset.[5]

The tanks met intense fire from machine guns and three were knocked out by field guns. A disturbing feature emerged in that the armour of the Mark IV tank appeared to be vulnerable to armour-piercing bullets. The Official History noted that

> In most cases three or four holes were made; but one tank reported 37 through its 8mm armour and in another the 12mm plate of the sponsons was pierced. Reports said 'The present armour plate is either bad material, or the enemy is using a better A-P bullet.'[6]

The infantry were unable to push forward against such strong opposition and by 3.30 p.m. the attack came to an end. North of Marcoing the Germans mounted a determined counter-attack on Noyelles but were driven out after a fierce street-by-street struggle.

The attack of IV Corps, which initially showed some promise, ended in disappointment. The 51st Division found that Flesquières had been abandoned overnight and the village was occupied at 6 a.m. The division's objective was the village of Fontaine, on the Bapaume–Cambrai road and about three miles from Cambrai, but once again there was a delay in sending orders to the tanks and at 10.30 a.m. the 154th Brigade went ahead without them; coming up against heavy fire from the Cantaing trench system, however, it was soon brought to a halt. Meanwhile the 1st Cavalry Division had moved from Trescault with the intention of bypassing Cantaing and Fontaine to the east and riding on northwards, but the check to the 154th Brigade at Cantaing prohibited any forward cavalry movement. Shortly after midday thirteen tanks appeared south-east of Cantaing and, accompanied by cavalry patrols, entered the village, followed by a company of infantry from the 6th Division. A battalion of the 154th Brigade arrived soon afterwards from the west and the village was occupied by 1.30 p.m. Although the divisional commander had ordered that no further advance should take place until the 62nd Division on the left had captured

Bourlon, the infantry, unaware of this order, seized Fontaine with the assistance of four tanks – a somewhat fortuitous capture that in the days to come would change to a desperate defence followed by loss and ultimately a particularly bloody attempt at recapture.

Bourlon village had been the principal objective of the 62nd Division. The attack was held up for twenty minutes awaiting tanks (their orders had yet again been delayed), but Anneux was captured with their assistance, the enemy putting up a fierce resistance. Heavy and sustained fire from machine guns in Bourlon Wood, however, eventually brought the advance to a standstill, and although a number of tanks managed to enter the wood the infantry were unable to follow them.

It had been an unsatisfactory day for the Third Army. The failure of the attack by III Corps effectively brought to an end the plan to pass cavalry across the St Quentin Canal. With only one bridge suitable for tanks, the canal had proved to be an insurmountable obstacle and this factor, combined with stubborn resistance from the enemy in the Masnières–Beaurevoir line, had been the principal cause of failure. Problems with communications had led to the delays in assembling tanks and these, in turn, had considerably delayed the assault, thus giving the enemy some breathing space. Even if the tanks had been up to time, it is questionable whether the initiative so spectacularly gained the previous day could have been maintained. The infantry and the tank crews were desperately tired and the advantage of surprise had been lost. Haig had originally imposed a limitation of 48 hours on the attack because it was anticipated that at its expiry German reinforcements would be arriving. (This was a correct assumption: two divisions had already arrived and a further two were beginning to assemble in the Cambrai area.) Dawn on the 22nd would see the end of the 48-hour restriction and Haig had then to decide whether to continue. In his judgement there was more support for continuation than for closing down. GHQ had believed, 'on somewhat slender evidence',[7] that the enemy was showing a tendency to retire and that reinforcements would merely replace casualties; moreover, Robertson had informed him that he could retain two divisions earmarked for Italy and the three divisions of V Corps had still to be used. The alternative was retirement, because any consolidation of the position reached would be threatened by enemy artillery on Bourlon ridge. However, with Haig's tenacity of purpose, so amply demonstrated in previous battles, it is not surprising that he decided on continuation. Accordingly, III Corps should hold a defensive line overlooking the canal crossings with the bridges prepared for demolition, and, despite IV Corps' disappointing progress on the 21st, he intended to concentrate on what he had always considered to be the main priority – the capture of the Bourlon ridge.

The orders issued by IV Corps for operations on the 22nd were for consolidation rather than a renewal of the offensive, particularly as no tanks would be available, having been withdrawn for maintenance. The plan for the 51st Division to establish a defensive flank from Cantaing to Fontaine came to nothing because at 10 a.m. the enemy delivered a counter-attack on Fontaine. Because of the divisional commander's orders the previous day to limit the advance to Cantaing, the village was only thinly held, and after a desperate defence the survivors, with ammunition running low, were forced to retreat. The 62nd Division was counter-attacked and lost some ground, although this was mostly regained. The only success was on the extreme left, where the 56th Division captured Tadpole Copse. The neighbouring division, the 36th, advancing astride the Canal du Nord, achieved a foothold in Moeuvres but was ultimately forced back to its starting line.

Haig saw Byng in the late afternoon and stressed the importance of gaining the Bourlon ridge. He had heard from Robertson that

> . . . although exploitation of your splendid success is sound and desirable and is entirely approved by the War Cabinet, it is equally necessary when you are deciding the extent to which the endeavour to exploit should be continued that due regard be had to probable Italian demands and to a very unsatisfactory man-power position.[8]

Haig's hopes were now placed on operations planned for the next day, the 23rd, when a major effort would be made to capture Bourlon ridge. The main emphasis was on the operations of the 51st and 40th Divisions (the latter having relieved the 62nd Division). The 51st Division was to recapture Fontaine and push onwards round to the north of Bourlon Wood; possession of Fontaine would enable the 1st Cavalry Division to threaten Bourlon village from the north-east. The 40th Division was to take the wood and attack the village from the south-west. Ninety-two tanks would be available, 48 to the 51st Division and 32 to the 40th Division; the remaining twelve were to assist the 36th Division in its advance northwards astride the Canal du Nord.

Thus Bourlon Wood was about to add its name to the litany of woods on the Western Front in which so much blood had been shed since 1916. Rising steeply some 130 feet above the Bapaume–Cambrai road, this thickly wooded 600 acres forms the crown of the ridge; the village lies on the lower slopes north of the wood. Strongly defended, it was a daunting obstacle, but, once gained, it would not only dominate the approaches to Cambrai, it would also threaten enemy communications in the Arras sector.

In cold and windy weather the battle opened. The 152nd Brigade of the 51st Division advanced on Fontaine at 10.30 a.m. in the wake of a barrage lifting every ten minutes. Tanks entering the village from the south came under a hail of fire from machine guns and anti-tank guns and the infantry, following normal divisional practice, were too far behind and could not penetrate beyond the outskirts of the village. However, twelve tanks and infantry bypassed the village and, pressing on, reached the north-eastern edge of the wood. Meanwhile the tanks were hotly engaged in Fontaine, but, even with the arrival in the afternoon of additional tanks, the defence, now considerably strengthened, held.

Attacking at 10.30 a.m. with two brigades behind a creeping barrage, the 40th Division had better fortune. After a stiff fight subduing machine-gun posts, the 119th Brigade reached the Bourlon–Fontaine road running diagonally through the centre of the wood shortly before noon. An hour later, together with thirteen tanks they reached the northern edge of the wood, where they soon came under a heavy artillery bombardment that forced a short withdrawal. The enemy mounted a strong counter-attack in the afternoon, which was repulsed, and by the evening the brigade had been reinforced by two companies from the 120th Brigade. The 121st Brigade attacked the southern edge of the village, meeting heavy artillery and machine-gun fire, but, although several tanks and some parties of infantry entered the village, they were unable to dislodge the defenders. The objective of the 36th Division was Quarry Wood, mid way between Moeuvres and Bourlon. Its capture would materially have aided the 121st Brigade in its assault on the latter village but, although most of Moeuvres was occupied by late afternoon, the position could not be held.

By the afternoon Byng knew that Bourlon Wood had been captured and believed that there was still an opportunity for cavalry to push northwards. Haig, however, wanted to make sure of Bourlon ridge and he told Byng that, if necessary, cavalry should be dismounted 'in any numbers' if there was a possibility that the gains would be lost.

Overnight the Guards Division had arrived from V Corps with orders to relieve the 51st Division, and the operations for the following day, the 24th, centred on capturing Bourlon village. The attack on the village was to be delivered by the 40th Division, assisted by twelve tanks and two battalions of dismounted cavalry. The 119th Brigade in the wood had been reinforced overnight, but it was about to be put to a severe test. The enemy delivered two counter- attacks between 8.45 a.m. and 11 a.m., resulting in bitter fighting of a see-saw nature. The brigade put up a spirited defence, but the enemy managed to gain a foothold on the right flank and at 3 p.m. a strong attack from the north-east drove the defenders back to the middle of the wood. Even then,

> Outnumbered and very weary, in dire need of reinforcement and relief, the British maintained the struggle and prepared for a fresh effort. About 4 p.m. a confused but well-knit line of Welch, Welsh Fusiliers, Borderers, Highlanders and Hussars, with the battalion staff of the Fusiliers distributed where needed as section leaders,

and with the commanding officer, Lieut.-Colonel J. Plunkett in the centre, pressed forward and drove the Germans back down the northern slopes of the wood, there to be caught by the British barrage.[9]

Because the allotment of twelve tanks was not considered adequate, the decision was made to postpone the attack on the village until the next day. Difficulties in communication resulted in the 121st Brigade not receiving notice of the postponement until too late, and at 3 p.m. the attack went ahead. The tanks entered the village but the infantry were too far behind to take any advantage; the exception was a battalion of Highland Light Infantry which passed through the village to the railway a few hundred yards beyond. Because of the postponement of the attack, no further support was forthcoming and the three leading companies of the battalion were cut off. This led to the mistaken belief at divisional headquarters that the village had been captured, and the news was passed to IV Corps and Third Army in the late evening. Soon afterwards, however, a further message was received from the division to the effect that German prisoners had revealed that a counter-attack would take place the next day. The division proposed sending a further battalion to support the troops in the village and twelve tanks were needed. Although the tanks were promised, IV Corps was presumably unaware that no tanks would be available, they having once again been withdrawn for refitting and maintenance. The attempt to clear Bourlon village on the following day (the 25th) ended in failure. The three companies of Highland Light Infantry could not be reached and they ultimately had to surrender.

The situation was becoming critical. The troops in Bourlon Wood were being subjected to continuous shelling and counter-attacks, and the only reserves now available to the 40th Division were three dismounted cavalry battalions. Haig telegraphed to Robertson:

My orders to Byng are to complete capture of Bourlon position and such tactical points on its flanks as are necessary to secure it. The positions gained are to be held and troops to be ready to exploit any local advantage and follow up any retirement of the enemy. Nothing beyond above to be attempted. For purposes stated second and forty-seventh divisions and cavalry remain at his disposal for the present. Bourlon hill is a feature of great importance because it overlooks Cambrai and the approaches to the town as well as the country northwards to the Sensée marshes.[10]

Shortly before midnight on the 25th, IV Corps was instructed to capture the Fontaine and Bourlon villages not later than the 27th and consolidate a line extending in an arc from Cantaing to west of Bourlon.

On the 26th British heavy artillery opened a bombardment on the key points of Fontaine, Quarry Wood, Moeuvres, Inchy and Sains; Bourlon was excluded, in case any British troops were still in the village. A conference was held in the morning at Havrincourt involving the commanders of IV Corps, the Guards Division and the 62nd Division (relieving the 40th Division). However, Major-General G. Feilding, commanding the Guards Division, was not happy with the plan for the capture of Fontaine. He thought that it was too strong and that the advance of his six battalions would be enfiladed from the high ground at Rumilly and from Bourlon ridge. He recommended an attack on Rumilly as a vital preliminary to securing the ridge, and 'if resources were not sufficient for this it would be the best policy to withdraw from the low ground and establish a main line of defence on the Flesquières ridge.' Feilding's objections were brushed aside after Byng arrived at the conference: the attack should take place as planned, and this was confirmed by Haig, who by then had also joined the conference. (As will be seen later, there was an element of prophecy in General Feilding's objections.) Thus the Guards Division with twelve tanks was to capture Fontaine and the north-eastern part of Bourlon Wood, and the 62nd Division was to secure the northern edge of the wood and the village.

At 6.20 a.m. in the darkness before dawn on the 27th the attack began and General Feilding's worries about the strength of the defence in Fontaine village were soon to be realized. A battalion of Grenadier Guards of the 2nd Guards Brigade preceded by tanks fought its way into the village, suffering heavy casualties from artillery and machine-gun fire. The value of tanks in assaulting strongly wired, entrenched positions in open country had been well demon-strated, but in the close confines of a village street their vision was severely hampered, and, with the enemy putting up a fierce defence from houses and cellars, the vehicles were not only ill-equipped but ill-prepared:

> There was horrible slaughter in Fontaine, and I, who had spent three weeks before the battle in thinking out its probabilities, had never tackled the subject of village fighting. I could have kicked myself again and again for this lack of foresight, but it never occurred to me that our infantry commanders would thrust tanks into such places.[11]

The Coldstream Guards battalion on the left of the Grenadiers met strong resistance on the northern outskirts of the village but eventually reached the railway station beyond. A battalion of Irish Guards on the left of the Coldstream surged through to its objective of the north-eastern part of Bourlon Wood and established contact with the Coldstream. However, reinforcements were desper-ately needed. Grenadiers from the 3rd Guards Brigade were moved up in support, but the defenders in the village mounted a powerful counter-attack and the Guards were forced to make a fighting withdrawal back to their starting line.

The two brigades of the 62nd Division had no better success. The 186th Brigade had the task of clearing the northern part of Bourlon Wood and pressing on to the eastern edge of the village and the railway. Assisted by four tanks, it gained the main street of the village but could make no progress towards the railway because of heavy fire from the enemy entrenched beside the railway line. As earlier referred to, the heavy artillery bombardment of the previous day had not included Bourlon village and, on the left, the 187th Brigade, preceded by fifteen tanks, entered the village, only to be confronted by a formidable array of defences. The tanks and infantry were immediately assailed on all sides by machine-gun and artillery fire, to such an extent that ultimately only five tanks returned. Although the fighting in the village continued for two hours, it was a hopeless situation and there was no alternative but to withdraw.

The failure of the attempts to capture Fontaine and Bourlon villages signalled the end of the offensive and the decision was made to consolidate the positions reached and prepare the Flesquières ridge for defence:

> None could view with satisfaction the events of the past seven days: so many attacks had failed, so many casualties had been suffered and so much hardship endured by the troops, in attempting to force a definite issue and to break a resistance of which the strength appeared to have been consistently under-estimated. And as a result, although the highest part of the ridge, the wooded hill, had been won, the enemy still looked down from the shoulders of the ridge upon the British battery positions in the Cantaing–Anneux–Graincourt plain.[12]

The Germans had had an anxious day on the 27th and were disappointed that the British still held Bourlon Wood. Nevertheless, with reinforcements arriving, their thoughts had already turned to the possibility of a counter-offensive: Crown Prince Rupprecht, commander of the Northern Group of Armies, told Ludendorff on the 27th that 'there [had] never been such an opportunity'.

The conclusion of the offensive had produced a salient some nine miles wide and four miles deep. The weakest area was on the north side, where the shoulders of Bourlon ridge remained in enemy hands. Apart from a short section where the front crossed the St Quentin Canal between Masnières and Marcoing, the eastern and southern side lay to the west of the canal, which, as most of the bridges had been destroyed, was thought to make the position of III and VII Corps relatively secure.

During the main offensive the role of VII Corps had been limited to carrying out subsidiary operations consisting of artillery bombardments and attacks of a purely local nature. As the battle continued further north, the corps commander, Lieutenant-General Sir Thomas Snow, became aware of increasing enemy activity on his front, which convinced him that an attack was in preparation. The frontage of his corps of some ten miles extended from Pontruet (the junction with the French) northwards to the Banteux ravine, where it joined III Corps. A junction between any military formation tends to be a weak link in attack or defence, and he became increasingly worried about the defence of the ravine. His concern over enemy preparations led him to warn the commanders of the 55th and 24th Divisions (the former division was responsible for the defence of the Banteux ravine) that an enemy attack could be expected on the 29th or 30th 'with its centre of gravity on the Banteux ravine'.

According to the Official History, 'This accurate forecast made little impression upon Army or III Corps headquarters.' On the 28th General Snow again warned Third Army headquarters of the likelihood of an enemy attack, but 'The Third Army issued no warning order, ordered no movement of reserves, took no steps to ensure that troops in the rear areas should be readily available.' Almost half the tanks employed in the offensive had been destroyed and the survivors were in the process of being withdrawn for the winter for essential repairs and maintenance. The Guards and 62nd Divisions had been relieved, although still in the area, and three fresh divisions had arrived. Indeed, there was a curious sense of relaxation abroad. Based on GHQ Intelligence, it was believed that the Germans had suffered such losses in Flanders and at Cambrai that they would be unable to launch a powerful counter-offensive and that if any attack were mounted it would be in the north against Bourlon Wood.

However, General Snow's forebodings were about to be realized. The German preparations for the counter-offensive had been completed by the 27th, on which date Rupprecht issued his orders for the attack fixed for the 30th. The principal thrust would be an attack from the south in the direction of Metz with the object of recapturing Flesquières and Havrincourt. Following this there would be an attack from Bourlon in a southerly direction. Thus, if both attacks succeeded, the salient would be bitten off at its base. A short preliminary bombardment was planned, using gas shell and smoke over a maximum of one hour, and then the assaulting infantry would outflank strongpoints and deal with them later when sufficiently enveloped – like an incoming tide sweeping round children's sand-castles, only to overwhelm them as the tide rises. (Less than four months later this tactic would be used again, but to infinitely greater effect.)

On the 28th the Germans opened a preliminary bombardment, drenching Bourlon Wood with gas shells, but the 29th was quiet, with no indication of the storm that was to come. Owing to a misunderstanding never satisfactorily explained, a request to III Corps for a heavy artillery bombardment of German positions south of Banteux at 6.30 a.m. on the 30th did not take place. Moreover, at 2 a.m. on the 30th the 29th Division had requested III Corps to put down a concentration of heavy artillery fire on Crèvecoeur and the nearby canal crossings at 6.30 a.m., but again no action was forthcoming.

At 6 a.m. in the darkness of the morning of the 30th the enemy's artillery opened what appeared to be a desultory bombardment on the position held by the 55th Division, but this gradually increased in intensity until it covered the whole of VII Corps' front. The guns of VII Corps, too few in number, replied, but they had little effect in stemming the German advance. The main blow was delivered between Vendhuille and Banteux and fell on the 166th Brigade of the 55th Division holding the extreme left of the VII Corps front. The enemy infantry, advancing under cover of swarms of low-flying aircraft and armed with light machine guns and flame-throwers, swept aside the brigade's resistance and entered the village of Villers Guislan behind the old British front line. The artillery in the village, after firing over open sights on the advancing infantry, was forced to retreat, leaving behind nearly sixty guns and howitzers (with their dial sights and breech-blocks removed). A hasty defence was improvised by the 55th Division, and for the time being the enemy was prevented from making further progress. The only troops adjacent to the area were the 4th and 5th Cavalry Divisions, who were ordered to Villers Faucon with the task of counter-attacking the German flank between Villers Guislan and Gouzeaucourt. During the afternoon further reinforcements – two more cavalry divisions and the 21st Division (from the First Army) – were allocated to VII Corps.

Further north, the 12th Division, on the right of III Corps, was positioned astride the Peronne–Cambrai road with its right brigade (the 35th) situated immediately north of the Banteux ravine. This brigade was bypassed in the German advance and, learning at the last moment of the capture of Villers Guislan, had no alternative but to retire. Meanwhile Gouzeaucourt and Gonnelieu had also been captured, and it became evident that if the advance continued in the direction of Metz, a village immediately south of Havrincourt Wood, the Germans would have reached the mid point in the base of the salient. The war correspondent Philip Gibbs was on his way to Gouzeaucourt when he learned from a gunner officer that his battery had been captured and that the enemy were already in the village:

> I went northward and saw that places like Hermies and Havrincourt, which had been peaceful spots for a few days, were under heavy fire. Bourlon Wood beyond was a fiery furnace. Hell had broken out again, and things looked bad. There was a general packing up of dumps and field hospitals and heavy batteries. In Gouzeaucourt and other places our Divisional and Brigade Headquarters were caught napping. Officers were in their pyjamas or in their baths, when they heard the snap of machine-gun bullets. I saw the Guards go forward to Gouzeaucourt for a counter-attack. They came along munching apples and whistling, as though on peace manoeuvres.[13]

Fortunately not all the tanks had left the area – the II Tank Brigade was still at Fins. Thirty-six tanks were quickly made ready and moved off before 1 p.m. in the direction of Gouzeaucourt. The Guards Division had been in reserve near Havrincourt Wood and the commander of the 1st Guards Brigade, learning of the fall of Gouzeaucourt, decided to attack the village. Three battalions and some dismounted cavalry stormed it, driving the enemy out and, in the process, retrieving guns and ammunition that had earlier been abandoned.

As has been seen, the full force of the enemy counter-offensive had fallen on VII Corps, but III Corps was not to escape unscathed. Its division on the far right (the 12th) had suffered heavy losses in men and guns as a result of the bombardment and was driven back to the area around La Vacquerie. The 20th Division in the centre was in an even worse plight. Both brigades were taken completely by surprise and overwhelmed before they could take any defensive action. Only one battalion put up any resistance, but this was ultimately to be of little avail. The two brigades of the 29th Division were across the St Quentin Canal between Masnières and Marcoing. The collapse of the 20th Division had allowed the Germans to pass through south of Les Rues Vertes on their way to Marcoing, and in consequence there was a grave danger that the two brigades across the canal would be cut off. Although the enemy had not initially entered Les Rues Vertes in great strength, its occupation would render the position of the 86th Brigade in Masnières untenable, but by the gallant and determined actions of small parties of men the village was cleared of the enemy and organized for defence. Meanwhile the Germans continued their advance on Marcoing but were then resolutely counter-attacked by the 88th Brigade, who forced a retreat.

The Germans had no benefit of surprise in their operations against IV and VI Corps on the north of the salient: their advance was soon observed from the ridge west of Bourlon Wood. With the exception of a battalion holding the ridge, both brigades of the 47th Division of IV Corps were positioned in the wood, this division having taken over the defence of the wood from the 62nd Division during the night of 28–29 November:

> The 62nd Division, acting under orders from the Corps, insisted on the whole of the 141st Brigade being sent into Bourlon Wood to relieve their brigade. In protest against this Major-General Gorringe [commander of the 47th Division] urged that to crowd seven battalions (four of 141st Brigade, one of 140th Brigade and two of dismounted cavalry) and forty-seven machine guns into the wood, which already contained one battalion of the 59th Division on the right, would only invite excessive casualties without increasing the value of the defence ... The protest was overridden, and on the night of November 28th–29th seven battalions were all in position in the wood. The enemy bombarded heavily with gas-shells during the night, and the 141st Brigade suffered many casualties.[14]

On the 30th, however, the defence in the wood was reduced to four battalions, but they were not seriously engaged. Nevertheless, a battalion in support in the wood was so affected by gas that its strength was reduced to a mere seventy officers and men:

The gas in Bourlon Wood hung in the trees and bushes so thickly that all ranks were compelled to wear their respirators continuously if they were to escape the effect of gas. But men cannot dig for long without removing them, and it was necessary to dig trenches to get any cover from the persistent shell-fire. Throughout November 30th there was, therefore, a steady stream of gassed and wounded men coming to the regimental aid-posts. Their clothes were full of gas, and as the medical officer could not dress wounds without removing his respirator, he, too, felt the effects. No fewer than seven medical officers went to hospital gassed as a result of this dilemma.[15]

The direction of the main German advance was southwards from Quarry Wood to the west of Bourlon Wood. The battalion on Bourlon ridge was heavily attacked and driven off the crest, and although some ground was recovered later when reinforcements arrived, the crest of the ridge was lost. The 2nd Division stood in the path of the attack, and despite strong artillery resistance, causing heavy casualties to the oncoming waves of infantry, the Germans still advanced. There were many desperate acts of defiance by pockets of British infantry, some of them fighting to the end. The 56th Division on the western flank of the Bourlon front had also to beat off a determined attack, and there was fierce fighting in the communication trenches of the old German Hindenburg support system, but the advance was stayed. By the end of the day it was apparent that the German attack from the north had failed. The German view of the attack , as expressed by Rupprecht, was that although 'success [was] not as great as we hoped, it [had] nevertheless given the British a blow.' It was intended to resume the offensive the following day, with the objective of the Beaucamp–Trescault heights.

Haig had met Byng before noon on 30 November and told him that reinforcements were on the way – three divisions plus heavy and field artillery brigades. The first of these reinforcements (two divisions) would arrive the following day, but Byng decided to launch a counter-attack in the early hours of the morning of 1 December in the hope of pre-empting the expected resumption of the German counter-offensive. VII and III Corps were to attempt to regain the old British front line south of the Peronne–Cambrai road; the Cavalry Corps was to co-operate with III Corps in attacking Gauche Wood and Villers Guislan with the aid of tanks. Zero hour was fixed for 6.30 a.m. In the event, the attacks by cavalry proved abortive owing to the inability to prepare tanks in time and inadequate artillery support, and both dismounted and mounted cavalry advances were soon frustrated by machine-gun fire. However, dismounted Canadian cavalry units reached Gauche Wood, to find that it had already been captured earlier by the 1st Guards Brigade. The 3rd Guards Brigade was to be assisted by twenty tanks in its attack on Quentin ridge and the village of Gonnelieu. The tanks lost direction in the darkness and the Guards attacked the ridge without them. They immediately met fierce machine-gun fire and suffered grievous losses until a lone tank arrived to flush out the enemy machine-gunners. The 4th Guards Brigade also had Gonnelieu as an objective, but the village was already filled with enemy troops massing for an attack, and although the brigade managed to enter the village it was ultimately forced to withdraw. Nevertheless, when the brigade re-formed it was able to prevent the enemy advancing from Gonnelieu.

Meanwhile time was running out for the 29th Division across the St Quentin Canal. The Germans put down a heavy bombardment on Masnières, followed by an attack along the near side of the canal against Les Rues Vertes. This was repulsed, but it was becoming evident that the position could not be maintained much longer. On the following day, 2 December, the bridges across the canal were prepared for demolition. The 86th Brigade had been withdrawn, thus abandoning Masnières, and the British front had shrunk to a total width of about 2,000 yards straddling the canal

The next day saw the end of the German counter-offensive: the commander of the German 2nd Army considered that the attack had 'run itself out'. Nevertheless, La Vacquerie was wrested from the British grasp, and a powerful attack on troops in the canal bend west of Marcoing eventually forced the defenders back across the canal. In the early hours of the following morning the canal bridges were blown.

The German attack on 30 November had forced Haig to face the possibility of a withdrawal from the Marcoing–Bourlon salient. It would be a painful decision to take, but no fresh reserves were available and he realized that the salient would be vulnerable in the event of further enemy attacks. By the 4th he had made up his mind and on that day he instructed Byng to commence a withdrawal to a defensive line roughly corresponding to the Hindenburg support system. This line ran from south of Marcoing through Flesquières to Hughes Trench east of the Canal du Nord, where it deviated from the Hindenburg support line and joined the old British front line at Demicourt. He telegraphed to Robertson:

> The present line could be held, but in view of the enemy's present activity it would use up troops which, in view of your instructions and the man-power situation, I do not feel justified in devoting to it. My available reserves to meet serious attack are very limited, and the troops need as much rest as possible after their strenuous exertions since April . . .[16]

By the 7th the withdrawal to the 'main line of resistance for the winter' had been successfully completed.

* * *

Liddell Hart described the end of the battle as 'A sombre sunset after a brilliant sunrise'. The sunrise had indeed been brilliant: the combination of the unregistered artillery bombardment at zero hour and a massive armada of tanks had enabled the formidable Hindenburg position to be overrun within four hours and an advance to be achieved of about four miles, but by early evening most of its impetus had been lost. This was a familiar and depressing repetition of past set-piece offensives, when, despite the careful planning and preparation made for the initial assault, the success of the breakthrough failed to be exploited. At Cambrai the role of exploitation had been given to the cavalry – its first real opportunity since 1914 – but, according to the Official History, 'not more than one brigade crossed the old British front line on the 20th November'. After reaching his objective at Marcoing and impatiently awaiting the cavalry, a Tank Corps officer described the eventual encounter:

> ... after walking for nearly an hour we met the vanguard of the Cavalry. It was at the village of Ribécourt, a place that had been in our hands since seven o'clock that morning. And what was the Cavalry doing? Why, carrying out the regular tactics for advancing by stages into an enemy's country! – troop halted in sunken road behind the village, two scouts sent forward to reconnoitre, one of them returns to report to the officer. No wonder they were late! I was furious with that young Cavalry officer ... But it was no good; it was all too late. The Cavalry squadrons were only just crossing No Man's Land and it was nearly 2 p.m., just six hours after the barbed wire entanglements had been cleared for them by special tanks detailed for that purpose. We heard afterwards that the head of the Cavalry column did not start until noon from Fins, which was four miles behind our original front line![17]

In his *History of the Great War*, the historian C. R. M. F. Crutwell wrote: 'The inaction of the two cavalry divisions has never yet been intelligibly explained.' A view advanced in the Official History was that

> A number of senior officers, however, remembered how vulnerable were bodies of horse to the fire of even a few machine guns, and, with some reason, were more fearful of wire than ever they had been on the hunting field. They therefore favoured the cautious approach and attached too much importance to the enemy's random shooting.

Apart from the spirited advance by a squadron of Canadian cavalry across the St Quentin Canal on the first day, the main use of cavalry thereafter had been in a dismounted role.

The failure to capture Flesquières, partly due to the eccentric behaviour of the 51st Division's commander in devising his own system of infantry/tank co-operation, had been a critical factor in Bourlon's not being gained on 20 November. It had been Haig's objective and was an immensely strong position, against which Fuller had not wanted to use tanks in a frontal assault, and it was particularly unfortunate that the tanks came up against enemy artillery specially trained in anti-tank defence. Although these batteries had been attacked from the air at 7 a.m., the mist and the smoke of battle, aggravated by rain, had prevented further attacks. Moreover, the bombardment by heavy artillery of the position, which had not been as effective as it might have been, had ceased at 9.15 a.m. and then, ten minutes later, moved on beyond the village. Another important factor, demonstrating the vulnerability of links between formations, was that Flesquières had been on the boundary between III and IV Corps. A division from each corps had bypassed the village, leaving its rear exposed to attack – which, in all probability, would have been successful. But there were delays in communication, particularly inter-corps, and the opportunity was lost.

With the momentum dissipated, the next day degenerated into a slogging match to capture the objectives set for the previous day. Apart from the capture of Anneux and, fortuitously, Fontaine (although the latter was lost the following day), the plan to pass cavalry across the St Quentin Canal foundered because of the failure to secure the Masnières–Beaurevoir line. Thus Bourlon village remained beyond reach and any hope of exploiting the initial success vanished. The reserves had been inadequate and the strength of German resistance underestimated, particularly at Bourlon village. Although the two enemy divisions bearing the brunt of the attack had suffered heavy losses, the arrival of a division from the Eastern Front had bolstered the faltering defence, particularly east of the St Quentin Canal, which, in the event, proved to be an insuperable barrier. Thus the way to Cambrai from the south had been blocked. From then until the closing down of the offensive on the 27th, the only success had been the capture of Bourlon Wood, when, even at this late stage, Byng had entertained hopes of the cavalry pushing northward. It was not to be. Instead, there were fruitless and costly attempts to capture Bourlon village and recapture Fontaine.

The German counter-offensive begun on 30 November had been almost wholly delivered by divisions withdrawn from other sectors of the Western Front, many of whom had served at Passchendaele. After the horrors these units had undergone in fighting the perpetual defensive battles of 1916 and 1917, it may not have occurred to the British High Command that the opportunity to return to the offensive would have provided a welcome boost to morale. Ludendorff, in his memoirs, thought that

> The success was the more remarkable because it was in the main achieved by half-tired troops . . . We regained a good deal of ground we had lost and some new ground as well. We had won a complete victory over a considerable part of the British Army. It was a good ending to the extremely heavy fighting of 1917. Our action had given us valuable hints for an offensive battle in the west if we wished to undertake one in 1918.

Ever since Neuve Chapelle the conclusion of a major offensive on the Western Front had always left the British in possession of the ground they had wrested from the enemy. There had never been a withdrawal such as had occurred at Cambrai. It is somewhat ironic that if the offensive had been stopped after forty-eight hours (the original limitation imposed by Haig) and a defensive position established on Flesquières, the result would have been acclaimed as a notable victory. Indeed, the commander of the Guards Division had suggested this on 26 November, but the capture of Bourlon was considered to be all-important. The German view, as expressed by Rupprecht, was that 'it was our biggest success over the British since 1915, at Ypres' (although the circumstances at 'Second Ypres' were not quite comparable).

After the celebratory ringing of London's church bells, the news of the reverse came as a shock to the British public and questions were raised in Parliament and the Press. The War Cabinet ordered an inquiry into the circumstances, noting the

> . . . discrepancy between the nature of the German success and the reports which had been consistently received from official sources in regard to their weakness and the deterioration of their morale.[18]

The outcome was that no fewer than four inquiries took place. Byng had to undertake two, as the first resulted in more information being demanded by the War Cabinet. He maintained that the German counter-offensive had not come as a surprise, his reserves were in a position to meet the attack and there were not sufficient grounds on which to question the competence of the commanders concerned. He attributed the reverse to the lack of training of junior officers, NCOs and men and thought that the staunchness of machine-gunners 'left much to desired.' Byng's statement that there had been no surprise clearly flew in the face of the warnings given by the commander of VII Corps, and Haig, although endorsing Byng's findings, sought to temper the criticism of the troops by emphasizing that they were tired, having had no relief since 20 November, and had been overwhelmed by sheer weight of numbers. Nevertheless, although accepting responsibility for the reverse, he thought that 'the enemy should not have succeeded in penetrating any part of our defence'.

The matter refused to die, and the War Cabinet appointed one of its own members, General Smuts, to hold an independent inquiry. He had a difficult, if not impossible, task. Conclusions other than those already reached could conceivably have resulted in a crisis of confidence in military leadership, and Smuts concluded that 'no one down to and including corps commanders was to blame'. He supported Byng in believing that 'the trouble was . . . with junior officers, N.C.Os and men' and considered that their training should be given immediate attention. On 15 January the House of Commons was informed accordingly, but further debate was effectively stifled by the statement that it was 'highly detrimental to the public interest to have a public discussion on the breakdown which undoubtedly occurred'. Finally, Haig on his own initiative set up a court of inquiry in France on 21 January. It was presided over by two corps commanders and a divisional commander (none of whom had been concerned in the offensive), who took evidence from the commanders of the divisions principally involved (the 12th, 20th and 55th) and a number of junior officers. It might be thought that Byng's Chief Staff Officer, who had received the warning from VII Corps, would have been an a vital witness, together with the commanders of VII and III Corps and their chief General Staff Officers, but all these were, in the words of the Official Historian, 'notable absentees'. Although the proceedings lasted until the 29th, the conclusions reached were not markedly different from those that had gone before, although, significantly, it was admitted that 'the Third Army's attention had been engrossed by the Bourlon front'.

To sum up on this unhappy affair, with all its ingredients of a cover-up, the facts were that the German attack on the fronts of III and VII Corps had come as a surprise and that the warnings given to Third Army had been disregarded. At this distance in time it is difficult to reconcile the emphasis placed on the need for training junior officers, NCOs and men with the fact that the German advance in the Bourlon area had been observed and successfully repulsed. Two of the three divisions involved had just come into the line, contrasting with the situation in the south where the assault had surprised tired divisions denied relief or reinforcement since 20 November. Other things being equal, it is difficult to believe that the fighting qualities of these divisions were any less than those in the north.

In his biography of Haig, John Terraine considers that 'The set-back at Cambrai represents the lowest ebb of Haig's career . . . It weakened his prestige and position at a time when he needed every support he could get.'[19] According to his diary entry for 26 December, Haig told Lord Milner that

> . . . if L.G. [Lloyd George] did not wish me to remain as C.in C. in the interests of the country and in order to obtain success in the war, it would be much better that I should go at once, rather than that L.G. should proceed with his policy of undermining the confidence which troops now feel in their leaders . . .[20]

Haig had been severely criticized by some Members when the results of the Smuts inquiry had been released to the House of Commons, but, dearly as Lloyd George would have liked to replace him, his removal would have had unpredictable political and military consequences. Instead, the axe fell on some of Haig's staff, notably Kiggell, his Chief of Staff, and Charteris, his Director of Intelligence – the last so often criticized for feeding Haig with misleading and over-optimistic forecasts of the enemy's strength and morale.

If the narrow view is taken, Cambrai, despite the brilliance of the success on the first day, was a failure because it ended in a position of stalemate. The amount of ground won by the British was about the same as that ultimately recovered by the Germans, and British casualties were some 47,000, with those of the enemy about the same. Haig had believed that Cambrai had prevented German reinforcements from being diverted to Italy, but the Caporetto offensive was already being scaled down because of the approach of winter. The five divisions that Haig had been forced to send to Italy had, in the event, served no real purpose other than to bolster Italian morale, but they would have been invaluable at Cambrai. Haig lamented their absence, and it could be argued that without them he attempted too much with too little. Nevertheless, Cambrai should be seen in the wider context. It was the last in the long series of conventional siege-warfare offensives on the Western Front. Cambrai was the watershed,

> . . . pointing and paving the way to the victorious method of 1918, and to take the still longer view, it is seen to be one of the landmarks in the history of warfare, the dawn of a new epoch. Thus we may say that the joy-bells, if immediately wrong, were ultimately right.[21]

Notes to Chapter 7

1. J. F. C. Fuller, quoted in Liddell Hart, A. H., *A History of the World War 1914–1918*, Faber & Faber (London, 1930)

2. Browne, D. G., *The Tank in Action*, Blackwood (London, 1920)

3. Quoted in Cooper, Bryan, *The Ironclads of Cambrai*, Pan Books (London, 1970)

4. Bacon, A. F. L., *Wanderings of a Temporary Warrior*, Witherby (London, 1922)

5. Miles, Captain W., (comp.), *Official History of the War: Military Operations, France and Belgium 1917*, Vol. III, HMSO (London, 1948)

6. *Ibid.*

7. *Ibid.*

8. *Ibid.*

9. *Ibid.*

10. *Ibid.*

11. J. F. C. Fuller, quoted in Cooper, *op. cit.*

12. Miles, *op. cit.*

13. Gibbs, Philip, *The Realities of War*, Heinemann (London, 1920)

14. Maude, A. H., (ed.), The 47th (London) Division 1914–1919, Amalgamated Press (London, 1922)

15. *Ibid.*

16. Cooper, *op. cit.*

17. Foot, S., *Three Lives*, Heinemann (London, 1934)

18. Lloyd George, D., *War Memoirs*, Odhams (London, 1938)

19. Terraine, J., *Haig – The Educated Soldier*, Hutchinson (London, 1963)

20. Blake, Robert, (ed.), *The Private Papers of Douglas Haig 1914–1919*, Eyre & Spottiswoode (London, 1952)

21. Liddell Hart, *op. cit.*

8

The Last Act: 1918

Our general situation requires that we should strike at the earliest moment, if possible at the end of February or beginning of March, before the Americans can throw strong forces into the scale. We must beat the British.—General E. Ludendorff, November 1917

THE EVENTS of the last year of the war brought to an end the deadlock on the Western Front. They are here dealt with only briefly, because in a sense they fall outside the scope of this book, which is primarily concerned with the unavailing attempts by the British Army over the three previous years to break the German line and achieve a strategic victory. However, there is a certain irony in the fact that, on the face of it, it was the German Army that found the key to the breakthrough – though was ultimately to lose it.

It was expected that the Germans would launch an offensive on the Western Front in 1918. The armistice reached with the Russians in December 1917 had allowed the Germans to commence the transfer of divisions to the Western Front, and by the end of January the number had increased from 150 to 175, with further arrivals bringing the total at the end of March to approaching 200. In contrast, the Allies' strength on the Western Front had fallen to slightly over 170 divisions (including nine American divisions) due to the demands of the Italian Front. In December Haig had pressed for drafts to bring his infantry up to establishment, calculated to be 40 per cent short by the end of March. Although there were ample reserves in the United Kingdom to achieve this target, the War Cabinet would only sanction a partial reinforcement, not only because of the demands of other theatres, but also because, with Passchendaele and Cambrai of recent unhappy memory, they were fearful of another costly Haig offensive.

To add to Haig's difficulties, he had been forced, under protest, to take over twenty-five miles of line from the French left, and this was completed by the end of January. The consequence of the take-over had been seriously to overstretch the Fifth Army's position on the British right, since it now held a third of the entire British front with scant compensation in the way of additional resources. The reasoning at GHQ was that this was an acceptable risk: there was room to give ground in the south, whereas any room for manoeuvre in the north was circumscribed by the nearness of the Channel coast. Moreover, the Fifth Army's southern boundary joined with the French, from whom, it was believed, assistance would be forthcoming in the event of a powerful German attack.

Haig was uncertain about the location and strength of the German attack. He told his Army commanders on 3 December that 'We must be prepared to meet a strong and sustained hostile offensive'. However, he told the War Cabinet on 7 January that he did not believe the Germans would embark on a large-scale offensive: he thought that they would launch 'attacks of limited scope, such as against Châlons, Arras or some salient'. He also considered that 'the best defence would be to continue our offensive in Flanders. . .' Nevertheless it was clear that consideration would have to be given to fighting a defensive battle, and three zones were designated, 'Forward', 'Battle' and 'Rear'. This system of defence in depth had been based on 1917 German practice wherein, to obviate heavy casualties being suffered in the preliminary bombardment, the Forward Zone was thinly held, with the purpose of merely delaying the assault; if ultimately penetrated, the offensive would be checked by the main force in the Battle Zone. But the British mistakenly allocated a third of their infantry to the Forward Zone, and due to a shortage of labour the construction of the Rear Zone defences was little more than an intention rather than an achievement.

Ludendorff was also uncertain where the attack should be delivered: he had to choose from an offensive against Hazebrouck code-named 'St George I', a subsidiary attack near Ypres ('St George II'), one at Arras ('Mars') and one at St Quentin ('St Michael') His preference was for 'St Michael':

If this blow succeeded, the strategic result might indeed be enormous, as we should separate the bulk of the English army from the French and crowd it up with its back to the sea.

On 21 January he made the final decision: it would be 'St Michael'.

On Thursday 21 March the storm broke. Three German armies launched a massive attack in dense fog on the position held by the British Fifth and Third Armies. This position extended from La Fère on the River Oise, the junction with the French, to just south of Arras, but the principal blow fell on the Fifth Army on the right wing of the British line.

The German attack was prefaced by a five-hour artillery bombardment on a forty-mile front from over 6,000 guns and howitzers using high explosive and gas – the greatest concentration of firepower yet seen on the Western Front. Then, looming through the fog, came the spearhead of specially trained stormtroops using the infiltration tactics successfully employed on the Eastern and Italian Fronts in 1917 and to a limited extent at Cambrai. Armed with light machine guns and flame-throwers, they swept around obstacles, leaving points of resistance to be dealt with by the moppers-up: their objective was to attack the artillery. The infantry of the Fifth Army, severely shaken by the suddenness and ferocity of the bombardment, suffered terrible casualties. Where garrisons were surrounded they defended to the last, but, blinded by the fog and with signal communications cut to brigade and division, there was little alternative but to withdraw to the Battle Zone. But here the bombardment had been equally destructive: battery positions had been drenched with gas and communication centres and headquarters destroyed. By nightfall the Germans held the whole of the Forward Zone and in places had reached the gun lines in the Battle Zone. Further north, the Forward Zone of the Third Army had also been breached, its infantry forced back to the rear edge of the Battle Zone.

Over the following days the situation developed into the second great crisis of the war. The Fifth Army, having borne the brunt of an assault from an overwhelming force, had virtually disintegrated, and although the German advance had been slowed by passage over the ruins of the Somme battlefields, by the evening of the 26th they had already captured Albert – an advance of over 20 miles – and were poised to strike at Amiens. Pétain, in response to Haig's request, had moved up six French divisions on the 23rd in order to assist the Fifth Army, but they could do little to influence a position which was already collapsing.

The crisis brought about the fateful Anglo-French Conference at Doullens on the 26th, when it was agreed that General Foch would be charged with the co-ordination of the action of the Allied armies on the Western Front. (His powers were increased a week later to embrace 'the strategic direction of military operations'.) However, the German advance was fast losing momentum. Ludendorff had opened the 'Mars' offensive in the Arras sector on the 28th against the junction of the Third and First Armies, but the defenders, well positioned in strong defences and aided by good visibility, fought off the attack and the operation was cancelled. Thwarted, Ludendorff shifted the emphasis of the offensive back to the south, where the deepest penetration had been achieved. The objective was Amiens, but the Allied defence had stiffened and, apart from limited gains made at the end of March and in early April, the tide of the advance had been halted within nine miles of the city. This, the greatest and most dramatic offensive of the war, had failed, as much because of the defeat at Arras as of the exhaustion of the German divisions and the difficulties in supplying them across the devastation of the old Somme battlefields. German casualties had been massive – about 300,000, compared with the Allied total of 240,000.

Ludendorff then decided that, owing to the shortage of fresh divisions, the subsidiary thrust near Ypres ('St George II') would have to be abandoned. Hence

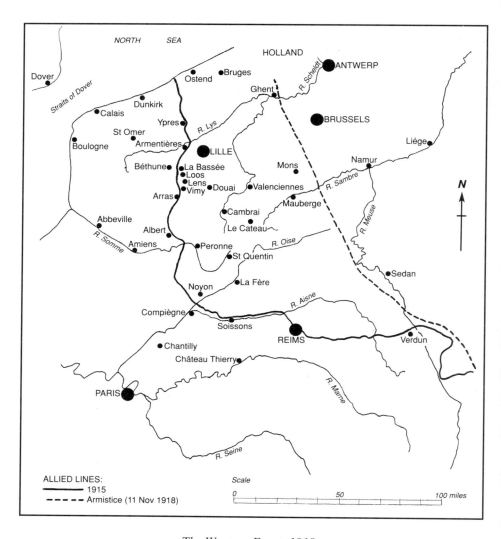

NORTH SEA

HOLLAND

Dover

Straits of Dover

Ostend
Bruges
Ghent

R. Scheldt

ANTWERP

BRUSSELS

Liége

Dunkirk
Calais
Ypres
St Omer
Boulogne
Armentières

R. Lys

LILLE

Namur

Mons

R. Sambre

R. Meuse

N

Béthune
La Bassée
Loos
Lens
Vimy
Arras
Douai
Valenciennes
Mauberge

Abbeville
Albert
Amiens
Peronne
St Quentin

Cambrai
Le Cateau

R. Somme
R. Oise

Sedan

Noyon
La Fère

Compiègne
Soissons

R. Aisne

REIMS
Verdun

Chantilly
Château Thierry

PARIS

R. Marne

R. Seine

ALLIED LINES:

───── 1915
- - - - Armistice (11 Nov 1918)

Scale

0   50   100 miles

The Western Front, 1918

'St George I', renamed 'Georgette', would be the next great blow, directed against Hazebrouck by way of Armentières and Bailleul. The plan was to employ the 6th and 4th Armies, the 6th to strike against the British First Army's position from the La Bassée Canal to Armentières on 9 April and the 4th the following day to assault the Second Army's position from Armentières northwards.

Once again there was fog on the morning of the 9th and a heavy bombardment similar to that of 21 March fell on the left wing of the First Army. Part of the assault was by four divisions against three brigades of Portuguese troops (Portugal, Britain's oldest ally, had entered the war in 1916). They were soon routed, and, pouring through the gap, the enemy had advanced over three miles by the evening. The attack of the German 4th Army the following day was, as usual, prefaced by a heavy bombardment. Initially there was strong resistance, but the three British divisions were heavily outnumbered and ultimately forced to withdraw. By the evening of the 10th the enemy had crossed the River Lys, Armentières had been evacuated and there was fierce fighting in the village of Messines.

Although the Germans made little progress on the 11th, Haig's appeal to Foch for French reserves to stem the German tide initially met with a refusal. He was told that the British Army 'must hold on where it stood'; Foch was saving the French Army for the counter-offensive. The crisis prompted Haig to issue an Order of the Day in which he stressed that 'There must be no retirement. With our backs to the wall . . . each one must fight on to the end . . .' However, Foch changed his mind and the next day ordered reserves from the French 5th Army to assemble near Amiens. But by the 19th the German 6th Army had been halted five miles from Hazebrouck and, apart from limited gains in the north by the German 4th Army, causing General Plumer to shorten his line fronting Ypres (thus giving up the gains achieved at such terrible cost in 1917), Operation 'Georgette' had come to an end. Although it could not be foreseen at the time, it had also brought to an end Ludendorff's hope of driving the British Army back to the Channel.

Ludendorff's next blow was against the French in the Aisne sector. This was intended to be a diversionary attack, with the object of attracting Allied reserves from the north preparatory to the launch of another offensive against the British. The position on the Chemin des Dames was held by sixteen divisions (including five British divisions resting from the March and April battles), but they were opposed by an attacking force of some forty divisions. The German bombardment opened at 1 a.m. on 27 May and nearly three hours later the attackers broke through the Allied front; such was the speed of the advance that there was no time to destroy the Aisne bridges. By the evening the bulk of the advance was some five miles beyond the Aisne, and it continued the following day. By 3 June the

Germans had reached the Marne at Château Thierry, an advance of thirty miles, but in the process had produced a narrow and vulnerable salient. There they halted, less than forty miles from Paris. A second diversionary thrust was made six days later west of the Chemin des Dames, and although an advance of about six miles was achieved it was brought to a halt by French and American counterattacks. Ludendorff called off the attack on the 13th.

However, Ludendorff was still intent on a Flanders offensive, and in yet another diversion he planned an attack on the French position in Champagne. The battle of the Chemin des Dames in May had produced a large salient to the west of Reims, part of its apex resting on the Marne to the east of Château Thierry. This was destined to be the heaviest of the diversionary attacks, employing three and half armies (fifty-two divisions) and designed once again to draw Allied reserves from Flanders. But the French, with thirty-four divisions (including British, American and Italian), were prepared.

The German objective was the Marne, and on 15 July, after a comparatively short preliminary bombardment, the attack began. East of Reims the advance was disrupted by French artillery fire, but although the lightly held forward zone was penetrated, the German attack was halted in the battle zone. Some success was gained south-west of the city when a precarious bridgehead was established over the Marne. Nevertheless, by the following day it was apparent that the German attack had stalled, and Ludendorff became anxious for the safety of the troops beyond the river. Indeed, the German advance had not only stalled, it had failed. The French (including British and American divisions) were poised for the counter-attack and on the 18th the drive forward began. An immediate success was gained on the western face of the salient, where the enemy was driven back some four miles, and although progress became slower over the following days a significant proportion of the ground lost in May was recovered by the end of July. By early August the salient had ceased to exist and with it, in effect, German hopes of victory on the Western Front. German casualties since March had been over a million men, and the decision was made to stand on the defensive until such time as the offensive could be resumed.

Foch now believed that the time had arrived for an Allied counter-stroke. Reinforcements to the British Army had been steadily arriving during May and June, and the absence of significant enemy activity in the British sector had allowed a period of comparative rest. On 8 August a combined force of British, American and French divisions, accompanied by a tank force of over 600 machines (of which 420 were fighting tanks), struck the 'nose' of the German salient fronting Amiens. Spearheaded by Canadian and Australians, the attack was generally successful. The German defences were penetrated to a depth of nearly eight miles, but what was out of all proportion to the ground gained was the effect on the defenders and Ludendorff himself: after the war he wrote that 'August 8 was the black day of the German Army in the history of this war.' The attack had been unsuspected, his front line troops had been decimated, 15,000 prisoners had been taken and there had been a serious collapse in morale, leading to some acts of insubordination. British casualties had been light, but there had been a heavy loss in tanks, with only 150 available for the following day. Over the next two days progress was slowed against stiffening resistance, and since a further advance would mean crossing the old Somme battlefields, there followed a pause to regroup.

Allied pressure was maintained during August, particularly in the last week, and by early September most of the ground gained by the Germans had been lost to them. Almost everywhere the German armies were falling back, occasionally counter-attacking, but for the most part fighting stubborn rearguard actions. The German armies were in fact near to collapse: insubordination continued to grow and morale was fast disintegrating, not only in the armies but on the home front. The spectre now haunting Ludendorff was not just of further French and British pressure but also of an American army on the Western Front amounting to nearly a million and a half men.

By the end of September Foch had decided that the time had come to mount attacks 'employing all the Allied forces in convergent action'. The successes in the summer had made progress, but the huge German salient that had existed for most of the war on the Western Front remained much as it had always been. Attacks were planned consecutively over four days beginning on 26 September – Franco-American on the underbelly of the salient near Reims, predominantly British on the St Quentin–Cambrai front in the centre and Franco-British and Belgian on the left from Armentières to the Channel.

The attack on the right achieved an average advance of about three miles, although the Americans were confronted with the difficult wooded country of the Argonne. The next day, the 27th, the British First and Third Armies made good progress despite the obstacle of the Canal du Nord and reached the outskirts of Cambrai. Further north the Passchendaele Ridge, scene of the bitter fighting in 1917, was regained, and the French and the Belgians pushed on towards Brussels. On the 29th the British Fourth Army crossed the St Quentin Canal and breached part of the Hindenburg Line defensive system.

Although the Franco-American offensive on the right wing had not achieved the headway expected, partly due to American inexperience, the attack in the centre by the British had been eminently successful: the Fourth and Third Armies had breached the Hindenburg Line's defences and reached the open country beyond. Nevertheless, the pace of the advance was slowing. The distance from the railheads was causing problems with supply, aggravated by worsening weather and the devastation caused to roads and railways by the retreating enemy. Despite these difficulties, however, the Allied advance continued throughout October against patchy German resistance.

The Allied attacks in September, particularly the penetration of the Hindenburg Line by the British, persuaded Ludendorff that an armistice was now imperative. Despite the initial reluctance of the new German Chancellor, Prince Max of Baden, the German and Austrian governments approached the United States president, Wilson, with a request for the opening of armistice negotiations. Wilson's reply contained Fourteen Points for acceptance, including the withdrawal of all troops from occupied territory. These were accepted without demur by Germany on the 12th in the belief that the conditions would enable its Army to withdraw to the German frontier, there to stand on the defensive. However, a second note from Wilson dispelled these hopes: the terms of the armistice would not be negotiated between heads of state but dictated by the Allied commanders. On 20 October Prince Max accepted Wilson's conditions. Hindenburg considered them unacceptable and endeavoured to persuade his army commanders to fight on, but this could not be tolerated by the government. Although Hindenburg was not relieved of his command, Ludendorff was forced to resign seven days later.

Germany was now on the brink of collapse: the Navy had mutinied on 29 October; rioting, fomented by army deserters, occurred on the home front; and there were demands for the Kaiser's abdication. Austria and Turkey had accepted an armistice on 3 November, and on the 9th Germany was proclaimed a republic. The next day the Kaiser abdicated and crossed the Dutch border into exile. On 11 November Germany signed an armistice, and at 11 a.m. the guns on the Western Front fell silent.

9

Retrospect

I T WILL BE evident that in the years 1915–17 the British High Command never solved the crucial problem of exploiting a breakthrough to the extent of gaining a strategic victory. There are a number of reasons for this, but one of the most important was Britain's total unpreparedness to fight a continental war of the scope and duration that it ultimately became.

In August 1914 Britain's tiny expeditionary force of 120,000 was dwarfed by French and German mobilized strength of two and half million with combined reserves of eight million. Nevertheless, this token force was considered adequate to guard the left flank of the French Army in what was initially believed to be a short war; the popular view was that it would all be 'over by Christmas'. Indeed, the capacity of the small British munitions industry was adequate to sustain only a short and mobile war, and shell production was concentrated on shrapnel rather than high explosive because of its effectiveness against troops in the open – it was useless against troops under cover or against fortifications. The expectation of a mobile war was reflected in the fact that in August 1914 British heavy artillery consisted of a mere sixteen guns, the predominant artillery pieces being the 13pdr and 18pdr field guns. Both highly mobile weapons, they complied with the prevailing tactical doctrine that the artillery would provide covering fire as the infantry advanced and, with direct observation, engage enemy artillery. Thus, of necessity, artillery had to be in the open, a situation which was soon to be shown as untenable in the face of machine-gun and artillery fire. With the end of the war of movement, the demand for high-explosive shell and heavy artillery became vital, but it was not until 1917 that the munitions industry was able to provide ammunition and guns in sufficient quantity and of adequate quality.

By the end of 1914 the BEF had suffered grievously, thereafter becoming primarily a civilian army and one hastily and inadequately trained for the battles yet to come. The Somme battles were fought by Territorials and New Army volunteers, their casualties ultimately replaced by conscripts. However if the British Army had become an unprofessional army, its senior commanders were professional in the sense that, with very few exceptions, they were all Regular Army; but this does not necessarily imply that they possessed the degree of professionalism needed to cope with conditions on the Western Front. The hierarchical order that had existed in the peacetime army meant that officers were promoted simply because it was their turn or because they were able to enlist patronage. Not surprisingly, this state of affairs did not always reward competence, and the outbreak of war found some senior officers in commands for which they were unfitted in terms of either temperament or experience. However, as the war progressed, many of these were weeded out and sent home, perhaps on the grounds of incompetence or perhaps because, for whatever reason, they were considered to be lacking in the 'offensive spirit'.

The battles of Neuve Chapelle and Loos in 1915 had fallen short of their objectives, but their accumulated experience appeared to demonstrate that the enemy's front could be pierced, provided that a long and methodical bombardment, in particular by heavy artillery, preceded the attack: it was also realized that an offensive on a wide front lessened the danger that enemy artillery might enfilade the flanks of a narrow attack. However, to assemble an attacking force for an offensive on a wide frontage required a substantial increase in the British Army's strength, accompanied by a similar increase in heavy artillery and ammunition. It also required a long period of preparation lasting weeks or, indeed, months, and the works required could not fail to be observed by the enemy, with the consequence that surprise was forfeited.

It was clear that the preliminary bombardment had to be heavy enough to destroy the enemy's front defences, but, for example, the timetable after the final bombardment before zero hour on the opening of the Somme offensive dictated that the bombardment lift to the next line of defence irrespective of whether the first line of defence (or its successors) had been captured. Thus the emphasis was on the destruction of defences rather than the provision of covering fire for the infantry, with the result that when the bombardment lifted from the German front trenches there was time for the defenders to emerge from their deep shelters with their machine guns. The solution formally adopted later in the series of Somme battles was the introduction of the creeping barrage which moved forward in short lifts, behind which the infantry advanced at a distance of about 100 yards. Always assuming that the preliminary bombardment had effectively created gaps in the wire entanglements, the infantry, advancing from one objective to the next behind a moving curtain of fire, had a reasonable chance of reaching the enemy's trenches before he could man the parapets. It will be evident, however, that the creeping barrage required great accuracy of delivery by the artillery, but the infantrymen welcomed its protection even though they suffered casualties where it fell short.

The Germans, thwarted in the attempt to gain a decision in the west, turned to the east with the object of knocking Russia out of the war. However, the Allied assaults on the Western Front in 1915 were harbingers of things to come. The Germans, accepting that their decision to stand on the defensive in the west would undoubtedly mean further attacks delivered with an increasing weight of artillery bombardments, set about constructing defence in depth with strong successive lines out of effective reach of all but the heaviest artillery. Thus the attacking infantry, after achieving a breach (if not driven back by counter-attacks from the positions won), were faced with a series of obstacles that could only be removed when the artillery was brought forward to recommence the bombardment. This, however, presented a fresh set of problems. The preliminary bombardment at the outset of an offensive was delivered from carefully sited gun positions, with reliable communications established to the headquarters of the attacking formations – even to the forward observation officers in the front line. In moving the guns up, however, these advantages were lost. Not only had guns to be brought forward over cratered ground and cluttered roads – if, indeed, these still existed – but new positions had to be established, usually in the devastation of the battlefield. The task of bringing up ammunition and supplies encountered the same difficulties, as did re-establishing lines of communication, which, at best, would be precarious. All this caused delay; the impetus of the attack was lost and time was given to the enemy to bring up reserves and mount counter-attacks.

It was Cambrai that appeared to offer the solution. Surprise was gained by the absence of the preliminary bombardment: the assembly of nearly five hundred tanks for the assault had been unobserved and, moreover, the path forward for both tanks and infantry was over comparatively uncratered ground. Even so, despite the ease with which the formidable Hindenburg Line had been crossed and the open country beyond reached, the following days saw the advance gradually coming to a standstill. This was as much to do with meeting enemy reserves as with the exhaustion of the tank crews and infantry and, above all, the lack of reserves to capitalize on the success achieved on the first day.

Although each offensive had been approached in a spirit of optimism that the lessons learned from the previous offensive would ensure success, the failure to attain the objectives set poses the question, was nothing learned? A qualified answer is that much was learned. For example, great strides had been made in the use of artillery, in particular the development of sound-ranging and flash-spotting, coupled with air observation in locating enemy batteries. The employment of the wave formation in infantry assaults was changed in favour of attacks in small groups, and greater reliance was placed on automatic weapons such as the machine gun and Lewis gun rather than the rifle and bayonet. Then came the tanks. Viewed at first with open hostility by many senior commanders, they demonstrated their value at Cambrai and again in 1918, but they were too slow and too limited in range to pursue the enemy and occupy territory; this, ultimately, was the task of the infantry.

It was the Germans, however, who broke the long stalemate on the Western Front. After a concentrated hurricane bombardment lasting only five hours, their great offensive in March 1918 fell on the front of the overextended British Fifth Army. The bombardment was followed by specially trained stormtroops employing the infiltration tactics used at Cambrai, and in six days they had advanced twenty-five miles on a frontage of fifty miles, effectively dividing the British and French Armies and causing the second great crisis of the war. The depth of penetration exceeded by far anything yet achieved by the Allies and appeared to indicate that the key to opening the door on the Western Front had at last been found. It was not, however, to be. The Germans had won a tactical, but not a strategic, victory: the sheer pace of their advance had outrun their artillery and supplies, and their divisions were close to exhaustion. This, the most dramatic offensive stroke of the war, ended in early April when they came up against a stiffened Allied defence before Amiens. Thus, in the final analysis, their experience mirrored the problems that had beset the British and the French.

Although the events of 1918 fall outside the scope of this book, they have a certain relevance when considering a proposition (albeit gained in hindsight) that, despite the massive growth in the destructive power of armaments, the German defence, even after initial adversity, would always have prevailed against Allied attacks on the Western Front through the years 1915 to 1917. A deadlock had been reached, and it required some special factor beyond the capacity of the Allies to break it; paradoxically, this was to be provided by the Germans. The underlying principle behind the British offensives had always been Haig's philosophy of 'the wearing out fight of varying duration', designed to exhaust the enemy's reserves before the main blow could be delivered. This is precisely what Ludendorff had in mind when launching the series of 1918 offensives, and although at their outset in March the Allies came close to disaster, it is ironic that the 'wearing out fight' eventually had a greater impact on the attackers than on the defenders – in other words, it was the principle of 'wearing out' in reverse. In Haig's Final Despatch, dated March 1919, he considered that 'the victories of the summer and autumn of 1918 will be seen to be as directly dependent upon the two years of stubborn fighting that preceded them'. Although it is indisputable that the Germans had suffered heavily on the Somme and at Passchendaele, Haig's conclusion overlooks the fact that it was only after the enormous losses suffered by the Germans in the 1918 offensives, and the accompanying drop in morale, that his far-reaching successes at Amiens in August and the Hindenburg Line in September were brought about.

The question then arises, would the stalemate have continued through 1918 (and even beyond) if the Germans had not gone over to the offensive in March 1918? The answer, obviously, can only be guessed at. The year 1918 saw the British (and French) tank forces expanded both in quantity and quality, and it saw the introduction of the Mark V tank, an improvement over the Mark IV, and a medium (and faster) tank, the Whippet. There had been a steady build-up of American divisions, substantial reinforcements to the British Army had arrived from the United Kingdom and the French were recovering from the effects of the 1917 mutinies. On the other hand, the German Army, always tenacious in defence, had been substantially reinforced from the Eastern Front. All the portents could have been that Allied assaults on the pattern developed at Cambrai would have brought gains, albeit at the cost of heavy casualties. It is highly probable, therefore, that an Allied victory in 1918 would not have come about. There is no doubt that German morale would have suffered, both in the Army and on the home front, but if the decision had been made to relinquish territorial gains in France and Belgium and retire to the Rhine, the knowledge that the homeland was being protected would have provided a moral uplift. Although ultimately an Allied victory would have been certain, it is possible that it could have been postponed, perhaps even until 1920.

Select Bibliography

Barnett, Corelli, *The Swordbearers: Studies in Supreme Command in the First World War*, Hodder & Stoughton (1981)

Bidwell, S., and Graham, D., *Firepower*, George Allen & Unwin (1982)

Blake, Robert, (ed.), *The Private Papers of Douglas Haig 1914–1919*, Eyre & Spottiswoode (1952)

Blunden, Edmund, *Undertones of War*, Collins (1965)

Campbell, P. J., *The Ebb and Flow of Battle*, Oxford University Press (1979)

Chapman, Guy, *A Passionate Prodigality*, Nicholson & Watson (1933)

Churchill, Winston S., *The World Crisis 1911–1918*, Odhams (1938)

Clark, Alan, *The Donkeys*, Hutchinson (1961)

Cooper, B., *The Ironclads of Cambrai*, Souvenir Press (1967)

Coppard, George, *With a Machine Gun to Cambrai*, Imperial War Museum (1980)

Crutchley, C. E., (comp.), *Machine-Gunner 1914–1918*, Bailey Bros & Swinfen (1973)

Cruttwell, G. R. M. F., *A History of the Great War* 1914–1918, Oxford: Clarendon (1934)

De Groot, G. J., *Douglas Haig 1861–1928*, Unwin Hyman (1988)

Edmonds, Brigadier-General Sir James, *A Short History of World War I*, Oxford University Press (1951)

———, (comp.), *Official History of the War: Military Operations, France and Belgium 1915*, Vol. II, Macmillan (1928); *1916*, Vol. I, Macmillan (1932); *1917* Vol. II, HMSO (1948)

Ellis, J., *Eye-Deep in Hell*, Fontana (1977)

Falls, Captain Cyril, *The First World War*, Longmans (1960)

———, (comp.), *Official History of the War: Military Operations, France and Belgium 1917*, Vol. I, Macmillan (1940)

Farrar-Hockley, A. H., *The Somme*, Pan Books (1966)

———, *Goughie: The Life of General Sir Hubert Gough*, Hart-Davis, MacGibbon (1975)

Fussell, P., *The Great War and Modern Memory*, Oxford University Press (1975)

Gough, General Sir Hubert, *The Fifth Army*, Hodder & Stoughton (1931)

Graves, R., *Goodbye to All That* (Penguin Books (1960)

Hankey, Lord, *The Supreme Command 1914–1918*, George Allen & Unwin (1961)

Holmes, R., *The Little Field-Marshal: Sir John French*, Jonathan Cape (1981)

Hutchison, Lt. Col. G. S., *Warrior,* Hutchinson (1932)

Keegan, J., *The Face of Battle,* Penguin Books (1978)

Liddell Hart, B. H., *A History of the World War 1914–1918,* Faber (1934)

Lloyd George, D., *War Memoirs,* Odhams (1938)

Macdonald, L., *Somme,* Macmillan (1984)

Manning, F., *The Middle Parts of Fortune,* Granada Publishing (1977)

Middlebrook, M., *The First Day on the Somme,* Fontana (1975)

Miles, Captain W., (comp.), *Official History of the War: Military Operations, France and Belgium 1917,* Vol. III, HMSO (1948)

Moran, Lord, *The Anatomy of Courage,* Sphere Books (1968)

Nicholls, J., *Cheerful Sacrifice: The Battle of Arras 1917,* Leo Cooper (1990)

Norman, T., *The Hell They Called High Wood,* William Kimber (1984)

Powell, G., *Plumer: The Soldier's General,* Leo Cooper (1990)

Prior, P., and Wilson, T., *Command on the Western Front,* Blackwell (1992)

Severn, Mark, *A Subaltern on the Somme in 1916,* J. M. Dent & Sons (1927)

———, *The Gambardiers,* Ernest Benn (1930)

Sixsmith, E. K. G., *Douglas Haig,* Weidenfeld & Nicolson (1976)

Spears, Brigadier-General E. L., *Prelude to Victory,* Jonathan Cape (1939)

Talbot-Kelly, R. B., *A Subaltern's Odyssey,* William Kimber (1980)

Terraine, J., *Douglas Haig – The Educated Soldier,* Hutchinson (1963)

———, *The Road to Passchendaele,* Leo Cooper (1977)

———, *The Great War 1914–1918,* Arrow Books (1977)

———, *The Smoke and the Fire,* Sidgwick & Jackson (1980)

Travers, T., *The Killing Ground,* Allen & Unwin (1987)

Vaughan, E. C., *Some Desperate Glory,* Frederick Warne (1981)

Warner, P., *The Battle of Loos,* William Kimber (1976)

———, *Passchendaele,* Sidgwick & Jackson (1987)

Winter, D., *Death's Men: Soldiers of the Great War,* Allen Lane (1978)

———, *Haig's Command: A Reassessment,* Viking (1991)

Wolff, L., *In Flanders Fields,* Pan Books (1961)

Index